Approaching the Dhamma

APPROACHING THE DHAMMA

BUDDHIST TEXTS AND PRACTICES IN SOUTH AND SOUTHEAST ASIA

ANNE M. BLACKBURN
JEFFREY SAMUELS
Editors

BPS PARIYATTI EDITIONS SEATTLE

BPS Pariyatti Editions
P.O. Box 15926
Seattle, WA 98115, USA
1-800-829-2748
www.pariyatti.com

ISBN 1-928706-19-3

10 09 08 07 06 05 04 03   5 4 3 2 1

Library of Congress Cataloging-in-Publication Data

Approaching the Dhamma : Buddhist texts and practices in South and Southeast Asia / Anne M. Blackburn and Jeffrey Samuels, editors.

Includes bibliographical references and index.
ISBN 1-928706-19-3 (alk. paper)
1. Dharma (Buddhism) 2. Sri Lanka--Religious life and customs. 3. Spiritual life--Buddhism--Southeast Asia. I. Blackburn, Anne M., 1967- II. Samuels, Jeffrey.

BQ4195 .A66 2003
294.3--dc21

Printed on acid-free paper.

CONTENTS

In affectionate and respectful celebration of

GODWIN SAMARARATNE
(1932-2000)

"Let one be in the habit of friendly relations,
of competent conduct let one be.
Being of abundant joy thereby,
one shall make an end of suffering."

*"paṭisanthāravutty assa ācārakusalo siyā
tato pāmojjabahulo dukkassantaṃ karissati."*

Dhammapada, Verse 376.

Introduction

Approaching the Dhamma is a collection of essays in honor of the late Godwin Samararatne. Although he was involved in various scholarly works, Godwin became best known as a meditation teacher, a role into which he grew over a prolonged period of time during the 1970s.

Godwin was born on September 6th, 1932 into a large family of seven children. During his youth, he studied at Dharmaraja College, a leading Buddhist school in Kandy, where, according to his teachers, he was quite mischievous, though good natured. In 1956, Godwin took a position as a librarian at the public library in Kegalle. After serving there for several years, Godwin shifted to the public library in Matale, and then later again moved, this time to Senanayake Library in Kandy.[1]

While in Kandy, Godwin began to see an old Dharmaraja school friend who had become a monk shortly after graduating from there: Venerable Sevali. At the time, Venerable Sevali was living in the famous Kanduboda meditation center outside of Colombo. While working at Senanayake Library, Godwin also joined a small group of lay people interested in Buddhist doctrine and meditation. This group met twice a week: once to discuss the primary and secondary Buddhist texts on meditation that they were reading, and once to practice meditation. During this period in his life, Godwin took time to visit several forest hermitages, such as Kanduboda and Mitrigala, to meet meditation adepts and to deepen his own practice.

The small Buddhist studies group continued to meet twice a week for several years. During one of the meetings, one member of the group who happened to own a tea plantation in the mountains above Kandy suggested that the group create a Buddhist study and meditation center for lay people. Under the sponsorship of the tea plantation owner and another group with which Godwin was associated—Mr. Ratnakara's Friends of the Good Teachings (*Sadaham Mithuru Samuluwa*)—land was purchased and several buildings were constructed. This became known as the Nilambe Meditation Center.

When the buildings were completed in 1979, Godwin was asked to run the center. He agreed to give it a try. In his usual humorous manner, he stated: "At that time, I was a librarian and still single. So, they asked me if I would like to stay there and see what happens. So I said that I will try it. And now I am continuing to try it. That was 1979. And that is how I became a meditation teacher. It just happened."[2]

In the early years of the Nilambe center, Godwin did not teach meditation; even though he made himself available for consultation to the students there, his role was mostly confined to that of caretaker. In this capacity, Godwin invited many lay and monastic meditation teachers to come to the center to conduct retreats. The first retreat held in the center was run by Joseph Goldstein, the co-founder of the Insight Meditation Society in Barre, Massachusetts.

It was not long, however, before Godwin also fell into the role of meditation teacher. His humorous and gentle approach in helping people along the path to enlightenment and away from the experience of suffering led Godwin to become highly sought after as a teacher. His popularity as a meditation teacher and as an emissary of Buddhism soon spread throughout Sri Lanka and beyond to Africa, Asia, Europe, Australia, and the United States.

Rather than teaching a single meditation method, Godwin adapted his teachings to meet the needs of individual meditators. The meditation topics that he assigned to his students ranged from certain forms of tranquility (*samatha*) meditation, mindfulness of the inhalation and exhalation (*ānāpānasati*), cultivating bare attention in which one watches whatever arises, insight meditation (*vipassanā*), and meditation on certain themes such as death and dying (*maraṇānussati*). Underlying all of these techniques however, was the meditation that played a large role in Godwin's life and teaching—meditation on loving-kindness (*mettā bhāvanā*). In the various retreats he led, Godwin returned again and again to this type of meditation, as he felt that love was a great antidote to self-centeredness and hatred.

Like other remarkable meditation teachers, Godwin did not confine his practice to his meditation cushion. He lived his teachings. Many of those who happened to meet Godwin noted his sense of equanimity and his inner peace. Godwin's practice of loving-kindness meditation also bore fruit in his everyday life through his involvement in various social service projects. From the early days of Nilambe, Godwin always remained concerned about being too removed from everyday life; thus, he divided his time between the center and Kandy. In the former setting, he taught meditation and helped his students overcome spiritual suffering. In the latter setting, he involved himself in helping poor people, unemployed women, and the ten precept nuns (*dasa sil mātāva*s) in Sri Lanka. He accomplished this through a variety of activities such as supplying financial aid to students, supplying eye glasses to poor people, building a training center where poor unemployed girls and women could be taught income-generating skills, and helping to raise the quality of life for Buddhist nuns or ten precept mothers.

Godwin died on March 27, 2000 from liver failure that was the result of contracting hepatitis in his youth. Godwin's undying sense of love and compassion remained with him until his last breath and he continually saw people and advised them even during the period before his death. Though most people would have experienced such a death with pained expressions, Godwin radiated compassion, friendliness, sympathetic joy, and especially equanimity up until the moment of his death. In fact, one close friend of Godwin remarked that the peace which flowed from his every pore may have even been responsible for his immediate death: as he lay there in his hospital bed, his body slowly shutting down, he maintained a smile on his face, perhaps fooling the doctors about the severity of his condition.

Godwin lived and died according to his practices and beliefs. He was a scholar, meditator, social worker, and most of all, a spiritual friend to many in Sri Lanka and beyond.

Part One

Godwin Samararatne possessed a rich sense of humor and a vibrant intellectual curiosity. These qualities allowed him to enjoy conversation with people working from a wide range of intellectual perspectives and caused him to support the very diverse research endeavors of his friends and colleagues. Samararatne's unusual combination of irony, compassion and acumen helped to shape research and reflection undertaken by each contributor to this volume. We are confident that he would have relished the diversity of positions represented here as well as the sensitivity with which the contributors elucidate Buddhist texts and practices in their South and Southeast Asian contexts. As a learned practitioner of meditation working in a variety of cultural contexts, he would have understood the need to make Buddhist texts and practices accessible to readers within, and beyond, the community of scholars concerned with the study of Buddhism.

In the first section of the ensuing essays, distinguished scholars Richard Gombrich, Gananath Obeyesekere, Venerable Bhikkhu Bodhi and John Ross Carter address crucial, and often complex, problems related to the interpretation and understanding of Buddhist texts and practices. The opening essay by Richard Gombrich, "Obsession with Origins": Attitudes to Buddhist Studies in the Old World and the New," provides an important intervention in an on-going debate over whether, and to what extent, it is possible to discern in Pāli texts evidence of early or original Buddhism and of the Buddha's own ideas about proper practice and the ideal path to liberation. Gombrich develops an account of American social scientific preoccupations with the contemporary and unstable meaning of texts and what he calls "a revulsion against history" (p. 5). This account is then used as a foil against which to develop specific and constructive claims about how Pāli texts can be read by those who wish to gain insight into the early contexts of South Asian Buddhism and the ideas of Gotama Buddha. In the face of inconsistencies and contradictions within Pāli *tipiṭaka* texts, Gombrich asks: "How, then, are we to proceed if we want to get closer to the Buddha himself than simply accepting the bulk of the Canon as an authentic record of his words?" (p. 9).

Crucial to Gombrich's answer is a distinction between stratifying texts (unlikely to contain the Buddha's exact words) and stratifying the ideas within the texts (many of which are likely to originate with the Buddha himself). In this way it is possible to delineate patterns of exposition consistent with what Gombrich has elsewhere described as the "originality, intelligence, grandeur and—most relevantly—coherence" of the four *nikāya*s and the central body of monastic rules.[3] This, however, is still a first step in the effort to determine the content of the Buddha's teachings. Identifying the structure of and context for ideas likely to be the Buddha's own is the critical stage in the determinative process. Gombrich underscores the importance of dialogical structure to the Buddha's *tipiṭaka* teachings and identifies as one of the Buddha's key pedagogical techniques the process of redefining the terms of his interlocutors in order to express central Buddhist teachings. Developing examples from Gombrich's own work and that of a colleague, Joanna Jurewicz, the essay shows that by attending to the redefinition of terms important to the Buddha's Brahmanic interlocutors we can gain a clearer understanding of the Buddha's ideas, the environment in which they were first expressed, and the varied approaches used to communicate them.

In his inspired treatment of the *Mahāparinibbāna Sutta*, "The Death of the Buddha: A Restorative Interpretation," Gananath Obeyesekere is careful to situate elements of this narrative about the Buddha's death within the cultural context inhabited by Gotama Buddha and his early followers. Obeyesekere (in an approach to this extent compatible with Richard Gombrich's attention to the Brahmanic context of *sutta* dialogue), charts a series of cultural associations between caste and gender status, food purity, and sexual pollution that would have been meaningful to the audience by and for whom the *sutta*'s narrative was first developed. Obeyesekere's primary aim, however, is neither an historian's account of Gotama Buddha's death nor an adjudication of inconsistencies visible in the *Mahāparinibbāna Sutta* to determine the ideas most likely to have originated with the Buddha himself. Instead, with homage to Nietzsche's claim that the death of religions occurs when "the feeling for myth" is replaced by historical claims (p. 18), Obeyesekere seeks to restore a feeling for the myth of the Buddha by offering a symbolic analysis of the Buddha's death as narrated within the *sutta*.

At the heart of this reflection on the "symbologic" (p. 33) of the Buddha's death is a comparison of the Buddha's birth and death narratives and an exegesis of the immediate cause of death: consumption of a poisonous dish offered by Cunda. Obeyesekere argues that "[t]he meal from Cunda has as profound a significance for Buddhism (or once had) as the last supper of Christ for Christianity, even though their soteriological meanings are different" (p. 28). Death as a result of consuming impure food offered by a person of low caste status in a rural backwater underscores, from this perspective, the humanity of the Buddha and Buddhism's universal message about the impermanence of all things. When read against the (literally) marvelous accounts of the Buddha's birth this emphasis on humanity is particularly significant. The symbolic last word in Obeyesekere's reading lies with the omnipresence of aging and death rather than with the promise of transcendence for one, or for some. Importantly, Obeyesekere explores the ways in which inconsistencies within the *sutta*'s account of the Buddha's death reveals evidence of historical debate about whether the Buddha's humanity or transcendence is to be emphasized in the unfolding of Buddhist 'tradition.' Obeyesekere at once attempts to recreate elements of this debate, to place within it the "Euro-rational" interpretations of Buddhism which have in his view helped to destroy its "feeling for myth" and to develop his own "hermeneutical interpretation" rooted, at least in part, in the experience of contemporary Sri Lanka's shocking violence (p. 18).

With the essay by Venerable Bhikkhu Bodhi, our attention is drawn to another *sutta* from the Pāli *tipiṭaka*. Once again, this close examination of a single text raises broader issues about how we are to interpret foundational Buddhist texts. Venerable Bodhi examines the *Kosambī Sutta*, a *sutta* in which the triangular conversation between the monks Saviṭṭha, Musīla and Nārada leaves the reader uncertain about the sort of knowledge constitutive of arahantship. Musīla and Nārada both claim to have personal knowledge of the same cluster of doctrinal matters that would characterize liberation yet the latter denies that he is, in fact, an *arahant*. Venerable Bodhi's exploration of this problem leads him to examine *nikāya* accounts of stages on the path to liberation, and to look closely for *nikāya* references related to cognitive and meditative experience, and the differences between them. The distinction between *dhamma*-followers and faith-followers emerges as a key to Venerable Bodhi's interpretation.

Significantly, this approach to the problem develops what we might think of as an intertextual apparatus for exegesis of the *Kosambī Sutta* by examining a cluster of related ideas about cognition, meditative experience, and liberation across a broader range of *sutta*s. With this subsequently expanded sense of what might be implied in the divergent positions of the *Kosambī Sutta*'s key monastic figures, Venerable Bodhi develops a new reading of the *sutta*. According to this reading, Musīla and Nārada exemplify the encounter with *nibbāna* characteristic of, respectively, a trainee (*sekha*) and an *arahant*, rather than as figures representative of meditation and cognition as opposing paths to liberation. Venerable Bodhi's reading of the text has serious implications for scholars interested in matters such as the early history of forest monasticism and the distinction between textual learning and practice. The importance of the essay is considerably broader, however. Venerable Bodhi suggests that attention to the "underlying groundwork of interconnected ideas" within the *sutta*s (developing an intertextual apparatus) is required in order to "decipher the texts in accordance with their implicit intention" (pp. 47-48). His words have challenging implications for those who seek to understand authoritative Pāli textual positions on a range of issues, including ethics and gender.

The final essay in Section One, by John Ross Carter, offers a subtle meditation on the nature of "understanding," asking "what might be occurring when we speak of ourselves as reaching an understanding… most comprehensively, of another person, especially another person in that person's religious life" (p. 69). The question posed by "On the Search for Interreligious Understanding" is a fundamental one, demanding reflection on that process which may occur without self-consciousness as one develops comparisons between religious traditions, texts and practices or engages in some form of interreligious dialogue. Carter develops a theological account of the study of religion grounded in the Aristotelian notions that "to understand ourselves we must understand the world" and that a religious life is a life lived through morally responsible relationships to other persons (p. 79).

Carter offers a striking argument in favor of scholarly focus on religious persons and "the centers of value in terms of which they, themselves, find personal integration, responsible relationships with others, and orientation to the world" (pp. 83). In the context of this volume, it is particularly interesting to note Carter's view that it is inadequate (a moral and a descriptive failure) for scholars to acquire rigorous knowledge of any single Buddhist phenomenon (such as a symbol, a practice, or a concept) without attending to the ways in which such a phenomenon sustains moral relationships and offers "a cohesive supportiveness" (p. 73) for Buddhist persons. The account of "understanding" developed by Carter also has critical (in both senses) implications for the practice of liberal or inclusivist interreligious dialogue and for "New Age" appropriations of Buddhism and other religious traditions.

Part Two

In the second section of this volume, "Ritual and Cosmology," Donald Swearer, Jeffrey Samuels, and Asanga Tilakaratna explore a Thai ritual oriented toward remembering the Buddha, the role of ritual performance in contemporary monastic training in Sri Lanka, and place of gods in Theravāda Buddhist canonical and post-canonical texts respectively. Though the particular subject matter of each essay differs, they share a similar goal in showing the historical and contemporary importance of rituals and the gods in the Theravāda tradition, particularly in the lives of lay people and monastics.

In the opening essay of this section, titled "In the Presence of the Buddha," Donald Swearer examines one from a variety of Buddhist rituals focused on recollecting and remembering the Buddha: the Thai Buddhist image eye-opening ceremony.

By exploring the manifold features of the ritual, Swearer illustrates the various ways in which the Buddha's presence becomes aurally, visually, and performatively present to the ritualist-monks and lay audience.

The particular features of the ritual that Swearer examines are the texts, images, and narratives recited and recollected. Looking closely at the narratives and the temple images, for instance, Swearer shows how the various facets of the Buddha's life (e.g., the bodhisattva perfections, the four sightings, and so on) lead the audience to become "actors on the stage of a sacred history" (p. 98) for whom the various events surrounding the Buddha's life and previous lives become something to be emulated. Swearer also suggests that the recitation of certain formulae (*mantra*s) and magical incantations (*dhāraṇī*s), combined with certain ritual gestures and doctrinal recitations, lead to an identification of the body of the Buddha with certain aspects of the Buddha's teaching (*dhamma*). Swearer poignantly concludes his article by pointing out that the image-consecration ritual goes far beyond casual recollection of the Buddha: it may actually serve to infuse one's mind with the very life and teachings of the Buddha so as to overcome, within oneself, certain mental hindrances and poisons.

In his article titled "Establishing the Basis of the *Sāsana*: Social Service and Ritual Performance in Contemporary Sri Lankan Monastic Training," Jeffrey Samuels explores the role of ritual performance in a recently created Sri Lankan monastic training institution—the *sāmaṇera* training center. By exploring the events leading up to the institution's establishment, its training curriculum, and its several leaders' understandings of ideal monastic service, Samuels illustrates how ritual performance becomes identified as a form of social service for the novices undergoing training in the centers.

To arrive at his conclusion, Samuels first explores how the *sāmaṇera* institution arose out of the perception of a decline in Buddhism, particularly in regards to monastic propriety and ritual performance. By turning to a more detailed examination of the training curriculum, Samuels shows the pedagogical function that ritual performance plays in the training of *sāmaṇeras* as well as how ritual performance shapes and even concretizes the monastic identities of the young monks as ritualists. Finally, by exploring head monks' and founders' understanding of ideal monastic service as ritual performance and the role that ritual performance plays in the continuation of the *sāsana*, Samuels' article illuminates the creative range of interpretations and ideas held by the contemporary *saṅgha*.

The third contribution in section two is Asanga Tilakaratna's article on "Buddhist Non-theism: Theory and Application." In this important contribution to the field, Tilakaratna argues that the complete denial of a creator god in the Buddhist tradition does not necessarily preclude the absence of god-like aspects. By examining a host of canonical and post-canonical texts, Tilakaratna reconciles the tension between non-theistic tendencies in the Theravāda tradition with the "lived reality of the religion of ordinary men and women" for whom belief in a god gives a sense of security and protection (p. 127).

In accomplishing his aim of examining how the Theravāda tradition accommodated the needs of ordinary people without necessarily compromising its cosmological and ethical standpoints, Tilakaratna first explores the Pāli canonical sources where the concept of god is unequivocally denied. Then, through an investigation of several canonical and post-canonical references pertaining to three important gods of the Theravāda tradition—Brahma, Yama, and Sakka—Tilakaratna illustrates how the tradition is able to incorporate three important aspects usually associated with god—virtue, righteousness, and goodness—without necessarily positing the existence of a creator god. In his conclusion, Tilakaratna conveys the religious and philosophical implications of this development by asserting that while the Theravāda tradition attributes certain theistic features—divine intervention, compassion, and goodness—to several important gods, these qualities and functions need not conflict with the basic Buddhist tenet that "one's greatness ultimately depends on one's inner purity" (p. 144).

Part Three

The third section of this volume, "Rebirth and Mental Culture," draws together historical and contemporary studies of Buddhist meditation, rebirth and psychotherapy. In an impressive range of contributions, P.D. Premasiri, George Bond, Susan Reed, Erlendur Haraldsson and the late Godwin Samararatne explore diverse aspects of meditative practice and mental refinement. In the opening essay, "The Ultimate Goal of Early Buddhism and the Distinctive Characteristics of Buddhist Meditation," P. D. Premasiri provides an incisive account of Buddhist meditative practice as described in the Pāli sources of the *tipiṭaka*. Premasiri carefully explores the historical context in which Buddhist meditation developed, attending to the similarities and contrasts visible in Buddhist *bhāvanā* and the yogic traditions which preceded it.

Crucial to Premasiri's account is the distinction between *samatha* (tranquillity) and *vipassanā* (insight) meditation as elaborated in the *Sutta Piṭaka*. His essay explains the importance of insight meditation to a Buddhist "middle way" between the metaphysical extremes of eternalism and materialism and illuminates the problems which the Buddha and his first followers associated both with *samatha bhāvanā* and yogic practice. In an important development, Premasiri uses the "fundamental distinction" between *samatha* and *vipassanā* (p. 157) to underscore the view that Buddhist mental culture cannot be linked properly to a metaphysical position that accepts a God-concept (see Tilakaratne's essay, above) or the idea of a permanent soul.

George Bond, long an observer of contemporary Buddhist meditation and social service movements in Sri Lanka, explores innovative approaches to meditation developed in 20th-century Sri Lanka as well as the social context for such innovation. Bond's essay, "Reconstructing the Path: Two Cases from the Lay Meditation Movement in Sri Lanka," examines the life and work of lay meditation teachers Godwin Samararatne and D.C.P. Ratnakara. Bond examines the attitudes of these teachers toward Theravādin textual and monastic authority, public ritual and social service.

Bond emphasizes that both the late Samararatne and Ratnakara privileged experience over textual and monastic authority in ways that constituted a critique of a *saṅgha*-based "Buddhist orthodoxy" (p. 169). At the same time, however, Bond's essay shows that Samararatne's approach to meditation retained a strong deference to ideas put forth in the Pāli *tipiṭaka* and early commentaries while Ratnakara developed novel sources of authority through a "*dhamma*" received through revelations to Mrs. Ratnakara. Samararatne's commitment to meditation as a healing practice and force in the emotional transformation of lay life stands in interesting contrast to the Ratnakaras' greater interest in social service and the attainment of *nibbāna* in one lifetime.

Susan Reed's annotated 1997 interviews with the late Godwin Samararatne provide a fascinating extension of the preceding essay. Against the backdrop of Bond's comparative social and historical account of lay Buddhist meditation in contemporary Sri Lanka, Reed provides a rare first-person distillation of ideas on cross-cultural Buddhist meditation, medicine, and psychotherapy. In two far-ranging interviews, Reed and Samararatne discuss a series of questions arising from Reed's anthropological interests in culturally specific formulations of illness and emotion and from Samararatne's commitment to meditative practice as a response to physical and mental illness.

The resulting exchanges provide a valuable record of Samararatne's approach to physical and emotional pain, his treatment of neurotic behaviors (including depression and phobia), and his conception of meditation as a form of self-reliant psychotherapy. Reed's careful commentary and bibliographic annotation create from these interviews a source from which to reflect on a range of issues important to meditation teachers and psychotherapists in Asia and beyond. These include: the differences characteristic of South Asian and non-South Asian meditative experience; culturally specific constructions of the self, emotion and illness; and the cross-cultural applicability of Freudian and other Euro-American psychoanalytic perspectives. Reed's essay highlights Samararatne's unusual understanding of meditation as psychotherapy, rooted in Asian and Euro-American interpretations, and his commitment to meditative techniques as tools for emotional transformation. Samararatne's remarks on intimate relationships and "spiritual friendship" (pp. 212-214) speak to contemporary Euro-American concerns about the place of meditative practice and domesticity in a lay *saṅgha*.

Fittingly, this final section closes with an essay that extends an examination of mental refinement from a single-life perspective to that of a rebirth process. This essay, "Children Who Speak of Memories of a Previous Life as a Buddhist Monk: Three New Cases," by Erlendur Haraldsson and the late Godwin Samararatne, exemplifies the commitment of both authors to careful social scientific and medical research into problems raised by authoritative Pāli Buddhist texts.[4]

Haraldsson and Samararatne recount their investigation of three cases from Sri Lanka in which a young child claimed to recall life as a Buddhist monk and displayed behavioral traits common to monastics. The essay reports the recollections articulated by the children and their families, distinguishing between cases in which the attempt to verify the child's account may have affected the account itself, and cases in which a complete recollection was obtained from the child before initiation of a verification process. The authors discuss interviews with family members and independent witnesses, conducted in order to gain a fuller understanding of the child's behavior, as well as their own observations, and attempt to identify deceased monks who fit the child's recollections. The behavioral emphasis is a striking feature of study, which queries the reasons for consistent monk-like behavioral manifestations and explores possible sources for a child's repertory of gestures, phrases and emotions common to advanced monastics.

We are privileged to conclude this commemorative volume with Venerable Bhikkhu Bodhi's reflections on "Acharya Godwin Samararatne."[5]

A Note on Style

The editors have endeavored to standardize styles of spelling, punctuation, and use of diacritical marks within each essay. We have not attempted to homogenize these matters across the volume, however, since it includes contributions from diverse textual communities. The majority of technical terms are given in Pāli, but some authors use also Sanskrit, Thai and Sinhala terms. All abbreviations for Pāli texts follow the Critical Pāli Dictionary.

Notes

1. The editors would like to thank Visakha Wickremeratne for providing much of the information about Godwin's early years.
2. Personal communication with Godwin Samararatne.
3. Richard F. Gombrich, *Theravāda Buddhism: A Social History from Ancient Benares to Modern Columbo* (London: Routledge and Kegan Paul, 1988).
4. The Editors are grateful to the *Journal of the Society for Psychical Research* for permission to reprint this article originally published in 1999.
5. The Editors express their thanks to the *Daily News* (Colombo), for permission to reprint this obituary originally published on 19 April, 2000.

Acknowledgements

The Editors are grateful to a number of individuals and institutions for assistance in the preparation of this volume. We are indebted to Ben Turner and Julie Schaeffer at BPS Pariyatti Editions for their compassionate and careful preparation of the book, to the Venerable Bhikkhu Bodhi for his assistance with the publication arrangements, and to Harilal and Visakha Wickremesmeratne for encouraging our work on the volume. We appreciate the responsiveness of our contributing authors and would like to acknowledge, with regret, the absence of an essay by Professor (Mrs.) Lily de Silva, due to scheduling difficulties.

Anne M. Blackburn would like to acknowledge the following institutions in particular: the Department of Religious Studies at the University of South Carolina, the Helen R. Whiteley Center at the Friday Harbor Laboratories (University of Washington), and Wolfson College, Cambridge University. She expresses her thanks to Richard Gombrich, H. L. Seneviratne and Donald K. Swearer for their guidance at various stages of the project. John Clayton's loving presence and editorial experience eased many moments of composition and edition, as did his gift of companionable walks along the Cam.

Jeffrey Samuels would like to acknowledge the support and financial assistance received from the Department of Philosophy and Religion as well as the Faculty Research Committee at Western Kentucky University, the Department of Religious Studies at the University of Virginia, and the Sri Lankan Fulbright Commission in Colombo.

Part One

Interpretation and Understanding

"Obsession with Origins":

Attitudes to Buddhist Studies in the Old World and the New

Richard Gombrich

Godwin Samararatne was a most unusual man, a precious blend of wisdom and compassion. As this implies, he had a lively, albeit understated, sense of humour. Once in Oxford he gave a talk on his experiences as a meditation teacher to aspirants both from the West and from Sri Lanka. There were two differences, he said, between the two groups. Among those who failed to achieve the progress in meditation that they had hoped for, the Westerners always failed because they tried too hard, the Sri Lankans because they did not try hard enough. On the other hand, the Westerners usually laid the blame for their problems on their parents; it never occurred to a Sri Lankan to do that. He chuckled.

Godwin was a devout (not to say exemplary) Buddhist, and at the same time keenly interested in and appreciative of the academic study of Buddhism. He and I shared values; and one of them was academic research, ferreting out the truth. When Godwin helped me in the research which led to *Buddhism Transformed*, a work which by documenting deviations from tradition has offended some chauvinists, he knew exactly what he was doing, and delighted in it. On many American campuses the kind of work that he helped me to do would be regarded as dubious, perhaps even politically incorrect. For many, Buddhism has alas become a "feel good" subject: students are allowed to enthuse about "what Buddhism means to me", rather than to describe, analyse and construct testable hypotheses. This was not Godwin's way.

I feel no need to defend academic study *per se*, but I hope it may be appropriate, writing in Godwin's memory, to criticise a recent academic trend. Unlike Godwin on western meditators, I am probably exaggerating when I ascribe a certain current attitude to Buddhist studies to the New World—by which of course I mainly mean the United States—and contrast it with a more traditional view which I believe continues to be common, though not universal, in the Old World, and which I propose to defend. My purpose in making the distinction, like Godwin's, is not to contribute to the sociology of ideas, but to make a deeper contribution to the subject matter. Let me therefore be content to fix my point of departure by means of a couple of anecdotes.

A research student of mine in Oxford wrote a splendid thesis on an important theme in the Buddha's teaching as it appears in the texts of the Pāli Canon. Her method was traditional but her findings highly original. Soon after she had published this thesis as a book she encountered at an academic gathering another ex-student of mine who, some 15 years earlier, had first written an excellent doctorate and then published an excellent book on a related theme; he had then emigrated to take employment in North America. Her hopes of an interesting discussion with her predecessor were dashed when he said to her, "Why this obsession with origins?"

Not long after this I found myself invited to lecture at a well-known American university a few days after the beginning of the academic year. Colleagues from other universities in the vicinity assembled to dine with me before my first lecture. All of them had just given their first lecture in an introductory or survey course about Buddhism. So I asked them, "Did any of you in your opening lecture say anything at all about the chronology of Buddhism?" A brief silence. Then someone replied, "No. Why should we do such a thing?" "Because if you don't know which came first, A or B, you can't tell whether A could have been the cause of B. And I am interested in causal questions." Their faces told me that they could see little hope for this old-fashioned European.

Though this can be presented as an American / European contrast, it is probably more accurate to see it as a sign of the predominance of social science and an interest in the present over the humanities, including textual study, and an interest in the past. There is however an overlap because I think that American social science is hegemonic world-wide. The reasons for what amounts to a revulsion against history, at least as history is traditionally understood, are complex, and it is not my purpose to examine them thoroughly. Post-modernism is obviously an important factor: the idea that we give meaning to texts by reading them has been taken to utterly absurd lengths which can subvert the very concept of documentary evidence. What interests me more in this context is an attitude which strikes me as particularly American: an egalitarianism, closely linked to political theory, which in defending the rights and dignity of each individual comes to mistrust any claim to authority. The political principle of one man one vote, has been sadly misapplied in the politicised academy. The Buddha and the ancient Indian emperor Asoka were individual human beings who died long ago; why should their opinions have any greater claim on our attention than those of any other individual Buddhist?

This view, which sees itself as "anti-authoritarianism", seems to be particularly at home nowadays in anthropology. If I travel to a distant land, anything that anyone there tells me is claimed to be equally "valid", which means equally worthy of attention and respect. It follows that there can be no such thing as a stupid or ignorant informant, for everyone has an equal right not merely to express their opinion but to have that opinion taken seriously. Anthropologists are in favour of doubt, but that doubt must be directed towards oneself ("reflexive anthropology"), not towards one's informants.

Let me illustrate this attitude from a well-known book on Sinhalese Buddhism by an intelligent (and very nice) British anthropologist, Martin Southwold. Like me Southwold lived for about a year in a Sinhalese village, and like me he was charmed by his neighbours and had a good time. It cannot have been from his neighbours, however, that he acquired the view that in such matters as religion, which concern all mankind, there can be no authority, so that every man's opinion is of equal value; that view he certainly took to Sri Lanka with him. Unfortunately, however, it involved him in a paradox: if the Buddhist villagers themselves believe that their religious ideas and practices are given to them by an authority, they must be wrong. So it suddenly turns out that informants *do* make mistakes—though apparently only in this respect.

Southwold writes:

> The term "Buddhism" is used in any or all of four senses, referring to four distinguishable kinds of thing:
>
> 1. Buddhendom, Buddhist civilisation, society and culture as a whole.
> 2. What within this appears to be specifically a religion.
> 3. The doctrines of that religion.
> 4. The teaching of the Founder, the Buddha himself.
>
> Now Buddhists themselves appear to relate these in reverse order. The origin and core of Buddhism is the Buddha's teaching; this is the basis of Buddhist doctrine; this is the basis of the religion; and this is the basis of Buddhist civilisation. I am not clear how far Buddhists do say just this—nor, to the extent that they do, how far they have been influenced into doing so by European ideas. No matter; this is what nineteenth-century Europeans would have 'heard' them saying, because it precisely corresponded with their understanding of the structure of their own

> religious civilisation, of Christendom. [1]

He continues:

> ...it is more likely than not that Buddhism did originate from the teaching of the historical Buddha...but we cannot know anything, or at best not nearly enough, about the historical Buddha and his teaching. So, even if this approach is well founded and methodologically proper, we cannot usefully follow it, and must either find another or despair...Thus the primary reality is Buddhist civilisation, Buddhist society and culture, a way of life of real men. This generates Buddhist religion, as a construction which orders and legitimises, in symbolic form, that civilisation. This in turn is systematised in Buddhist doctrine. And to legitimise the doctrine and the religion that lies behind it, these are attributed to Lord Buddha, who thus emerges as a projection of, perhaps an impersonation of, the prior and more basic elements of the system. No doubt the historical Buddha was the origin of the whole system; but he is unknowable.[2]

Godwin, who on my visits to Sri Lanka would guide me around various Buddhist cult groups in order to observe "the way of life of real men", would have found this uproariously funny. But the main point, as Southwold is fully aware, is that he is contradicting the views not only of Godwin Samararatne but of all his informants. Any belief in authority or hierarchy simply cannot be accepted. In fact traditional Buddhists in Sri Lanka have their own schema to represent "Buddhism in life": *pariyatti, paṭipatti, paṭivedha.* These three Pāli words mean learning (this refers to learning Pāli texts), practice and realisation. They form a hierarchy, each being a prerequisite for the next: without knowledge of the texts there can be no correct practice of morality and mental cultivation, and without such practice no one can achieve realisation, *nibbāna.* According to tradition the texts in question are "the word of the Buddha" as it was formulated and recited for memorisation at the first Council shortly after his death.

To some extent Southwold is simply under a misapprehension about fact, for he writes that the scriptures "were composed by monks several centuries at least after the Buddha's death," [3] probably confusing "composed" with "written down". Modern scholarship takes a position somewhere between Southwold and the traditional view. It is virtually certain that there was no writing in India at the time of the Buddha, so that for two to three centuries after his death the record could only be preserved orally. There seems to be no reason to doubt that chronicle (*Mhv* XXXIII, 100-102) which claims that the Canon was committed to writing in Sri Lanka rather late in the first century B.C. This refers to the version in Pāli, peculiar to the Theravādin tradition; we have no comparable record of the writing down of scriptures in other dialects, and our earliest physical evidence to survive is fragmentary manuscript material from the far north-west of India probably dating from the second century A.D. While the chronicle is referring to the organised writing down of the whole Canon, there is no reason to think that particular texts might not have been written down up to two centuries earlier, for the inscriptions of Asoka, the earliest dated examples of Indian writing,[4] date to the middle of the third century B.C.

On the other hand, the Vedic tradition, in which a huge body of textual material was orally preserved by brahmins without the use of writing for perhaps as long as two millennia, shows that not only was such a feat possible in ancient India, but the Buddhists had a model before them.[5] They organised the *saṅgha* into groups with responsibility for preserving particular collections of texts; and the events which we usually refer to as Councils were primarily communal recitations, rehearsing and thus checking the material. I suspect that the so-called Second Council which must have been held about seventy years after the Buddha's death,[6] was particularly important for formulating the Canon that we now have, except for the *abhidhamma*.

The Buddhist Canon is a very large body of textual material, showing considerable sophistication and coherence.

It survives in several versions (mostly in Chinese and Tibetan translations) and the variation in versions of texts which are universally agreed to be comparatively early are many but on the whole rather trivial. It is inconceivable that this large body of material could have been composed and agreed on as authentic once Buddhism had spread over a large geographical area, as we know that it did under the emperor Asoka. The common textual heritage must therefore date back to within about 150 years of the Buddha's death, which I have shown to have taken place around 405 B.C.[7]

On the other hand, there are certainly inconsistencies and even contradictions within this material. The simplest explanation for this is multiple authorship: many different individuals contributed their own recollections of the Buddha's teaching. These individuals came from different backgrounds before they were converted to Buddhism, and arrived with different assumptions. Moreover, the Buddha himself may have been inconsistent on some relatively inessential matters. Certainly, since he preached for 45 years, and made a point of adapting his presentation to his audience, he must have put things in very many different ways—as the tradition itself claims. Besides this, one can obviously not rule out the possibility of textual corruption—and in some cases it is a virtual certainty.

How, then, are we to proceed if we want to get closer to the Buddha himself than simply accepting the bulk of the Canon as an authentic record of his words? To begin with, we should be alive to the inconsistencies and view with scepticism the efforts of the traditional commentators either to ignore them or to argue them away. Then, if the inconsistency is serious, we may want to decide which view is more likely to have been the Buddha's own. This leads us to attempt some stratification of the material. Stratification has acquired an extremely bad name. Because it has often been done badly, the stratifier clearly following his own prejudices, the general consensus has become that it should not be attempted at all. I strongly disagree.

We have to distinguish between stratifying the texts exactly as we have them and stratifying the ideas they contain. Because the oral tradition has tended to level out modes of expression and to shift passages, whether stock phrases or entire sequences of paragraphs, from text to text, we are most unlikely to have access to the Buddha's precise words. Access to his ideas is however another matter, and indeed those ideas may include key terms, as for example when he is quoting.

The Pāli canonical texts show the Buddha in dialogue with a large number of individuals, some of them brahmins, some of them ascetics with theories of their own, or their followers. The Buddha always listens to the other man's point of view and then responds, often by cross-questioning, before expounding his own views. It is not common for him to respond simply with a flat contradiction. Sometimes he begins by talking as if he accepted what the other man has said, but then steers his exposition round to give a quite different meaning to what has been said. Often he goes to great lengths to change the meanings to key words. For example, everyone knew that brahmin was a hereditary status. Giving a false etymology of the word, the Buddha said that a true brahmin was somebody who had banished evil. This is much like saying in English that being a gentleman is not a matter of birth but of conduct.

Since the reinterpretation of being a brahmin is explicit in the text, everyone knows about it. But it is astonishing how few interpreters have noticed the extent to which the Buddha uses this tactic. A crucial move, for example, was his redefinition of *kamma*, which means "action" and referred in particular to ritual action, to mean intention—which indeed is the very opposite of action.[8] Moreover, as the wordplay with *brāhmaṇa* shows,[9] the Buddha liked to move from the literal to the metaphorical, and used both irony and wit.

Johannes Bronkhorst has done valuable work in showing how the Buddha argued with the Jains.[10] It is all the more disappointing that in his recent summary of the Buddha's teaching he should write: "It is not impossible that the Buddha was familiar with the content of some *Upaniṣads* or parts thereof, and with other Vedic texts."[11] Whereas in the Jain case we can clearly see the Buddha's reaction to ideas, but cannot trace quotations from their texts, because their textual tradition is comparatively deficient and very few, if any, texts go back to the time of the Buddha, we can actually trace passages in the *Upaniṣads*, especially the *Bṛhadāranyaka*, to the which the Buddha was alluding.

Over the last decade I have produced several publications drawing attention to such references, and I hope to continue the series. However, the most startling discovery in this respect is not mine. At the conference of the International Association of Buddhist Studies held in Lausanne in August 1999, Dr. Joanna Jurewicz of the University of Warsaw showed that the formulation of the *pratītyasamutpāda*, the Buddha's chain of dependent origination, is as it is because it represents the Buddha's answer to Vedic cosmogony, and indeed to the fundamental ontology of brahminical thought.

Let me be clear about the nature of this fundamental discovery. The chain of dependent origination has to be understood on two levels, the general and the particular. At the general level, it embodies the Buddhist claim that nothing exists without a cause and that indeed there are no "things" existing in total isolation from other "things"; there are only causal processes. As Prof. Paul Williams once put it to me, for Buddhism there are no nouns, only verbs. Over the centuries Buddhists came to regard the Buddha's teaching as "the middle way" in this sense: that he proclaimed neither the existence of things in their own right, which we would now call essentialism, nor some kind of nihilism, but that the world of our experience is a world of flux and process. This process is also a middle way in that it is neither random nor rigidly determined, for it leaves room for free will. This "middleness" gave its name to the school of philosophy founded by Nāgārjuna, *Madhyamaka.*

On the other hand, the particular interpretation of the chain of dependent origination has been contested among Buddhists from the earliest days. There simply is no one agreed interpretation. Moreover, in the *locus classicus* for this doctrine, the *Mahā Nidāna Sutta*, the text begins (*D* II, 55) with a unique feature. Ānanda happily tells the Buddha that he has understood the chain of dependent origination, and the Buddha reprimands him, saying that it is extremely difficult to understand. The Buddha normally is shown in texts as doing his very best to make himself clear, and I know of no parallel to his statement here that this teaching of his is profound and difficult to understand. I interpret it to mean that those who first formulated the text and recorded the teaching did not understand it themselves.

It is not surprising that this obscure teaching appears in several variant forms. In the commonest form, however, the chain has twelve links, and it is this form that Dr. Jurewicz has explained. That there are other forms seems to me to be no argument against her interpretation. The part of the chain which has caused the most difficulty is the first four links: ignorance conditions volitional impulses, which condition consciousness, which condition name and form (which she shows to refer to individuation). Since she has given a convincing interpretation of why these terms are used, they must have been there in the original teaching.

Since Dr. Jurewicz's article has been published,[12] I shall not here attempt to reproduce her very rich argument, but only to give its gist. The Buddha chose to express himself in these terms, she said, because he was responding to Vedic cosmogony as represented particularly in the famous "Hymn of Creation", *Ṛg Veda* X, 129, and in the first chapter of the *Bṛhadāranyaka Upaniṣad*, but also in the *Śatapatha Brāhmaṇa* and other *Upaniṣads*. In this cosmogony a close correspondence, amounting originally even to an identity, between the microcosm and the macrocosm is assumed. At first there is nothing, not even the distinction between existence and non-existence, for there is no consciousness which could be aware of existence. Then somehow—it cannot be explained—a volitional impulse initiates the process of creation or evolution. The first result is pure consciousness. Initially is consciousness alone, not consciousness *of* anything. Then it cognises itself. From this reflexivity, in which there is still only one entity, develops an awareness of subject and object, and then this in turn leads to further individuation, until we reach the multiplicity of our experience: individuation both by name, in linguistic category, and by appearance, perceptible to the senses.

The first four terms of the Buddha's chain correspond to this process, and the rest of his chain carries it through further, still in line with Vedic ideas. However, the end of the chain—decay, death, grief and lamentation—is a climax which turns round and subverts all that has gone before. For Vedic thought, the Absolute which cognises itself and so generates the world is the *ātman*, which is at the same time the self of every sentient being. Let me quote Jurewicz:

> The Buddha preached at least some of his sermons to educated people, well versed in Brāhmaṇic thought, who were familiar with the concepts and the general idea of the Vedic cosmogony. To them, all the terms used in the *pratītyasamutpāda* had a definite meaning and they evoked definite associations. Let us imagine the Buddha enumerating all the stages of the Vedic cosmogony only to conclude: 'That's right, this is how the whole process develops. However, the only problem is that no one undergoes a transformation here!' From the didactic point of view, it was a brilliant strategy. The act of cutting off the *ātman* ... deprives the Vedic cosmogony of its positive meaning as the successful activity of the Absolute and

> presents it as a chain of absurd, meaningless changes which could only result in the repeated death of anyone who would reproduce this cosmogonic process in ritual activity and everyday life.[13]

Usually when a new interpretation of a famous text is proposed, one does well to pose the sceptical question: "Why did nobody notice this before?" One of the beauties of Jurewicz's discovery is that the answer to this question is simple and obvious: at a very early stage the Buddhist tradition lost sight of the texts and doctrines to which the Buddha was responding. And, I might add, irony does not weather well.

Note also that this interpretation of dependent origination does not subvert the Buddhist tradition or run counter to traditional Buddhist ideas. On the contrary, it enriches them, giving precise meaning to what was previously obscure by adding substance and detail to the Buddha's "no soul" doctrine. Moreover, it is a powerful example of the Buddha's famous "skill in means", a term which originally referred precisely to his skill in adapting his presentation to his audience.

To me this gives two strong reasons for being "obsessed with origins". Firstly, we acquire more understanding of someone who must have had one of the most brilliant and interesting minds in the whole of human history. If it is élitist to be more interested in his thought than in the thought of any person the anthropologist meets in the street, or even in the local monastery, I am happy to be an élitist.[14] Secondly, by seeing how original meanings have been lost and changed, we are able to give Buddhism a history—and thus incidentally to corroborate the Buddha's claim that all compounded things are impermanent. I think Godwin would have liked it.

Notes

1. Martin Southwold, *Buddhism in Life* (Manchester: Manchester University Press, 1983): 113.
2. Ibid., 126.
3. Ibid., 113-4.
4. Harry Falk, *Schrift im alten Indien* (Tübingen: Narr, 1993).
5. R.F. Gombrich, "How the Mahāyāna Began", *The Buddhist Forum* I, ed. T. Skorupski (London: SOAS, 1990): 21-30.
6. R.F. Gombrich, "The History of Early Buddhism: Major Advances Since 1950", *Indological Studies and South Asia Bibliography: A Conference 1986*, ed. A. Das (Calcutta: National Library Calcutta, 1988): 12-30. (See p.17).
7. R.F. Gombrich, "Dating the Buddha: A Red Herring Revealed," *The Dating of the Historical Buddha* (Die Datierung des Historischen Buddha) pt. 2, *Symposien zur Buddhismusforschung*, IV, 2, ed. Heinz Bechert (Göttingen: Vandenhoeck & Ruprecht, 1992): 237-259.
8. R.F. Gombrich, *Theravāda Buddhism: A Social History from Ancient Benares to Modern Colombo* (London: Routledge and Kegan Paul, 1988): 66-69.
9. In fact the Buddha punned on a Prakrit form of the word, *bāhaṇa*.
10. See especially Johannes Bronkhorst, "The Buddha and the Jains Reconsidered", *Asiatische Studien* XLIX, 2, (1995): 333-350.
11. Heinz Bechert, et al., *Der Buddhismus I: Der indische Buddhismus und seine Verzweigungen* (Stuttgart. Kohlhammer, 2000): 47.
12. J. Jurewicz, "Playing with Fire: The Pratītyasamutpāda from the Perspective of Vedic Thought". *Journal of the Pāli Text Society* XXVI (2000): 77-103.
13. Ibid., 100-101.
14. See Southwold, *Buddhism in Life*, 115-6.

The Death of the Buddha:

A Restorative Interpretation

Gananath Obeyesesekere

One can speak of the "the death of the Buddha" in at least two senses. First, on the model of "the death of God" made famous by that great anti-Christ and herald of our modernity, Freidrich Nietzsche. Nietzsche's main point is that for the late 19th century in which he lived, the idea of god had lost its personal meaning and cultural significance irrespective of whether or not people actually continued to "believe" in him. So is it with contemporary Buddhism. It is not the loss of belief that is at issue but the decline of what I like to think of as the "spirit" of the doctrinal tradition: its values of compassion and kindness, its universalistic vision that obliterates social distinctions, its tolerance which even extends to "false beliefs," its good humor and its unique meditative *askesis* which can embrace in its vision all living creatures caught in the net of *saṃsāra*. To me Godwin Samararatne represents in his life and work that spirit of Buddhism, proving that the values enshrined in them have not totally died out though they are being increasingly swamped by the passionate and sometimes violent nationalism that has identified Buddhism with the religion of an imagined Sinhala nation-state. Though such disturbing forms of nationalism have been the fate of our times, I want to speak of the death of the Buddha in the second sense: that pertaining to the textual traditions of Buddhism that have been rationalized and literalized by European scholarship and now accepted as "truth" by native intellectuals. In this sense also Nietzsche has noted with great insight:

> For this is how religions usually die out: namely, when the mythical presuppositions of a religion are systematized as a finished sum of historical events under the strict rational eye of dogmatic conviction and when one begins to mount an anxious defence of their credulity, when therefore the feeling for myth dies out and is replaced by religion's claim to historical foundations.[1]

Let me look at the death of the Buddha as recorded in the great *Mahāparinibbāna Sutta* as a counter-response to those European scholars who, spurred by the spirit of *their* Enlightenment, have seen Buddhism through a "Euro-rational" lens that in turn tended to downplay the "feeling for myth." This is not to deny the powerful "rational imperative" that underlies Buddhist thought but to make the case that Buddhist doctrinal rationality ought to be counterposed with, or framed within, the feeling for myth that Nietzsche spoke about.[2] And while such a feeling is found in many places in the Buddhist texts, they appear most conspicuously in the manner of the hero's birth and death. Many scholars have noted the mythic significance of the former but have seen the death as an empirical event that actually occurred in history, rather than a parable or an event of a symbolical order that occurred in the *construction* of Buddhist history.

It does seem, on the face of it, that the death of the Buddha as recorded in the *Mahāparinibbāna Sutta* is an actual or empirically true event. The text clearly says that he grew old; that he ate a meal of soft, perhaps even stale, pork (or maybe mushrooms) given by Cunda, a blacksmith; that he had a severe indigestion compounded by diarrhea; and that he died soon after. This sounds real—it could happen to anyone. Here therefore, it is implied, there is a trace of the empirical Buddha that other texts try to hide. A minor problem pertains to the exact translation of the Pāli phrase *sūkara maddava*, "the soft flesh of the pig." A few modern day European translators have found the idea somewhat repugnant and, following some commentarial traditions in both Theravāda and Mahāyāna, have suggested that the Buddha died by eating mushrooms in a place trodden by pigs.[3] Rhys Davids, the great translator of Theravāda texts, following Neumann's example, thought that even mushrooms from a pig-trodden place was a rather distasteful way for the Buddha to die and in his translation of the *Mahāparinibbāna Sutta* he used the word "truffles" which, for the European consciousness, is surely the more civilized way of terminating one's existence.[4] And for modern bourgeois Buddhists directly or indirectly nurtured in European translations of their sacred texts, and also influenced by the new Hindu gurus in their midst, it is inconceivable that the Buddha, a pure Being and the epitome of non-violence, should die by eating pork, a substance whose foulness is further compounded by the fact that it is considered loathsome by the Muslim citizens in their midst. Therefore it had to be mushrooms; truffles they were not acquainted with. Yet it is the case that virtually every Theravāda Buddhist commentator of old, including those given to an idealistic view of the Buddha, have insisted on the minimal interpretation of *sūkara maddava* as "pork." So did ordinary people in Theravāda societies, such as Bishop Bigandet's monk informants in Burma and mine among Sri Lankan villagers—at least till recently.[5]

Both the intellectualist and the contemporary bourgeois interpretations of the death of the Buddha have to be taken seriously; they too are part of a historical debate on the nature of the Buddha. I shall deal with the nature of this debate later on but, for the moment, I want to defend the idea that the Buddha died by eating stale pork through a symbolic analysis of that event combined with an ethical stand that I think is consonant with the spirit of Theravāda Buddhism. I suggest that the manner in which the Buddha died has little to do with the empirical Buddha of modern Buddhists. It may well have been that the real or empirical Buddha died of eating pork (or mushrooms for that matter) but what is important is the preservation of this event in Buddhist memory. Historical or cultural memory preserves experiences that are significant to its own tradition and is not too different from individual memory in this regard. Moreover, it is certainly possible that empirically real events could simultaneously be symbolically real ones also. Consequently one must consider seriously the significance of Buddhist memory in *wanting* to preserve this tradition of his death, even though, I shall show later, it ended up as a truncated memory in the Buddhist commentarial tradition along with the countervailing tendency exacerbated in modern times of the Buddha dying, in Brahmanic fashion, by eating a vegetarian meal. And most importantly I want to suggest that the Buddha dying—irrespective of whether he ate pork or mushrooms—cannot be considered apart from the *mythic* persona of the Buddha as he is depicted in Buddhist texts.

THE BIRTH

The references to the miraculous birth of the Buddha are well known among ordinary folk in Buddhist societies and are depicted in a multitude of "texts" such as temple frescoes, popular and classic literatures and in songs sung in village healing rituals. I shall refer only to a few ancient texts of the Pāli Canon to give the reader a feel for the material. In the *Acchariyābbhutādhamma Sutta* ("The Discourse on Wonderful and Marvellous Qualities") the Buddha asks Ānanda, his personal attendant, cousin (father's brother's son) and favorite disciple, to relate to the assembled monks the miracle of the Buddha's birth.[6] According to Ānanda, the Buddha-to-be was born in the Tusita heaven, and, after his life span there was over, he decided to be reborn in the human world, "mindful and clearly conscious." He entered the Mother's womb, mindful and clearly conscious, and when this happened the earth itself trembled "and there appeared the illimitable glorious radiance surpassing even the *deva*-majesty of *deva*s."[7] As he entered the womb, four gods guarded the four quarters to prevent any human or non-human from annoying the Buddha-to-be or his mother. More miracles: The mother saw the Buddha-to-be in her womb as an emerald jewel, and the child was "complete in all his limbs, his sense organs perfect."[8] Moreover, as the Buddha is born "he issues quite stainless, undefiled by watery matter, undefiled by mucus, undefiled by blood, undefiled by any impurity ... ."[9] He is "pure and stainless" owing to the purity of both mother and son.[10] The text lists other miracles also, and mentions the fact that the Bodhisattva's mother dies seven days after he is born.[11] The *Mahāpadāna Sutta* makes it clear that all Buddhas, past and future, have the identical life history and all mothers of all Buddhas must die seven days after the birth of the Redeemer.

Clearly then, conception did not occur through sexual intercourse; moreover though Māyā, the mother of the Buddha, could not be converted into a virgin in the historical traditions of Buddhism, she does avoid sexual relations at the time of conception; and she conceives the Buddha when she was observing celibacy (i.e., the ten precepts on *uposatha* days one of which enjoins celibacy or *brahmacariya)*. Yet what about the necessity for the mother to die in seven days? Some Theravāda commentators say that this is to preserve the purity of the mother "because no other child is fit to be conceived in the same womb as a Buddha."[12] The most interesting answer is given in the *Mahāvastu*, the famous text of the Lokottaravādins or Transcendentalists, which says that it is due to sexual rather than childbirth pollution. "'I will descend', says he [the Bodhisattva], 'into the womb of a woman who has only seven nights and ten months of her life remaining.' And why so? 'Because', says he, 'it is not fitting that she who bears a Peerless One like me should afterwards indulge in love.'"[13]

In which place was the Bodhisattva born? Most popular and doctrinal texts agree that he was born in a grove of *sala* trees in Lumbini. Let me present one well known version. The queen, Mahāmāyā, informs Suddhodana, her husband, of her desire to visit her parents' home at Devadaha to give birth to her child—a perfectly normal custom in both India and other patrilineal societies.[14] Suddhodana consents, decorates the road between Kapilavastu, his capital, and Devadaha with plantain trees, pots full of water, and banners and streamers. "Now between the two towns there is a pleasure grove of Sala-Trees, called the Lumbini Park, belonging to the citizens of both towns. At that time all the trees were one mass of blossoming flowers from the root to the topmost branches. In between the branches and the flowers swarms of bees of five varieties and flocks of birds of many species moved about warbling in sweet tones."[15] The Bodhisattva is born in a liminal space, neither in the home of the mother nor of the father but in between, in a space that belonged to the citizens of both towns. The implication is clear enough: the hero does not belong to his father or mother but to the people or the world in general. The *sala* trees under which he was born are not the trees found in Indian forests but a mythic *sala* blooming from the root to the topmost branches. As he is born the infant Bodhisattva takes seven steps and from each step a lotus flower blooms, presumably to prevent dust from touching his feet; he also surveys *the four quarters of the world,* the locus of his transcendental and universal teaching.

THE DEATH

The *Mahāparinibbāna Sutta* is a long text and I shall only consider those sections relevant to my theme. I will begin with the arrival of the Buddha at Vesali or Vaiśali, the country of the Liccavis. He stays in the grove of Ambapālī, "mango-keeper," the courtesan of Vaiśali. Ambapālī visits the Buddha and the latter agrees to go to her house with his brethren for the morning meal. The citizens of Vaiśali try to bribe Ambapālī with a huge sum of money to give *them* the opportunity of offering alms to the Buddha, but she refuses. The life story of Ambapālī is not irrelevant to the present story: she was born spontaneously and found at the foot of a mango tree in the king's orchard. She was so beautiful that princes fought among themselves to possess her. To solve the problem of strife they all agreed to appoint her as the official courtesan of Vaiśali available to them all. She is highly regarded; yet also a bought woman.

After eating a meal of "sweet rice and cakes" at Ambapālī's, the Buddha asks some of his disciples to stay in Vaiśali for the rain-retreat (*vassa* or the rainy season) while he goes to Beluva, a village nearby with Ānanda, his attendant, and some other monks. The rainy season when monks cease their wanderings and stay in one place, often preaching, also brings the tropical monsoon, the harbinger of disease. "But when the Blessed One had entered upon the rainy season, there rose in him a severe illness, and sharp and deadly pains came upon him. And the Blessed One endured them mindfully, clearly comprehending and unperturbed."[16] But because he did not want to die without taking leave of the monk community, he thought: "Let me suppress this illness by strength of will, resolve to maintain the life process, and live on."[17] Ānanda, his faithful attendant, is anxious that the Buddha leave instructions as to the future of the order, and the Buddha gently chides him. "What more does the community of *bhikkhus* expect of me, Ānanda. I have set forth the *dhamma* without making any distinction of esoteric and exoteric doctrine; there is nothing, Ānanda, with regard to the teachings that the Tathāgata [Buddha] holds to the last with the closed fist of a teacher who keeps some things back."[18] He tells Ānanda that there is no need to have the truth dependent on any person, and then, in a key sentence, refers to his own frail condition. "Now I am frail, Ānanda, old, aged, far gone in years. This is my eightieth year, and my life is spent. Even as an old cart, Ānanda, is held together with much difficulty, so the body of the Tathāgata is kept going only with supports."[19] And then he makes the well-known statement that crystalizes the Buddhist quest: "Therefore, Ānanda, be lamps unto yourselves, refuges unto yourselves, seeking no external refuge; with the *dhamma* as your lamp, the *dhamma* as your refuge, seeking no other refuge."[20]

The scene now shifts to Vaiśali where, having robed himself, the Buddha goes on his begging rounds early in the morning. He comes back, and after eating his meal of rice, talks to Ānanda nostalgically about the beauty of the city and its delightful sites (for meditation). He senses that Ānanda is distressed by the prospect of his impending death and so he tells Ānanda: "Whosoever, Ānanda, has developed, practised, employed, strengthened, maintained, scrutinized and brought to perfection the four constituents of psychic power [*iddhi*] could, if he so desired, remain throughout a world-period [*kappa, kalpa*] or until the end of it."[21] With this episode we have one of the most obscure problems in the *Mahāparinibbāna Sutta*. The text implies that Ānanda missed the hint the Buddha gave, namely, he *could have really gone on to live for an aeon (kappa)* if only Ānanda had asked. But Ānanda was incapable of comprehending what the Buddha meant because his mind was possessed by Māra, the Malign One, Death himself. But more of this later.

If Ānanda failed to ask the Buddha to postpone his death till the end of the aeon, not so with Māra who soon afterwards insists that the Buddha die straightaway. He reminds the Buddha of a previous event when the Buddha, soon after his *bodhi* (Awakening), told Māra that he will die when the faith has been proclaimed to the world and the order of nuns and monks had been established. Now Māra tells the Buddha that all that is accomplished and it is time for him to die. The Buddha agrees; he does not fight with Māra on this occasion. "Do not trouble yourself, Malign One. Before long the *parinibbāna* of the Tathāgata will come about. Three months hence the Tathāgata will utterly pass away."[22] From this point onwards the Buddha converses with Ānanda at length on the signs attendant on the death of a Great Being, the Buddha included. But yet at the back of Ānanda's mind is the gnawing anxiety of the Buddha's impending death and now he implores him to postpone it for an aeon. But this is too late because the Buddha has already, very deliberately made a commitment to Māra to die within three months. But the Buddha consoles Ānanda with this profound Buddhist message. "Yet, Ānanda, have I not taught from the very beginning that with all that is dear and beloved there must be change, separation and severance? Of that which is arisen, come into being, is compounded, and subject to decay, how can one say: 'May it not come to dissolution!'" The Buddha says that his word has been given and he has no will to live longer and "that the Tathāgata should withdraw his words for the sake of living on is an impossibility."[23] He then adds the refrain that punctuates this text right along: "All component things are subject to decay. Therefore strive with earnestness."[24]

Since the Buddha knows that he is going to die in three months, the text could have ended in a variety of ways, for example, dying peacefully in bed! Instead the text tells us that the proximate cause of the Buddha's death was due to food poisoning and a severe indigestion after Cunda, the blacksmith, offers him some food. "And Cunda the metalworker, after the night had passed, had choice food, hard and soft, prepared in his abode, together with a quantity of *sūkara maddava,* and announced it to the Blessed One saying: "It is time, O Lord, the meal is ready."[25] The time has indeed arrived: Cunda was not aware of the irony of his utterance. This was the morning meal; before eating it the Buddha tells Cunda: "With the *sūkara maddava* you have prepared you may serve me; with the other food, hard and soft, you may serve the community of *bhikkhus*." He urged Cunda to bury the rest of the boar's meat, for no one else should and could eat it. The text continues: "And soon after the Blessed One had eaten the meal provided by Cunda, the metalworker, a dire sickness fell upon him, even dysentery, and he suffered sharp and deadly pains."[26] Even so he cautions his disciples not to blame Cunda, or cause remorse in him for having offered him the last meal. On the contrary, he should be told that his was an exemplary and meritorious act.

The text says that the Buddha suffered from severe diarrhea and dehydration and he tells Ānanda, "I am thirsty, Ānanda, and want to drink."[27] Undaunted by his illness the Buddha decided to go on his planned trip to Kusināra, there to die. But Kusināra is not quite the place for a great being to die! "Let it not be, Lord, that the Blessed One should pass away in this mean place, this uncivilized township in the midst of the jungle, a mere outpost of the province," insists the deluded Ānanda. More appropriate are the wealthier and nobler places such as Campā, Rājagaha, Sāvatthi, Sāketa, Kosambī and Benares.[28] But apparently the Buddha refused to agree with Ānanda and lay beside two *sala* trees, those very trees that witnessed his birth and, as then, blooming out of season, but now dropping flowers in homage over his dead body. His last words were: "Behold now, *bhikkhus*, I exhort you: 'Transient are all the elements of being! Strive with earnestness.'"[29]

As in all Buddhist traditions, this text reveals the decay, impermanence and imperfectability of the world and those in it. For me this aspect of the Buddha's dying has a profound meaning. Ānanda, the faithful disciple, is troubled by the Buddha's impending death, and the Buddha sensing his anxiety tells him that he could live for an aeon if he wishes to. Ānanda, rightly I think, does not urge him to do so. When finally he urges the Buddha to postpone his death he does so out of devotion to the Buddha. Ānanda, precisely because of his attachment, is blind to the truth and misses the irony of the Buddha's statement and its deeper significance: that is, the Buddha, like any other conditioned being, must perish, and by dying now, at eighty, he was affirming his ordinary mortality and human frailty. A further irony: the Buddha sides with Māra by agreeing to die! Even when Ānanda belatedly asks the Buddha to postpone his death, he does not recognize that his request is merely a *postponement*, because the Buddha is not an immortal god (and indeed no immortal gods can exist in Buddhism). By dying now, and yielding at last to Māra, he is denying any semblance of divinity and affirming his mortality and his identity with human beings and all of sentient existence. Ānanda is the one monk among the Buddha's elders who hasn't achieved *nibbāna* to become an *arahant*. He constantly misses the significance of the refrain: all conditioned things must decay and perish, or he only knows it intellectually and nominally. He represents an ordinary and touching devotion of the sort that existed throughout in the history of Buddhism, including the devotion of modern bourgeois Buddhists. Deep down Ānanda does not recognize that separation from loved ones, decay and dying, and transitoriness apply both to ourselves and the world and not even the Buddha is exempt from them. Hence the powerful metaphor of the old cart that needs constant repairs to keep it going.

The immediate cause of the Buddha's death is the stale food given by Cunda, the smith. Here again let me present an exegesis that makes sense in terms of the spirit of Buddhism and for the times we now live in. To convert stale pork into mushrooms is to miss the profoundly symbolic nature of the Buddha's dying. This act of accepting alms from Cunda reverberates into previous actions of the Buddha and leads us into the symbolic significance of the alms round. Begging from one and all by the Buddha and other mendicant monks of the time must be seen in relation to the prevailing Brahmanic ideology of that period.[30] According to Brahmanic norms commensality is with one's own caste fellows and to eat food of a lower-caste member results in pollution which in turn requires elaborate ritual procedures to restore one's normal ritual status. The Buddha and other wandering mendicants, in begging for alms from all and sundry, are symbolically proclaiming a public message: they are deliberately courting pollution and affirming our universal species-being and the irrelevance of caste for salvation. For anyone brought up in

South Asia would know that Cunda, the blacksmith, is the sinful maker of weapons of destruction, and belongs to a low caste; he is a *śūdra*. Once we recognize Cunda's symbolic action in this text, we can also see the significance of the previous act of eating—not from the nobles of Vaiśali, but from their courtesan, Ambapālī, the mango lady. But note that *amba* also means "woman." Like Marion Bloom in Joyce's *Ulysses*, she is one version of the universal female. She is the bought woman and, like Cunda, she is tainted. Yet, unlike Cunda, she is beautiful and highly regarded by the citizens of Vaiśali. She sells her body but she refuses to sell her right to give alms to the Buddha and his disciples. The Buddha eating from her is also a symbolic act, but it is not the act that leads to his dying. This must come from one lower still; and equally significant is the final place of lowly dying in the wattle and daub town of Kusināra.

Now it is easy to see the significance of the consumption of the last meal. The pig, needless to say, is the filthiest of all creatures (at least for South Asians), and what is more polluting than stale pork? No wonder pious devotees, then and now, want to convert it into mushrooms; but surely, as the Buddha said of Ānanda, they are blind and possessed by Māra! The meal from Cunda has as profound a significance for Buddhism (or once had) as the last supper of Christ for Christianity, even though their soteriological meanings are different. Here was the Buddha deliberately eating polluted food given by one of the low. The text tells us that the Buddha knew through his superior insight that the food was tainted even though it was dressed up, like the body beautiful itself. He therefore urged Cunda not to serve it to the other monks and to bury it afterwards. That which is offered by the layperson with devotion cannot be refused, even if it causes one's own death. But more than this: the Buddha, by deliberately eating polluted food from a low caste person and then dying in an ignominous place, annuls through his lowly death the symbolic meaning of his glorious birth.

BLAMING ĀNANDA: A DEBATE ON THE BUDDHA-NATURE

I now want to refer to an extraordinary interlude in the *Mahāparinibbāna Sutta,* sandwiched between the textual segments dealing with the Buddha's knowledge of his impending death and the Cunda episode. In this interlude, poor Ānanda, distressed by the approaching death of the Buddha quite reasonably urges the sick Buddha not to attain final release till he has made a statement about the order. Thereupon, as we have seen, the Buddha makes the very significant statement insisting that the order does not need him, that he has never withheld any information with a closed fist, that his body has already decayed like a worn out cart, and that the monks themselves should live like islands or lights unto themselves with no external refuge except the *dhamma*.

At this point the "second recitation" ends and there is a break in the text. The third recitation is a movement away from the human nature of the Buddha to the superhuman. In it the Buddha comes to the Capala shrine and there informs Ānanda that because of his supernormal powers he could postpone his death for a whole aeon or *kappa/kalpa* but poor Ānanda does not take the hint. This seems perfectly sensible on Ānanda's part because he is still influenced by the Buddha's very human and humane voice of the preceding recitation. But now the Buddha takes on another voice through the agency of an interlocutor (who in this text is appropriately anonymous.) Here the deluded Ānanda takes the hint at last and asks the Buddha to delay his death by an aeon for hadn't the Buddha himself proclaimed his capacity to do so? Now we have the Buddha's (uncharacteristic) reply in Rhys Davids' aptly terrible Victorian prose: "Then, O Ānanda, thine is the fault, thine is the offence—in that when a suggestion so evident and hint so clear were thus given thee by the Tathāgata, thou wast yet incapable of comprehending them, and thou besoughtest not the Tathāgata, saying: 'Vouchsafe, lord, to remain during the aeon for the good and the happiness of the great multitudes, out of pity for the world, for the good and the gain and the weal of gods and men.' If thou shouldst then have so besought the Tathāgata, the Tathāgata might have rejected the appeal even to the second time, but the third time he would have granted it. Thine, therefore, O Ānanda, is the fault, thine is the offence."[31] Not satisfied with this onslaught on Ānanda, the Buddha repeats the phrase "thine is the fault, thine is the offence" four times, each time reminding Ānanda of an occasion when he should have asked the Buddha to postpone his death; for surely on the third appeal he would in fact have agreed! In effect these repetitions nullify the existential significance of recitations one and two and also recitation four on Cunda, all dealing with conditionality, impermanence and the picture of the aging Buddha waiting for his body, the old cart, to come to a halt. No wonder Rhys Davids was puzzled and says that these statements "seem to be in marked contrast, if not in absolute contradiction," to the two previous recitations (or sections of the text).[32]

The British Buddhist Maurice Walshe, the most recent translator of our text, attempts to resolve the problem by rendering *kappa* or *kalpa* as "century," the full life-span of a person in the Buddha's time and some commentarial traditions apparently agree with him.[33] In Walshe's rendering the Buddha would simply have added twenty years to his life because he was being pestered by Ānanda. This translation makes the Buddha all too human, fitting nicely with the orientation of contemporary British Buddhists. But to achieve this Walshe has to give a dubious translation of *kappa/kalpa.* Moreover, his simplistic solution cannot account for the Buddha's uncharacteristically harsh chastisement of his favorite disciple, Ānanda. One therefore needs to take the text as it is and try to explain its perversity differently by positing the idea of "debate," that is, the contentious discourses that erupt in history and is responsible for this and other textual perversities.

Texts, one might say, contain precipitates of debates that have often enough occurred within a specific tradition and in the Buddhist dialogues they are filtered through the "fictional persona" of the "strategic interlocutor," sometimes an anonymous person, sometimes a known monk, often Ānanda, preeminently the custodian of Buddhist memory.[34] Hence these texts are prefaced by the phrase: "Thus have I heard." It therefore seems that the early debates among monks and layfolk about Buddhist knowledge and supernormal powers (as well as other kinds of information) could enter into the discourses of the Buddha by penetrating these guardians of Buddhist memory, themselves *dramatis personae* in deliberately constructed texts.

Debates are what primarily accounts for the "contradictions" that occur within a single text or between related texts. For example, there are texts like *Vāseṭṭha Sutta* that present a critique of caste (*varṇa*) and affirm species equality; yet, other texts, in debates with Brahmin status claims, affirm the superiority of the Buddha's own caste. This means that the first set of texts is in harmony with the spirit of Buddhism while the second is much more parochial. At other times a single text stratifies multiple debates and this is best exemplified in the *Mahāparinibbāna Sutta*. Because this text deals with a critical event, it is one which must have provoked arguments on the Buddha persona and the nature of his death among monks and layfolk and some of these debates are incorporated into the text itself. The text nevertheless constitutes an overall narrative unity even though each diacritical segment or recitation maintains its own integrity, permitting the scholar to speculate on its genealogy.

The episode blaming Ānanda is a response precipitated by the Buddha's previous ironic claim that he could live to the end of an aeon by virtue of his supernormal powers cultivated through meditation. It is provoked by the question: if the Buddha possessed the supernormal powers of an *arahant* why did he not postpone his death for the good of the world?

And surely this question itself must have been provoked by contentious arguments on this theme (and related ones) by Buddhism's opponents. A restorative interpretation must therefore place the "interpolation" within the context of debate and reaffirm the existential relevance of the textual segments that preceded and succeeded it. The preceding argument suggests that Buddhist memory is not only the memory of those who have "heard" the Buddha-word but also those who have had to listen to other significant voices of the time and strategically incorporate them into the body of a text, as examples of the voice of the Buddha.[35] The several voices that constitute the text—the idea of supernormal powers, the idealization of the Buddha, doceticism, the marks and features of the world conqueror—do not exist independently of each other but are connected through an associative chain of interrelated meanings or signifieds.

PORK, MUSHROOMS, TRUFFLES AND OTHER DELICACIES

My interpretation of the life and death of the Buddha poses some questions about the nature of interpretation itself. In an "explanation" one is, however qualifiedly, engaged in the discovery of a truth. So is it with any *theoretical* interpretation; one cannot legitimately say that one's theory is false; one might say that one thinks it is true and that one is not sure, but this tentativeness only implies that a truth (of whatever sort) is what ideally should be aimed at. By contrast, the kind of interpretation advanced here is inherently unstable, since it cannot yield a truth; it properly belongs to the domain of hermeneutics. In it I, as the exegete, take a particular position in relation to a text and try to "understand" (*Verstehen*) it, perhaps in the Diltheyan sense. In this instance I am attempting to understand the death of the Buddha or elements thereof in a special kind of way by carrying my own peculiar debate with others in the Buddhist tradition, sometimes with native thinkers, sometimes with those Indologists who present a

Euro-rational interpretation of Buddhism. The latter are, I think, bringing Buddhism within the frame and understanding of their own philosophical traditions. The question of truth is not germane to this issue either; these scholars are in reality presenting their own vision of Buddhism, as other schools of Buddhism did before them. Their mistake however is to imagine that they are presenting the true version when in fact all they are doing is presenting another one. Their truth claims are strictly analogous to the truth claims of the various schools of Buddhism. In dislodging the rationalist view of Buddhism I am not creating a truer Buddhism but rather one that I take is more consonant with the spirit of the Theravāda tradition and with our contemporary intellectual situation where we are beginning to question simplistic views of rationality. In this specific case I have presented an alternative reading of the Buddha myth, treating it as a myth *per se*, and possessing a symbologic of its own. Early Buddhist intellectuals probably advanced interpretations similar to mine but they are not extant in Theravāda commentarial works. I shall show, however, that they did argue about the details of the myth that seem to violate what they felt were central to their view of Buddhist soteriology.

I said earlier that Theravāda Buddhists had few arguments about the Buddha myth as a totality but they did argue whether the Buddha died of eating pork or mushrooms and, indeed, what kind of pork or mushrooms. Arthur Waley, in the article mentioned earlier, shows that the Chinese Buddhists as early as the beginning of the fifth century simply translated *sūkara maddava* as "mushrooms" and, in some instances, as a specially pure mushroom growing from a sandalwood tree. What is striking about this interpretation is that the pig is not a filthy animal for the Chinese! In the Chinese case I think that purity as an ethical value comes to the fore. How could the apostle of non-violence die of eating meat? That too is a "true interpretation" from Mahāyānist soteriological perspectives, because their texts emphasize the docetic and transcendental nature of the Buddha and many enjoin vegetarianism. In which case there is no discontinuity between the birth and the death, *both of which are pure.*

Unlike Mahāyāna, the interpretation of "pig's flesh" has been a problematic one for Theravāda and has produced a debate in that great tradition that is inherently unresolvable, because the position one takes is predetermined by one's conception of the Buddha nature. Ordinary villagers in Sri Lanka had no problem with the Buddha dying of eating pork, and even if they do not want to follow the anthropologist's interpretation of "soft" as "stale," they might, I think, be quite willing to recognize it as an impure substance. But the moment you deal with urban and educated bourgeois Buddhists, whether influenced by Rhys Davids or Sai Baba, pork is rejected for mushrooms. But this too is a "true" interpretation that suits the present mentality of the bourgeoisie. And it is clear that it was part of an old debate because the commentaries have had a field day weaving meanings around the term *sūkara maddava,* without radically moving from the core meaning of "pig." Thus we have: pig's flesh made soft and oily; plants sprouting from a pig-trodden place; a flavoring substance made of pig's flesh; wild boar meat from the market; the soft flesh of the same animal; the flesh of a single supreme pig or a prize pig, and so on.[36] What then is going on in these commentaries? Because the tradition is strong that the Buddha died of eating pig's flesh, there emerge a variety of debates that try to deny that the pork was stale (soft). Thus, on the one hand the pig gets converted into a prize pig that is nice and juicy (soft); on the other it becomes a kind of flavoring of the sort that nowadays people put into their curries. The commentaries in typical scholastic fashion, very much like 19th century European philologists, have become obsessed with the meaning and etymology of the word, and have forgotten or ignored the context in which that word appears. What I have done is to practice another kind of language game that *restores* the context, both the immediate one and the larger setting. The immediate context is that of the frail Buddha—a worn out cart— dying of eating stale pork from a *śūdra* blacksmith. In all Buddhist commentaries, as with the European Indologists' "truffles," this crucial figure is totally ignored or barely recognized. Also ignored is the ironic statement of the Buddha that no one should eat Cunda's offering of meat but the Buddha himself and that the leftovers should be thrown away and not given to the other monks. Soon after, the text tells us, the Buddha had severe diarrhea and deadly pains and then he dies.[37]

In Buddhist texts, foods are classed as "hard" and "soft" and a good meal to the Buddha should contain both types. Thus certain kinds of meat are "soft," that is they are tender and juicy and they do not cause diarrhea! The term "soft" in the last meal of the Buddha has therefore a double meaning; it looks soft but it is the softness of stale meat. The irony and the significance of the immediate context is what pious commentators have wanted to miss. They have also missed the larger context inextricably associated with Buddhist devaluations of caste, of purity-pollution and so forth in respect of its soteriological goals. Yet, having made this interpretation I am assailed by a slight doubt, a Buddhist *angst* as it were, for in these kinds of hermeneutical situations where there are no true or false interpretations, the scholar-anthropologist, like his rationalist predecessors, both European and South Asian, is a participant in a larger historical debate in which there can be no real boundary between the interpretation of the myth and the myth of the interpretation.

DEATH AND DOCETICISM: THERAVĀDA AND MAHĀYĀNA

I have made a case for looking at the Buddha myth as a totality. In the pure birth and the impure death we have left the world of the empirically real to the mythically real. One cannot deduce the empirical Buddha by rationalizing or literalizing the myth; this is also true for Jesus Christ. This does not mean that there was no empirical Buddha; the Indic tradition is replete with gurus and founders of religious sects. But even when we consider contemporary living gurus like Sai Baba, we are struck by the fact that for most devotees he is a mythic figure, most importantly by the very fact that he is defined as an *avatār* or manifestation of God himself. If he is God, then his earthly body is but a mere physical form of a divine essence. This idea is naturally reinforced by the felt devotion of the believer, a process one could call "idealization."[56] A parallel term is "doceticism" from the Christian tradition which held that Christ's body was a purely insubstantial or illusory phenomenon, and, as a part of the Godhead, he was in fact a kind of essence manifesting in the outward cover of a human body. There were strongly idealistic movements in Theravāda that in turn were influenced by docetic movements in both Hinduism and Mahāyāna Buddhism. Theravāda did however resist doceticism. The thrust of the major Theravāda traditions is to say that the Buddha was born outside of bodily processes known as an *opapātika* birth. In my view there is not the slightest doubt that there was an existent empirical being who later became the Buddha; in some of the texts spoken by the Buddha the empirical person seems to emerge briefly before being overpowered by the myth-making process.[39]

While the extrapolation of the empirical Buddha from the myth is a futile one, I think it possible to depict the *processes* that lead to the transformation of the historical Buddha into the Buddha of myth. These historical processes are of no concern to Buddhism as a faith; only to us scholars of religion. This shift in the strategy of analysis means that our interpretation is no longer confined to filling the *lacunae* in texts but in depicting the historical "causes" that lead to the transformation. However, these historical causes cannot be defined as variables; rather, in the manner of Max Weber, they have to be contextualized in the socio-cultural context in which they are implicated. In this endeavor one can agree with the rationalist scholars that the mythologization of the Buddha was based on "myth models" that existed in Indic thought prior to and after the earliest period of Buddhism in the sixth/fifth century BCE. They came from Brahmanic Hinduism and from traditions of Buddhism that were more or less contemporaneous with that of Theravāda, combined of course, as always, with a devotional religiosity that felt itself impelled to idealize the Buddha in a specific direction set by prior cultural traditions.

Here then is the main issue: In Hinduism, and in South Asian religions generally, all major gods are born outside of human processes. The Buddhists also adapted these ideas in their notion of *opapātika* births. In South Asian thought a further problem arises, that of pollution and purity. Ordinary birth is from sexual intercourse, conception in the female womb, and issuing forth in blood and mucus, all of which are polluting. Thus a problem in South Asian thought in general: how is a god or goddess, who is by definition pure, conceived and born in the impure womb? The answer is clear: a pure deity cannot be born in the normal way and so you have the endless myths of Hinduism where the deities are born outside of ordinary bodily processes, unmediated by intercourse, and undefiled by the womb's impurities. By contrast, demons and inferior spirits are born out of blood and impurity and violence.[40]

Theravāda Buddhism in its continuing dialogue with competing religions had to elevate the Buddha into a Hindu type of divinity and at the same time, paradoxically, affirm the historicity of the Buddha and his human existence. The latter requires that the Buddha be born of human parents and this is true even of the Sarvāstivāda tradition of Buddhism.[41] Hence the Buddhist resolution of the paradox as to whether the Buddha was a Brahmanic type deity or not: the Buddha was born of human parents in his mother's womb, but in a unique, unordinary way and undefiled by impurity.

The Theravāda view of the Buddha then is the precipitate of debates with both Brahmanical Hinduism and with other competing religions. These debates in turn influence, and are influenced by, a devotional religiosity that could not tolerate the idea that the very epitome of non-violence should die of eating pork, stale or otherwise, served by a low caste maker of weapons. The Theravāda traditions preserve the content of some of these debates, but it is in traditions that were close to Mahāyāna that doceticism appears full-blown. Consider the *Mahāvastu* once again, which, according to some accounts, made a bridge between the early Theravāda and the later Mahāyāna.[42]

These Transcendentalists believed in the supramundane nature of the Buddha, a total denial of the reality of his physical nature, and viewed him as pure essence. This essence is always existent manifesting in the outer form of previous and future Buddhas. With the development of this idea, there is a point by point denial of normal processes of birth and conception, elaborated to an extreme degree, much more so than the Theravāda versions. Here too the Buddha is conceived in a miraculous manner when Māyā had abstained from sexual relations with her husband.[43] However, the originality of the *Mahāvastu* lies in its discussion of Buddha's human life as "mere conformity with the world." In fact it is wrong to say that he is born of parents, for this is simply an illusion. But then a question is asked of the narrator of the text: if this was the case, how did the Buddha have a son, Rāhula, by his wife, Yasodhara, and did he not have intercourse with her? The answer: Rāhula also came from the Tusita heaven and entered the womb of his mother which was also pure and undefiled![44]

The final section in the *Mahāvastu* dealing with the attributes of the Buddhas ends in a paean of triumphant exultation.

> The conduct of the Exalted One is transcendental, his root of virtue is transcendental. The Seer's walking, standing, sitting and lying down are transcendental. ... The Buddhas

> conform to the world's conditions, but in such a way that they also conform to the traits of transcendentalism. ... It is true that they wash their feet, but no dust ever adheres to them; their feet remain clean as lotus-leaves. This washing is mere conformity with the world. ... ... They keep their dark and glossy hair close cropped, although no razor ever cuts it. This is mere conformity with the world.... Although the Sugata's [Buddha's] corporeal existence is not due to the sexual union of parents, yet the Buddhas can point to their fathers and mothers. This is mere conformity with the world. From Dipaṅkara onwards, the Tathāgata [Buddha] has a son, Rāhula, to show. This is mere conformity with the world.[45]

It is then virtually certain that the myth of the birth was influenced by debates with docetic tendencies in forms of Hinduism and Mahāyāna Buddhism. Doceticism or idealization also influenced the way the Buddha was perceived in some of the commentarial traditions and even by major Buddhist thinkers. Thus the great Buddhist commentator, Buddhaghosa, denies that the body of the Buddha is subject to decay. The references to aging in the canon merely mention "one solitary wrinkle the size of a hair and was seen only by Ānanda, his personal attendant"—ignoring the references in the *Mahaparinibbāna Sutta* and other key texts to the physical decrepitude of the Buddha.[46] Yet the tradition was so strong that the Buddha died of eating pork that even Buddhaghosa has to admit this fact. It is this dilemma that lead commentators to substitute things like prize pigs and nice, soft meat for stale pork. I do think, however, that if the idealizing or docetic tendencies are carried to its logical conclusion, you will not only have an unaging Buddha but also one who could not possibly have died of eating a foul substance served by one of the lowest of the low. A similar motivation lies behind the modern Buddhist bourgeosie almost universally affirming the purity of his death.

Other affirmations of the physical perfection of the Buddha would have occurred in prior periods in Buddhist history. This is evident from a reading of a portion of an *abhidhamma* text, *Kathāvatthu* or "Points of Controversy" which, adopting a strict Theravāda position, argues against heretics who treat the Buddha as a transcendental being. It affirms the historical nature of the Buddha as one who lived and walked among people preaching his doctrine. The whole of Book XVIII of this text is entirely devoted to a critique of the docetic view of the Buddha, affirming that "the Master was undefiled, not by being out of the world, but by the corruptions of heart with respect to the things of the world."[47]

This text records instances of the actual places visited by the Buddha and criticizes the idea that because the Buddha had conquered passion he felt no pity for human beings. And then in a wonderfully sarcastic critique of docetism it refers to sects known as the *Andhaka*s and *Uttarapāthaka*s for whom even "the excreta of the Exalted Buddha excelled all other substances." If that were the case, says our text, the Buddha would have "fed on perfumes" rather than on rice gruel; and if that proposition was true people would have used the substance to perfume their bodies and would have made cosmetics of them and, having nicely packaged them, would have offered them for sale in the bazaar![48]

The affirmation of the Buddha's humanity was important for the early Theravāda tradition in spite of the powerful countervailing debates mentioned earlier. The Buddha of its texts expressed the notion of our common humanness in the phenomenon of decay and impermanence expressed in bodily ageing, decrepitude and the inevitability of dying. One of the commonest meditation texts is known as *asubha* or *pilikul bhāvanā*, "meditation on revulsiveness," which urges the meditator to reflect on the body's putrescence and decay, not for its own sake, but as reflective of the nature of the world itself.[49] In this sense the true meditator (who is the quintessential Buddhist) must confront pollution directly and overcome it. This attitude to pollution was institutionalized in customary behavior. For example, a menstruating woman cannot perform *pūjā*s for the gods (derived from Hinduism) or enter their shrines; yet she can enter a Buddhist temple and participate in Buddhist rituals freely.[50] Thus, though the Buddhists of Sri Lanka were influenced by Hindu notions of pollution and purity, they felt that these notions were inapplicable to the realm of Buddhist worship. Consequently popular belief stated that it was an ill omen if one saw a monk at the commencement of a journey: he represented the phenomenon of pollution, death, and human decrepitude. While it is undeniable that the Buddhist preoccupation with impermanence and transitoriness permeated the Buddhist tradition, popular and doctrinal, right through the ages, it was also the case that the very being who taught that tradition was believed by Buddhist commentators to be exempt from those processes.

I do not know how far this idea prevailed in the monastic schools of Theravāda; given the imprimatur of Buddhaghosa one can assume that it was widespread. It was less so in the popular (folk) traditions. Yet, it is a troubling fact that, while there are depictions of the ascetic austerities undertaken by the Buddha prior to his *bodhi* or "Awakening" in the Buddhist sculpture that developed from the post-Mauryan period to our own times, there is nowhere, as far as I know, any artistic or literary representation of the ageing Buddha pointing to himself as an example of the idea that "decay is inherent in all component things." This key section of the *Mahāparinibbāna Sutta* has been virtually erased from Buddhist memory and all that is left is an etymology of a word.

Notes

1. Friedrich Nietzsche, *The Birth of Tragedy*, trans., Douglas Smith (New York: Oxford University Press, 2000): 61.
2. For a detailed examination of the place of rationality in Buddhism see Gananath Obeyesekere, *Imagining Karma: Ethical Transformation in Amerindian, Buddhist and Greek Rebirth* (Berkeley: University of California Press, in press).
3. The details of this controversy are found in Arthur Waley, "Did the Buddha Die of Eating Pork?" *Melanges Chinois et Bouddhiques* (July 1932): 343-54.
4. Ibid., p. 345. Neumann's is pure guess work and justified by grammatical possibilities only. "Neumann has shown that ... there occurs a whole series of words having "pig" as their first element; [on this analogy] Neumann takes *sukaramaddava* to mean 'pig's delight.' and assumes that it is the name of some kind of truffles." See also T.W. and C.A.F. Rhys Davids, trans., *Maha Parinibbāna Suttanta* ("The Book of the Great Decease), *Dialogues of the Buddha (Dīgha Nikāya)*, part ii, (Oxford: Pāli Text Society, 1989): 137-39.
5. See Reverend P. Bigandet, *The Life and Legend of Gaudama, the Buddha of the Burmese,* 4th edition, (London: Kegan Paul Trench and Trubner, 1912): 36.
6. "Discourse on Wonderful and Marvellous Qualities" (*Acchariyābbhutādhamma Sutta), The Collection of Middle Length Sayings (Majjhima Nikāya),* vol. iii, trans., I.B. Horner (Oxford: Pāli Text Society, 1990): 163-69.
7. Ibid., p. 165.
8. Ibid., p. 167.
9. Ibid., p. 168.
10. Ibid.
11. Similar statements are repeated in the *Mahāpadāna Sutta* of the *Dīgha Nikāya*. They are also elaborated further in later texts like the *Jātaka Nidāna* and the *Buddhavaṃsa*. These latter texts state that the Bodhisattva entered his mother's womb while she was observing the Buddhist vow of celibacy and reaffirm the fact that Māyā, his mother, must die seven days after his birth.
12. G.P. Malalasekera, *Dictionary of Pāli Proper Nouns*, vol. ii, (New Delhi: Oriental Books Reprint Corporation, 1983): 609-10.
13. *Mahāvastu*, vol. ii, trans., J.J. Jones, (London: Pāli Text Society, 1976): 3.
14. This is to ensure the psychological welfare of the mother during a critical phase in her life.

15. *The Story of Gotama Buddha (Jātaka Nidāna),* trans., N.A. Jayawickrama, (Oxford: Pāli Text Society, 1990): 69. Contemporary Buddhists have identified the *sala* tree with a tree growing in many temple premises with beautiful flowers growing from the trunk; unfortunately they are not aware that this tree, known also as the "cannon ball" tree, was introduced by the British from South America around 1881! Such is the power of "symbolic traditionalization." See Venerable Kirallē Ñānavimala, *Deśiya Vaidya Sabdha Kośaya* ["Dictionary of Indigenous Medicine"], (Ratnapura, Sri Lanka: Sastrodaya Press, 1970): 517.

16. Sister Vajira and Francis Story, *Last Days of the Buddha: The Mahāparinibbāna Sutta* (Kandy, Sri Lanka: The Buddhist Publication Society, 1988): 31. There are two better-known translations of the *Mahāparinibbāna Sutta*. The older version by T.W Rhys Davids is in *Dialogues of the Buddha (Dīgha Nikāya), part ii,* (Oxford: The Pāli Text Society, 1989): 78-191; and Maurice Walshe, *The Long Discourses of the Buddha, a translation of the Dīgha Nikāya*, (Boston: Wisdom Publications, 1995): 231-77. Unfortunately, one of the key terms, *sukara maddava,* as we shall see, is erroneously rendered by the former as "truffles" and by the latter with deliberate vagueness as "pig's delight." In what is probably an earlier version originally published in 1880, Rhys Davids used the more likely term "dried boar's meat" but later changed it. See T.W. Rhys Davids, *Buddhist Suttas*, (New York: Dover Publications, 1969): 72. Owing to these difficulties, my primary resource will be the translation by Sister Vajira and Francis Story.

17. Ibid.

18. Ibid., p. 32.

19. Ibid. A similar reference to the aging Buddha is found in another important text, *Mahāsīhanāda Sutta* ("The Greater Discourse on the Lion's Roar" of the *Majjhima Nikāya*. See *The Collection of the Middle-Length Sayings,* vol., i, trans., I.B. Horner (London: The Pāli Text Society, 1987): 109. The Buddha tells Sāriputta, a major disciple: "I, Sāriputta, am now worn, old, stricken in years, I have lived my span, and am at the close of my life, being round about eighty." See also the reference to the *Jāra Sutta* in note 49.

20. Ibid., p. 33. I have changed the text slightly. Vajira and Story translate *dīpa* as "island" which is also Walshe's usage. But the older translation of Rhys Davids which renders it as "lamp" seems to me to be more in the spirit of Buddhism. Perhaps "light" would even be better. "Islands unto yourselves" suggest a kind of spiritual isolation from others rather than pity for the world, whereas "lamp" or "light" suggest inward illumination.

21. Ibid., p. 34.

22. Ibid., p. 36. Here as elsewhere I substitute "Malign One" for "Evil

One" which is preferred by most translators. I doubt that Māra is the equivalent of Satan and that "radical evil" exists in Buddhism.

23. Ibid., p. 47.
24. Ibid., p. 49.
25. Ibid., p. 55.
26. Ibid., p. 56.
27. Ibid., p. 57.
28. Ibid. pp. 75-76.
29. Ibid., p. 86.
30. For some interesting insights into this period see, M.M.J. Marasinghe, *The Gods in Early Buddhism* (Kelaniya: Vidyalankara University Press, 1974).
31. Rhys Davids, *Dialogues,* i, p. 122.
32. Ibid, p. 126, n. 1.
33. Walshe, *The Long Discourses,* p. 246, p. 569, n. 400.
34. This is not to say that such characters are not historical figures; but I am interested in their role in the text.
35. It is impossible for me to deal with each of the diacritical segments of the *Mahāparinibbāna Sutta* in this essay, except to note that another debate recurs here and this is the theme of the world conqueror or world renouncer with the thirty-two marks and other features of greatness. Thus, perhaps owing to felt devotion, the idealization tendencies reappear in other segments of the text and the Buddha returns to the role assigned to him at birth: earthquakes resound at his death, the relics are enshrined in great glory and the devotional cult of the great man enters the myth-making process.
36. For details see, E.J. Thomas, *History,* p. 149, n.3; Horner, *Clarifier of Sweet Meaning*, pp. 393, 430 and her "Introduction," p. xxxix. My friend Richard Gombrich, personal communication, translates *eka-jettaka* from *Sumaṅgalavilāsinī* ii, 568 as "prize pig."
37. It should be remembered that in general the Buddha did permit the eating of meat unless it was explicitly killed for the consumer. See, *The Book of Gradual Sayings*, iv, trans. and ed. E.M. Hare (Oxford: The Pāli Text Society, 1978): 129.
38. I have borrowed the term "idealization" from Freud. For a discussion of Freud's distinction between idealization and sublimation, see Gananath Obeyesekere, *The Work of Culture* (Chicago: University of Chicago Press, 1990): 33.
39. For details see, *Ariyapariyesanā Sutta* and *Mahāsaccaka Sutta* in *The Collection of Middle Length Sayings,* vol. i, trans., I.B. Horner (London: Pāli Text Society, 1977): 207, 295 respectively.

40. Gananath Obeyesekere, "The Goddess Pattini and the Lord Buddha: Notes on the Myth of the Birth of the Deity," *Social Compass, xx* (1973): 217-29.

41. See, E.J. Thomas, *History*, p. 147. Sarvāstivāda refers to a Buddhist denomination closely related to Theravāda; its doctrines were written in Sanskrit whereas the Theravāda doctrines were in Pāli.

42. For a scholarly discussion of these issues, see Telwatte Rahula, *A Critical Study of the Mahavastu* (Delhi: Motilal Banarsidass, 1978).

43. For details see, *Mahāvastu,* trans., Jones, vol. ii, pp. 6-21.

44. Ibid., p. 121.

45. Ibid., pp.132-34.

46. The reference is to a conversation between the Buddha and Ānanda in the *Jāra Sutta, Saṃyutta Nikāya,* vol. v., trans., F.L Woodward (Oxford: Pāli Text Society, 1990): 191-92 where the physical decrepitude of the Buddha is clearly mentioned. Buddhaghosa in his commentary on *Sarātthappakāsinī* makes the point of the Buddha's bodily perfection. I am indebted to Bandula Jayawardene for pointing this out. For details, see "Buddhology," *Encyclopaedia of Buddhism,* vol. iii, (Colombo: Government Press, 1971): p. 497.

47. *Points of Controversy or Subjects of Discourse* (*Katha-Vatthu*), trans., Shwe Zan Aung and Mrs. Rhys Davids, (London: The Pāli Text Society, 1979): 323.

48. Ibid., p. 326.

49. For a psychological analysis of this text, see Gananath Obeyesekere, "Depression, Buddhism, and the Work of Culture in Sri Lanka," in *Culture and Depression,* ed. Arthur Kleinman and Byron Good (Berkeley: University of California Press, 1985): 134-52.

50. Some of these attitudes to Buddhism have been changing recently; see Richard F. Gombrich and Gananath Obeyesekere, *Buddhism Transformed: Recent Religious Changes in Sri Lanka* (Princeton: Princeton University Press, 1988) and H.L. Seneviratne, *The Work of Kings: The New Buddhism in Sri Lanka* (Chicago: University of Chicago Press, 1999).

Musīla and Nārada Revisited:

Seeking the Key to Interpretation

Ven. Bhikkhu Bodhi

I

Although the Pāli *sutta*s are noted for the exceptional clarity and simplicity of their teachings, to the thoughtful interpreter they can sometimes be as opaque and mystifying as a cryptogram. Not only are the texts themselves composed in a clipped laconic style that mocks our thirst for conceptual completeness, but their meaning often seems to rest upon a deep underlying groundwork of interconnected ideas that is nowhere stated baldly in a way that might guide interpretation. Instead of resorting to direct expression, the *nikāya*s embed the basic principles of doctrine in a multitude of short, often elusive discourses that draw upon and allude to the underlying system without explicitly spelling it out. To determine the principles one has to extract them piecemeal, by considering in juxtaposition a wide assortment of texts. Yet this method, if applied without due caution, can easily drag the unwary interpreter into the notorious hermeneutic circle: to gain access to the exegetical system underlying the *sutta*s one must understand them; to understand the *sutta*s one needs access to the underlying exegetical system. Given this quandary, it is hardly a cause for wonder that present-day scholars of early Buddhism arrive at such strikingly different interpretations of the *nikāya*s.

But the hermeneutic circle need not be a vicious trap. By proceeding heedfully, with the combined aid of intuition and reflection, we can often discover enough of the exegetical framework to help us decipher the texts in accordance with their implicit intention. In this paper I will apply this approach to the task of interpreting one especially knotty little *sutta* which seems almost as if it had been planted in the canon as an exam piece for fledgling expositors of the doctrine. The *sutta* I will discuss is found near the end of the *Nidāna-Saṃyutta*, The Connected Discourses on Causation.[1] Named simply after the place where it is set, the city of Kosambī, the *sutta* features a discussion between three monks, the Venerables Saviṭṭha, Musīla, and Nārada. The Venerable Ānanda is present as a bystander, but enters the discussion only at the end. Apart from Ānanda, who had been the Buddha's personal attendant, none of the other monks plays a prominent role in the *nikāyas*.

The *sutta* begins when the Venerable Saviṭṭha asks the Venerable Musīla: "Apart from faith, personal preference, oral tradition, reasoned reflection, and acceptance of a view by pondering it, does the Venerable Musīla have personal knowledge thus: 'With birth as condition, aging-and-death comes to be'?" To this, Musīla replies that he knows and sees this for himself. Saviṭṭha then poses parallel questions about each of the other propositions in the chain of dependent origination, first with respect to arising (in reverse order, down to "With ignorance as condition, volitional formations come to be") and then with respect to cessation (from "With the cessation of birth comes cessation of aging-and-death" back to "With the cessation of ignorance comes cessation of volitional formations"). Finally Saviṭṭha asks Musīla whether, apart from faith and so forth, he has personal knowledge that *nibbāna* is the cessation of existence, to which he replies in the affirmative.

This reply induces Saviṭṭha to draw what he thinks is the inescapable conclusion: "Then the Venerable Musīla is an *arahant*, one whose taints are destroyed." Musīla keeps silent. In the context of monastic discipline, such silence clearly implies assent. For if Musīla were not an *arahant*, and did not cherish any delusion of being one, it would have been incumbent on him to reject Saviṭṭha's inference; otherwise he would have been guilty of implicitly claiming a superior attainment, a serious breach of discipline.

At this point the Venerable Nārada enters the discussion, proposing that Saviṭṭha ask him the same series of questions that he had just asked Musīla. Saviṭṭha complies, and to each question Nārada answers in the affirmative, just as Musīla had done. Thus Saviṭṭha draws the same conclusion: "Then the Venerable Nārada is an *arahant*, one whose taints are destroyed." But here comes the surprise—and the setting of the puzzle—for Nārada denies that he is an *arahant*. He illustrates his situation with a simile: "Suppose, friend, there was a well along a desert road, but it had neither a rope nor a bucket. Then a man would come along, oppressed and afflicted by the heat, tired, parched, and thirsty. He would look down into the well and the knowledge would occur to him, 'There is water,' but he would not be able to dwell touching it with the body. So too, friend, though I have clearly seen as it really is with correct wisdom, '*nibbāna* is the cessation of existence,' I am not an *arahant*, one whose taints are destroyed."

At the very close of the *sutta*, the Venerable Ānanda, who has hitherto been silent, asks Saviṭṭha what he would say about the Venerable Nārada when he speaks in such a way. Saviṭṭha says, "Nothing except what is good and favourable." This seems to give the canonical imprimatur to Nārada's answers.

The riddle posed by the *sutta*, the challenge to interpretation, is this: How is it possible that both monks claim to have personal knowledge of the same compendium of doctrinal matters, the knowledge of which is apparently constitutive of arahantship, yet one accepts the ascription of arahantship to himself while the other denies it? The simile of the well is brought in to provide an answer, but all it gives is a hint, a touch of imagery, not a clear explanation in direct doctrinal terms. Thus the *sutta* ends on a note of mystery, challenging the interpreter to dispel the mist with a convincing resolution of the problem.

II

Among Western scholars, the challenge posed by the *Kosambī Sutta* was taken up long ago by Louis de La Vallée Poussin in his paper, "Musīla et Nārada: Le Chemin de Nirvāṇa."[2] De La Vallée Poussin does not explore the *sutta* at length but rather uses it as the preamble to a detailed examination of what he takes to be two rival conceptions of the path in ancient and scholastic Buddhism, namely the ecstatic or ascetic conception, which gives primacy to meditative experience, and the cognitive conception, which gives primacy to intellectual understanding. In his view, the two monks represent these two competing versions of the path. Musīla, by accepting the ascription of arahantship to himself merely through mastery of doctrinal knowledge, represents the cognitive version. Nārada, by rejecting the sufficiency of intellectual knowledge (as represented by Musīla), stands for the experiential, meditative version.

More recently, Richard Gombrich has focused upon the *Kosambī Sutta* in his book *How Buddhism Began*, in a chapter devoted to tracing a hypothetical "ancient debate" between the cognitivists and the meditators.[3] Gombrich sees the *Kosambī Sutta* as serving a largely polemical function. In his view it was included in the canon by the meditative faction to counter the cognitivist strain of thought expressed in the *Susīma Sutta*. The *Susīma Sutta* features a group of monks who claim to be *arahant*s yet deny possessing the formless meditations (*āruppa*) and the five spiritual powers (*abhiññā*); they say they have been "liberated by wisdom" (*paññāvimutta*). As Gombrich reads the text, these monks "have no meditative attainments" and "seem to claim Enlightenment without having meditated."[4] He thus sees the *sutta* as expressing the viewpoint of a faction in the *saṅgha* that held Enlightenment to be attainable without meditation, solely by *paññā*, which he interprets as "a process of intellectual analysis."[5] The *Kosambī Sutta*, in his opinion, offers a rebuttal of the *Susīma Sutta*, expressing the viewpoint of those monks who insisted that meditation was indeed needed to attain arahantship. For Gombrich as for de La Vallée Poussin, Musīla represents the view that arahantship can be achieved by intellection, Nārada the view that intellection must be superseded by meditative realization. Thus once again the two monks stand for competing versions of the path, and the *sutta* favours Nārada's view over Musīla's.

III

In my own understanding, the *Kosambī Sutta* has nothing to do with alternative conceptions of the path to arahantship and is not intended to endorse the standpoint of one party against another in some hypothetical contest between rival factions of monks. Although the canon may present different evaluations of the role of meditation in relation to the goal, the dichotomy of meditative and cognitive approaches to enlightenment is not the key to unlocking the riddle posed by our text. The key lies in an altogether different direction. To discover the correct key we have to make a detour along a by-path that will disclose to us different vistas of the Buddha's teaching. Though our journey will take us through territory that may seem remote from the concerns of the *Kosambī Sutta*, be assured that we will eventually return to it, hopefully with the correct key to interpretation in our hands.

Our excursion begins by noting that arahantship is the fourth and last of a four-stage scale used in the canon to classify individuals who have become irreversible in their progress towards *nibbāna*. The four stages are distinguished by way of the mental defilements eliminated at each stage and by the number of rebirths that remain. The first stage, stream-entry (*sotāpatti*), is attained with the breaking of the first three fetters: identity view (or view of self), doubt, and wrong grasp of rules and observances. The stream-enterer is assured of attaining *nibbāna* in a maximum of seven more lives passed either in the human world or celestial realms. The second stage, that of the once-returner (*sakadāgāmī*), is reached by the weakening of greed, hatred, and delusion; at this stage no fetters are eradicated, but the attenuation of the root defilements ensures that the once-returner will come back at most only once more to the sense-sphere realm and then make an end of suffering. At the third stage, the two fetters of sensual desire and ill will are snapped; the disciple then becomes a non-returner (*anāgāmī*), one who never returns to the sense-sphere realm but is spontaneously reborn in a higher sphere (the "form realm") and there attains *nibbāna*. Finally, at the fourth stage, the disciple breaks the five subtle fetters—desire for form-sphere and formless existence, conceit, restlessness, and ignorance—and thereby becomes an *arahant*. For the *arahant* there is no future rebirth anywhere. One who attains arahantship "by the destruction of the taints, in this very life enters and dwells in the taintless liberation of mind, liberation by wisdom, having realized it personally by direct knowledge."[6]

The simple scheme of four stages is sometimes subdivided into eight stages by drawing a distinction, with respect to each stage, between the person who has actually reached the stage and the one who is striving to reach it. The latter is described as one "practising for realization of (such and such) a fruit." Thus, when the distinction between the phase of full attainment and the phase of preparatory practice is taken into account, we arrive at a scheme of four pairs of persons comprising eight individual types: the stream-enterer, and the one practising for realization of the fruit of stream-entry; the once-returner, and the one practising for realization of the fruit of the once-returner; the non-returner, and the one practising for realization of the fruit of the non-returner; the *arahant*, and the one practising for arahantship (or for realization of the fruit of arahantship).[7] These eight types collectively constitute the Buddha's community of disciples in the eminent sense, the *sāvaka-saṅgha*, said to be "worthy of gifts, worthy of hospitality, worthy of offerings, worthy of respectful salutation, the unsurpassed field of merits for the world."[8]

We sometimes find, attached to lists of the four main stages of attainment, two additional types that are clearly preliminary to stream-entry. These are called the *dhamma*-follower *(dhammānusārī)* and the faith-follower *(saddhānusārī)*.[9] The spiritual faculties (faith, energy, mindfulness, concentration, and wisdom) of both are said to be weaker than those of the stream-enterer, and the faith follower's faculties are weaker than the *dhamma*-follower's; the latter is thus superior to the former. Yet both have to some degree acquired the five spiritual faculties, which sets them apart from the worldling, who is completely bereft of the faculties.[10] Although the *nikāyas* never expressly say that these two types are a subdivision of "the person practising for realization of the fruit of stream-entry" (an odd omission), this seems to be a reasonable inference.

The *dhamma*-follower and the faith-follower are distinguished by the way they enter the path. Whereas the former "accepts the teachings proclaimed by the Buddha after pondering them sufficiently with wisdom," the latter simply has "sufficient faith in and devotion to the Tathāgata."[11] Thus the two differ by way of their dominant faculty: the one gives precedence to wisdom, to a reflective attempt to understand the *dhamma*; the other gives precedence to faith, to personal devotion to the Buddha as the spur towards realization.

A small chapter in the *Saṃyutta Nikāya*,[12] consisting of ten *suttas* composed on the same model, sketches for us, however tersely, the process by which the two types of disciples progress towards the fruit of stream-entry. The first *sutta* will suffice for our purpose. The text states that the eye, ear, nose, tongue, body, and mind are impermanent, changing, and becoming otherwise.[13] One who has faith in these teachings and resolves on them thus is called a faith-follower, "who has entered upon the fixed course of rightness (i.e., the supramundane eightfold path), has entered upon the plane of the superior persons, and transcended the plane of worldlings." Such a person cannot do any deed that might lead to a bad rebirth and cannot die without having realized the fruit of stream-entry. The *dhamma*-follower has all the qualities ascribed to the faith-follower, but is described as one who accepts these teachings (on impermanence, etc.) after pondering them to a sufficient degree with wisdom. The *sutta* ends with the words: "One who knows and sees these teachings thus is called a stream-enterer, no longer bound to the nether world, fixed in destiny, with enlightenment as his destination."

This *sutta* shows us that at a certain point in the contemplative process the disciple undergoes an inward metamorphosis which ensures ultimate success in the endeavour to win the final goal. This metamorphosis involves a radical change of lineage: one leaves behind the ranks of the worldlings and enters the fold of the noble ones, bound to reach the fruit of stream-entry within that life itself. However, despite the transformative impact of this achievement, neither *dhamma*-follower nor faith-follower has yet actually *seen* the truth of the teaching. It is only when the preparatory path reaches its consummation that the disciple directly sees and knows the truth of the teaching. This direct cognition of the *dhamma* is, in fact, the event that marks the end of the preparatory path and ushers in the realization of the fruit.

Whether stream-entry is approached by way of wisdom, as in the case of the *dhamma*-follower, or by way of faith, as in the case of the faith-follower, the decisive factor that brings its attainment is knowledge, an act of knowing *(ñāṇa)* so direct and immediate that it is also described as an act of seeing *(dassana)*. In the *nikāya*s, the acquisition of this ocular knowledge is called "the breakthrough to the *dhamma*" *(dhammābhisamaya)* and "the gain of the *dhamma*-eye" *(dhammacakkhu-paṭilābha)*. One who has undergone this experience becomes "endowed with view" *(diṭṭhisampanna)*, the transcendent right view which is bound to culminate in the final knowledge of arahantship.[14]

The gaining of the *dhamma*-eye is usually described in the texts in a stereotyped passage in which the critical cognition is triggered off, not by systematic training, but by a discourse spoken by the Buddha or an enlightened monk. A typical example is the case of the householder Upāli, who had been a staunch follower of the Jains.[15] After a heated debate, the Buddha gives Upāli a graduated discourse on the *dhamma*. When he knows that Upāli's mind is favourably disposed and free of impediments, he then expounds to him the "teaching special to the Buddhas," namely the Four Noble Truths. Then, "just as a clean cloth with all marks removed would take dye evenly, so too, while the householder Upāli sat there, the spotless immaculate *dhamma*-eye arose in him: All that is subject to arising is subject to cessation." The next sentence is especially important: "Then the householder Upāli saw the *dhamma*, attained the *dhamma*, understood the *dhamma*, fathomed the *dhamma*; he crossed beyond doubt, did away with perplexity, gained intrepidity, and became independent of others in the Teacher's Dispensation." This indicates that by gaining the *dhamma*-eye the disciple sees, reaches, understands, and fathoms the truth of the Buddha's teaching *(diṭṭhadhammo pattadhammo viditadhammo pariyogāḷhadhammo)* to such an extent that he or she becomes "independent of others," even of the Buddha himself, in regard to the Master's message *(aparappaccayo satthusāsane)*. Though the stream-enterer's insight is far from perfect, such a one has seen the innermost core of the *dhamma*, the essential point from which all the more specific principles flow: the Four Noble Truths, the three characteristics, dependent origination, and so forth. The disciple has caught a glimpse of what the Buddha wished to convey, the critical truths which, when fully understood, issue in unshakeable liberation of the mind.[16]

IV

The *nikāyas* not only calibrate the course leading to liberation into four major stages and eight sub-stages, but also collapse this typology into a simpler twofold scheme. On one side of this divide are the *arahants*, those who have completed the training. On the other side are those who have entered the ranks of the noble disciples but have yet to bring the training to completion. Those in this latter category are collectively called *sekhas*, trainees, and the *arahant* is contrasted with them as an *asekha*, one beyond training.[17]

The word "*sekha*" does not seem to be used with an invariably technical meaning in the canon but exhibits some degree of flexibility in its applications. Sometimes it seems to have a broad enough range to include any disciples—but particularly monks—who have taken up the training in full earnestness. Even the commentaries recognize this variability when they say, "The good worldling, who is on the verge of attaining a path and fruit, is also called a trainee in the sense that he trains."[18] More typically, however, the category of *sekha* is restricted to those who have actually entered the supramundane path. Hence the commentaries regularly speak of the "seven types of trainees," namely those on the four paths and those who have realized the three lower fruits. There is some ambiguity in the *suttas* themselves as to whether or not the person practising for the fruit of stream-entry—that is, the *dhamma*-follower and faith-follower—should be counted among the *sekhas*. In so far as such disciples have entered the supramundane path and are training to realize the fruit, they are surely to be included. But other texts lay down a more stringent criterion for the *sekha*, penetration of the Four Noble Truths, and on this criterion the category of the *sekha* might have to be limited to those from the stage of stream-enterer up to those on the path to arahantship. For our purposes here the technical distinction between path-attainer and fruit-realizer can be ignored, and thus the *sekha* can be considered a collective term for stream-enterers, once-returners, and non-returners.

Having posited a dichotomy of *sekha* and *arahant*, the *nikāyas* set about defining the distinction between them, and they do so primarily in terms of their cognitive agility. Though the difference is expressed in diverse ways, the distinction that emerges is a consistent one which may be briefly stated thus: Both the *sekha* and the *arahant* have made the "breakthrough to the *dhamma*," sharing essentially the same understanding of the innermost truth of the teaching; but while the *sekha* still has to develop this understanding in order to win the goal, the *arahant* has completed its development and thus lives in the realization of the goal. The *sekha* "has work to do with diligence." The *arahant* has accomplished what had to be done and thus has nothing more to accomplish.

A simple statement of this distinction is found in a short discourse addressed to the Sakyan Mahānāma.[19] Here the Buddha defines the *sekha*'s wisdom as the correct understanding of the Four Noble Truths. Equipped with this wisdom, he continues, the trainee destroys the taints and enters and dwells in "the taintless liberation of mind, liberation by wisdom." This is the wisdom of the *asekha*, the one beyond training.[20] Elsewhere, in a debate with the sophist Saccaka, the Buddha frames the contrast in terms of the teaching of non-self *(anattā)*. The disciple "who carries out my instructions and responds to my advice"—the *sekha*—is one who sees (*passati*) the five aggregates as "not mine, not I, not my self." The *arahant* with taints destroyed is one who, "having seen" *(disvā)* the five aggregates thus, is liberated by non-clinging.[21] Still another text says that a noble disciple who correctly understands *(pajānāti)* the five aggregates by way of their origin, passing away, gratification, danger, and escape is a stream-enterer. One who having understood *(viditvā)* the five aggregates thus is liberated by non-clinging, is an *arahant*.[22] Those ascetics who have directly known the five aggregates, their origin, cessation, and the way to their cessation, and are practising for the fading away and cessation of the aggregates – "these are practising well and have gained a foothold in this *dhamma* and discipline" *(ye supaṭipannā te imasmiṃ dhammavinaye gādhanti)*; that is, they are *sekhas*. Those who have directly known all this and have realized the fading away and cessation of the five aggregates are "well-liberated consummate ones" *(ye suvimuttā te kevalino)*; that is, they are *arahants*.[23]

Examples could be multiplied, but these would only go to reinforce the same point, namely that the *sekha* and the *arahant* are distinguished, not by any particular item of knowledge that the one enjoys over and against the other, but by the degree to which they have developed their common insight into the essential principles of the *dhamma*. The *sekha* is still engaged in applying this knowledge to the task of inner purification from the taints, clinging, latent tendencies, and fetters. The *arahant* has used this knowledge to uproot all the defilements and thus dwells in the taintless liberation of the mind.

V

Now, having apparently travelled quite some distance from the *Kosambī Sutta*, we are about to turn around and head back to it. We will not return along the route on which we set out, but will take a different route that will lead us through some new territory that bears directly on the *sutta*. This new territory is dependent origination *(paṭicca-samuppāda)*. I do not intend here to embark on an explanation of the significance of this doctrine, which has been interpreted in so many different ways. My concern rather is with the bearings the doctrine has on the distinction we just drew between the *sekha* and the *arahant*.

Close scrutiny of the *Nidāna-Saṃyutta*, and other related texts, would show that the same conclusion we reached above regarding the Four Noble Truths, the doctrine of non-self, and the five aggregates also applies here. The understanding of dependent origination is common ground to both *sekhas* and *arahants*. They differ, not with respect to their insight into this doctrine, but with respect to the extent they have utilized that insight to reach the final goal.

It need hardly be mentioned that the *arahant* has clear direct knowledge of dependent origination, for this knowledge is indispensable to the development of liberating wisdom. But it would be a mistake to see such knowledge as peculiar to the *arahant*. In four *suttas* of the *Nidāna-Saṃyutta*,[24] the Buddha declares that when a noble disciple (or *bhikkhu*) correctly understands dependent origination, "he is then called a noble disciple (or *bhikkhu*) who is accomplished in view, accomplished in vision, who has arrived at this true *dhamma*, who sees this true *dhamma*, who possesses a trainee's knowledge, a trainee's true knowledge, who has entered the stream of the *dhamma*, a noble one with penetrative wisdom, one who stands squarely before the door to the Deathless." This encomium makes it clear that the understanding of dependent origination is the defining mark of the *sekha*, not of the *arahant*. It is "a trainee's knowledge, a trainee's true knowledge" *(sekhañāṇa, sekhavijjā)*, and one who has acquired it "has entered the stream of the *dhamma*" *(dhammasotaṃ samāpanna)* without necessarily having reached its consummation.

A parallel way of drawing this distinction is found in the *Sammādiṭṭhi Sutta*.[25] In this text, the Venerable Sāriputta takes up (in reverse order) each factor of the twelve-fold formula of dependent origination and treats it according to the fourfold pattern of definition, origin, cessation, and way to cessation. In each section of exposition, the *sutta* states that one who understands this fourfold analysis is "one of right view, whose view is straight, who has perfect confidence in the *dhamma*, and has arrived at this true *dhamma*." Though the text does not use the word "*sekha*," it is evident from the context that the *sekha* is intended as the one with right view. Each section then concludes by saying that when a noble disciple has understood this fourfold analysis, "he entirely abandons the underlying tendency to greed, he abolishes the underlying tendency to aversion, he extirpates the underlying tendency to the view and conceit 'I am,' and by abandoning ignorance and arousing true knowledge in this very life he makes an end of suffering." This clearly describes the *arahant*, who has applied right view for the purpose it is intended to serve.

VI

At this point in our journey we are ready to descend once again upon the *Kosambī Sutta*, and our long excursion has given us the clues we need to disentangle its riddle. It should now be clear why the Venerable Nārada wanted the Venerable Saviṭṭha to ask him the same questions he had put to the Venerable Musīla, and why he answered in the way he did. Nārada was not out to challenge Musīla's tacit assent to the status of arahantship, nor did he have hidden in the fold of his robe a different conception of the path to *nibbāna* than that held by Musīla. He recognized (or at least believed) that in concluding Musīla was an *arahant*, Saviṭṭha had drawn the right conclusion. But he also realized that Saviṭṭha had drawn this conclusion for the wrong reason, on the basis of a mistaken assumption. Saviṭṭha had assumed that direct cognition of dependent origination is the defining mark of the *arahant*. In making this assumption, he failed to realize that this cognition is also shared by the *sekha*. It is "a trainee's knowledge, a trainee's true knowledge." By claiming direct knowledge of dependent origination while rejecting Saviṭṭha's ascription of arahantship to himself, Nārada is saying in effect that knowledge of dependent origination, even direct experiential knowledge, is not a sufficient ground for arahantship. Such knowledge is indeed necessary, but it is not distinctive of the *arahant*; it is also held by the *sekha*, a status he implicitly ascribes to himself (the commentary tells us he was a non-returner).

There remains one problem facing the interpretation of the *sutta* I am advancing here. Saviṭṭha's questionnaire did not deal solely with dependent origination but also with *nibbāna*. Both Musīla and Nārada say that they have personal knowledge that *nibbāna* is the cessation of existence *(bhavanirodho nibbānaṃ)*, yet Musīla admits (by silence) that he is an *arahant* while Nārada denies this of himself. Nārada's simile of the water in the well suggests that something more than direct cognition of *nibbāna* is required to qualify as an *arahant*, but what exactly is needed is only hinted at metaphorically without being made explicit.

On the interpretation of the *sutta* proposed by de La Vallée Poussin and Richard Gombrich, Musīla and Nārada hold opposite views on this issue. Musīla, by his silence, suggests that mere personal cognition of *nibbāna* is sufficient to qualify a person as an *arahant*; thus he advocates insight as the chief factor of the path. Nārada, by his replies, is challenging Musīla's position and pointing to an alternative view of the path that gives precedence to deep meditative experience. Thus, in the view of these scholars, the *Kosambī Sutta* testifies to two conflicting currents of thought in the early *saṅgha*, throwing its weight behind the pro-meditative faction in their contest with the more compromising position of the cognitivists.

In my understanding, this interpretation of the *sutta* arises from the application of the wrong exegetical key. The right key to its meaning is not the tension between two competing visions of the contemplative path, but the contrast between the achievements of the *sekha* and the *arahant*. This reading of the text would make the positions of the two monks mutually compatible within a single coherent vision of the Buddhist way. On my reading, the two monks, Musīla and Nārada, do not disagree with one another; once again, the point is that Saviṭṭha has drawn a wrong conclusion, or, more properly put in relation to Musīla, has drawn a right conclusion on the basis of a wrong assumption. Nārada's answer, intended to clear up Saviṭṭha's misunderstanding, rests on the distinction between the *sekha* and the *arahant* that we delineated above. By stating that he has "clearly seen as it really is with correct wisdom that *nibbāna* is the cessation of existence," Nārada is indicating that he is at least a *sekha*. He is appealing to the deep underlying exegetical principle that direct cognition of *nibbāna* is an achievement already made by the *sekha*. By denying that he is an *arahant*, he is insinuating that an *arahant* has not only directly cognized *nibbāna* but is capable of experiencing it in a meditative state so powerful that one seems to be making bodily contact with it.

The interpretation of the *sutta* proposed by de La Vallée Poussin and Gombrich appears to draw support from the use of the expression "he dwells contacting with the body" *(kāyena phusitvā viharati)* in relation to certain elevated states of meditation. However, in relation to higher meditative states, this expression is generally used to describe mastery over the formless meditative attainments *(āruppa)*. The formless meditations are not necessary qualifications for arahantship. There may be masters of the formless meditations who are not even on the way to arahantship, and there are *arahant*s who do not enjoy the formless meditations. Yet Nārada's simile of the well implies that "bodily contact" with *nibbāna* is something to which all *arahant*s have access.

The expression "*kāyena phusitvā viharati*" occurs only rarely in the canon, but it is found in one passage that bears some relevance to the *Kosambī Sutta*. Significantly, this passage comes in a *sutta* which defines the criteria that can be used to distinguish between the achievements of the *sekha* and the *arahant*. The relevant portion of the text reads:

> A *bhikkhu* who is a trainee *(sekha)* understands the five spiritual faculties – the faculty of faith ... the faculty of wisdom. He does not yet dwell having contacted with the body that which is their destination, culmination, fruit, and final goal; but having pierced it through with wisdom, he sees.[27] This is a method by means of which a *bhikkhu* who is a trainee, standing on the plane of a trainee, understands: 'I am a trainee.'
> And what is the method by means of which a *bhikkhu* who is one beyond training *(asekha)*, standing on the plane of one beyond training, understands: 'I am one beyond training'? Here, a *bhikkhu* who is one beyond training understands the five spiritual faculties – the faculty of faith ... the faculty of wisdom. He dwells having contacted with the body *(kāyena ca phusitvā viharati)* that which is their destination, culmination, fruit, and final goal; and having pierced it through with wisdom, he sees. This is a method by means of which a *bhikkhu* who is one beyond training, standing on the plane of one beyond training, understands: 'I am one beyond training.'[26]

The *sutta* does not specify what it is that the *arahant* contacts with the body, but another *sutta* in the same collection says that the five faculties, when developed and cultivated, "have the Deathless as their ground, the Deathless as their destination, the Deathless as their final goal" *(amatogadhāni amataparāyanāni amatapariyosānāni)*.[28] Since the Deathless is *nibbāna*, the text quoted above implies that both the *sekha* and the *arahant* "see" *nibbāna* with wisdom, but the *arahant* alone can "dwell contacting it with the body."[29]

The ocular cognition of *nibbāna*, it seems, initially takes place with the first arising of the *dhamma*-eye at the peak-moment of the path to stream-entry; it is subsequently repeated with each breakthrough to a higher stage along the path. True to their characteristically taciturn style, the *sutta*s describe the content of the *dhamma*-eye only by way of the tantalizingly elusive phrase, "Whatever is of the nature of arising, all that is of the nature of cessation" *(yaṃ kiñci samudayadhammaṃ sabbaṃ taṃ nirodhodhammaṃ)*. Though the texts do not make explicit what this experience actually entails, from the description of the breakthrough to stream-entry (and the higher stages) as a penetrative realization of *all* Four Noble Truths, we can well suppose that with the arising of the *dhamma*-eye the disciple directly sees the truth of the cessation of suffering, which is *nibbāna*. This is supported by the treatment of the supramundane path-knowledge in the commentaries. Using a more technical and systematic model than the *sutta*s, the commentaries offer a detailed account of what takes place at each moment of penetration by the supramundane path. This account centres on the idea that with each major breakthrough, the mind performs four functions at a single moment, one with respect to each of the Four Noble Truths. It penetrates *nibbāna*, the noble truth of cessation, by taking it as object *(ārammaṇato)*. At the same time, it simultaneously penetrates the other three truths by way of function *(kiccato)*: the noble truth of suffering by fully understanding the five aggregates; the noble truth of the origin of suffering by stripping away successive layers of craving; and the noble truth of the path by developing the eight factors of the Noble Eightfold Path.[30] From this, we see that direct cognition of *nibbāna* becomes accessible to the disciple on the occasion of attaining stream-entry, the very first penetration of the *dhamma*. Thus direct cognition of *nibbāna* is not an achievement specific to the *arahant* but is also shared by *sekha*s.

On the interpretation I am advancing here, the *Kosambī Sutta* builds upon, and reinforces, a deep exegetical principle that distinguishes the *arahant* from the *sekha*. All *arahant*s arrive at their goal through the same threefold training in virtue, concentration, and wisdom. They never bypass the training in concentration but merely differ in the degree to which they pursue this phase of the path. The principal division is between those *arahant*s who gain mastery over the formless attainments (technically called *ubhatobhāgavimutta*, "both-ways-liberated *arahants*") and those who settle for a lower degree of concentration (technically called *paññāvimutta*, "liberated-by-wisdom *arahants*").[31] But this difference is irrelevant to the *Kosambī Sutta*. Regardless of their route of arrival at the goal, all *arahants* gain access to a meditative state in which they can experience *nibbāna* with a fullness and immediacy that surpasses the capacity of the *sekha*.

Sekhas can see *nibbāna* but they cannot enter and dwell in it; they stand squarely before the door to the Deathless and can peek inside, but they cannot pass through the door to partake of the ultimate bliss. Their residual defilements bar the way. *Arahants* have destroyed all defilements and thus gain admission to this state in which they can experience *nibbāna* as if touching it with the body. By eliminating clinging, by eradicating all the taints, latent tendencies, and fetters, the *arahant* can dwell in this profound experience of the Deathless just as tangibly as a man with a bucket can scoop up water from the well and dispel his thirst.[32]

Notes

1. S II 115–18.
2. Louis de La Vallée Poussin, "Musīla et Nārada: Le Chemin de Nirvāṇa."*Mélanges Chinois et Bouddhiques* V (1936–37): 189–222. I am grateful to William Pruitt for translating for me the relevant portions of this paper and for giving me some idea of the contents of the other parts. Several paragraphs are also translated in Richard F. Gombrich, *How Buddhism Began: The Conditioned Genesis of the Early Teachings* (London & Atlantic Highlands, N.J.: Athlone, 1996): 133–34.
3. See preceding note. Gombrich discusses the *Kosambī Sutta* at pp. 127–29, the *Susīma Sutta* at pp. 123–27.
4. Richard F. Gombrich, *How Buddhism Began*: 125 and 126.
5. See ibid., 96.
6. Texts that mention the four main stages are ubiquitous in the canon. I give here just a few main references: D I 156, II 92–93; M I 34–35, 141–42, 226, 465–68; III 80–81.
7. In Pali: *sotāpanna*, *sotāpattiphala-sacchikiriyāya paṭipanna*, *sakadāgāmī*, *sakadāgāmiphala-sacchikiriyāya paṭipanna*, *anāgāmī*, *anāgāmiphala-sacchikiriyāya paṭipanna*, *arahā*, *arahattāya* (or:

arahattaphala-sacchikiriyāya) paṭipanna. In a recent paper, Joy Manné translates *paṭipanna* as "attained to" and then complains that the distinction between "the stages and their fruits" is spurious and unintelligible ("Case Histories from the Pāli Canon II," *Journal of the Pāli Text Society XXI* (1995): 44, 87–88). Once *paṭipanna* is translated correctly, as "practising for" rather than "attained to," the problem vanishes.

8. A IV 292–93.

9. The *dhammānusārī* and the *saddhānusārī* are added to the four main stages at M I 142, 226, and S V 200. At S V 377 and 379 the terms are not expressly used, but the formulations indicate that they are intended. Sometimes the two are added at the end of more finely nuanced versions of the list, as at S V 201-2. Formal definitions of the two types are at M I 479, where, however, they are attached to a different sevenfold typology of disciples.

10. S V 202.

11. M I 479.

12. S III 225–28.

13. The other *sutta*s in the chapter make the same stipulations in relation to the six sense objects; the six classes each of consciousness, contact, feeling, perception, volition, and craving; the six elements; and the five aggregates.

14. On the breakthrough to the *dhamma*, see especially S II 133–39, which establishes the equivalence of the breakthrough with the gaining of the *dhamma*-eye and the attainment of stream-entry. S V 457–65 establishes that this breakthrough involves the penetration of the Four Noble Truths.

15. M I 379–80.

16. The exact relationship, however, of the *dhamma*-eye to the phase of path attainment is not clarified in the *nikāyas* and remains problematic. The texts that describe the arising of the *dhamma*-eye almost always show it as occurring in a new convert to the teaching, not in one already established on the path. Thus we can only draw inferences about its exact place in the process which leads from path attainment to the realization of fruition. The model used by the commentaries, based on the *Abhidhamma* theory of mind-moments, identifies the arising of the *dhamma*-eye with the attainment of the supramundane path, an event which exists for a single mind-moment followed immediately by the fruit, a sequence of two or three mind-moments. On this model, one is a path-attainer (as *dhamma*-follower or faith-follower) for a single mind-moment, after which one becomes a fruit-realizer. This model is hard to square with the *nikāyas*, which depict the path-attainer as engaging in activities (such as receiving alms) that require more than one mind-moment

to fulfil. We might try to reconcile the two models by interpreting the arising of the *dhamma*-eye as the culminating moment of a temporally extended path-process, occurring when the path-attainer has brought to maturity the constellation of mental factors needed for realization of the fruit. Even this proposal, however, has cracks and rough edges, and perfect congruity between the two models may finally be unachievable.

17. See A I 63 on the two types of persons in the world who are "worthy of gifts" (*dakkhiṇeyya*), the *sekha* and the *asekha*.

18. M I 37 (Sinhala-script Simon Hewavitarāne Bequest edition).

19. A I 220.

20. This same distinction underlies the contrast another text draws between "the person with a mind like lightning" (*vijjūpamacitto*) and "the person with a mind like a diamond" (*vajirūpamacitto*). See A I 124.

21. M I 234–35.

22. S III 160–61. The same thing is stated elsewhere in relation to the various types of faculties (*indriya*): about the five spiritual faculties at S V 193–94; about the six sense faculties at S V 205–6; about the five feeling faculties at S V 207–8. Manné, in the article referred to in note 7 above, takes the distinction between stream-enterer and *arahant* to be between *pajānāti*, understanding, and *viditvā*, which she renders "seeing" (p. 70). She does not seem to realize that *viditvā*, though from a different root, functions as the usual absolutive of *pajānāti*. The real distinction is between correct understanding and liberation from the taints through understanding.

23. S III 59–61.

24. S I 27, 28, 49, 50; II 42–45, 77–80.

25. M I 49–54.

26. S V 230.

27. *Yaṃgatikāni yamparamāni yamphalāni yampariyosānāni na h' eva kho kāyena phusitvā viharati paññāya ca ativijjha passati*. At *Kindred Sayings*, 5:205, Woodward translates the above as if the negative *na* applies to both phrases: "he dwells not in personal experience thereof, nor does he pierce through and through by insight and see them plain." If that were the sense, however, we would expect an additional *na*. Here the conjunction *ca* should be understood in the disjunctive sense, as the *Saṃyutta* Commentary confirms with its paraphrase: "He does not dwell having contacted that, having obtained that, with the name-body (*nāmakāya*, the corpus of mental factors); but (*pana* as a gloss on *ca*) he understands by reviewing wisdom, 'Beyond there is a faculty – the fruit of arahantship.' On the plane of the *arahant* he dwells having obtained this, and he

understands by reviewing wisdom, 'There is a faculty—the fruit of arahantship.'"

28. S V 232.

29. The commentary, as we see in the preceding note, identifies this, not with *nibbāna*, but with the fruit of arahantship. The reason, it seems, is that the commentator is reluctant to establish a connection between *phala* (in the expression *yamphalāni*) and *nibbāna* from fear this would imply *nibbāna* is the effect of a cause. But the commentator seems to have forgotten the line at S I 173 (= Sn 80) *evaṃ esā kasī kaṭṭhā sā hoti amatapphalā*, "When this plowing has been done it has the Deathless as its fruit."

30. See Vism XXII 92–97.

31. See especially M I 478–79.

32. This unique meditative state is spoken of only obliquely in the *sutta*s, but the texts that allude to it extol it as the ultimate fruit of the Buddhist path. It seems to be the topic of discussion at A V 7–10, 319–26. It also seems to be referred to in various ways in texts composed in verse, for example in the lines of the *Ratana Sutta* (Sn 228): *te pattipattā amataṃ vigayha laddhā mudhā nibbutiṃ bhuñjamānā*, "those who have reached the attainment, having plunged into the Deathless, freely enjoying the quenching (= *nibbāna*) they have obtained."

On the Search for Interreligious Understanding[1]

John Ross Carter

This is a preliminary inquiry into a human activity with which we have been familiar for long but which might not be entirely clear, a consideration of which might repay reflection. The scope of the inquiry is enormous; one would anticipate a thorough and an inclusive investigation to involve contributions by psychologists and philosophers, historians and theologians, major authorities working in several more recent intellectual pursuits: especially neurology. What I am proposing, however, in this brief chapter is that we give pause to consider what might be occurring when we speak of ourselves as reaching an understanding, an understanding of a proposition, a mathematical formula, a musical score, an instruction given to us, or a carpenter's skill, and, most comprehensively, of another person, especially another person in that person's religious life, particularly, in this case, in the religious life of Theravāda Buddhists or Christians. Let it be known at the outset, that this preliminary inquiry will remain incomplete, will hardly offer a definition of "to understand," surely will remain inconclusive. Its objective will have been achieved if serious consideration is given to the human process of understanding as a distinctively and authentically human activity, as a religious activity, not solely as a cognitive enterprise posing an epistemological issue, as David Hume (1711-1776) and subsequent generations of competent thinkers have considered it in the canon of the received tradition in the Western philosophical heritage.[2] This kind of understanding is central in understanding a religious tradition other than one's own, and in achieving this understanding one becomes religiously self-conscious not unlike the dawning of self-consciousness in the developmental process and growth of the human personality.

Consider this. A student ponders over a mathematical formula and cannot at all see the principle involved, fails to align the sequence of steps leading to the integration of the formula, and cannot at all discern the comprehensive structure of the formula or the foundation provided, consequently, by the formula for the next, more advanced, sequencing of mathematical principles. Now, consider a student who, with insight, sees the point of it all and realizes a delightful sense of contentment. Or, try as one might, a *rāga* remains opaque, a disconnected cluster of *ad hoc* sounds incapable of being discerned as providing musical structure, cadence and counterpoint in temporal sequence. Yet one marvels at *sitar* or *vīna* player who soars, as it were, with impressive freedom of improvisation entirely taken up in a delicate sense of joy, unimpeded by scale or rhythmic beat. What makes the difference between an arithmetician and a mathematician, on the one hand, and a musician and an accomplished performing artist, on the other? In both cases, it seems, while the former can reproduce what others have discerned, even created, the latter understands, sees through to the point of, mathematical order and musical genius. The former would be one who is capable of knowing something presented and learned. The latter would be one who understands, who has been enabled to give expression to a foundational structure of truth that, as it were, stands under him or her. The parallel would suggest that in the study of Buddhist religiousness, the former would represent one who has knowledge about the Theravāda Buddhist tradition. The latter would be one who understands Theravāda Buddhists.

We can recall the observation, now wide-spread and perhaps trite, that there is a response referred to as an *ah-ha* moment, an instant, perhaps, when something becomes clear, when the point is seen, when comprehension arises and one learns, knows, indeed, understands for oneself what is presented or has arisen. It is in this very familiar and broad dimension of human experience, not entirely dissociated from a religious realization, that I would like to place this brief inquiry on the search for understanding—of the world, of oneself, of others, including others of differing religious traditions, and, ultimately, of transcendence.

The Theravāda Buddhist tradition has been studied by outsiders for well over a century, and a great deal has been learned: languages, literary heritages, customs, practices, institutions, and much more. Philologists have made their important contributions, as have historians, linguists, anthropologists, historians of religion, sociologists, theologians, political scientists, and one could continue. Their work has been enormously significant in adding to our knowledge. But wherein does this work cohere? What is the foundation for the appearance in space and time of the items or topics of these studies? In my judgment, the subjects being studied by means of these disciplines are rooted in the persons being studied, whether of the 11th century or today, and the search for understanding must, to be comprehensive, involve an understanding of persons, which understanding, in so far as it is realized by another person who is engaged in the study, is not unlike a religious activity.

Within religious studies, whether in the frame of reference known as history of religion or that of Christian theology, intellectual progress seems to have stalled: our academic disciplines have tended to offer us important but disparate details and theological approaches have been diverted to internal debates. It is not possible to tell the meaning of that which is being studied or to present something in understandable terms without involving how the meaning is grounded in persons and how what is made understandable has become understood by persons. It is in the dimension of inquiry in which persons are engaged in understanding persons in their religious life that the process of understanding becomes a religious act.

Aristotle nudged this notion by showing us how the process of reflection is participatory in the inherent intelligibility of the cosmos. The person engaged in that activity of coming to understand, which, of course, would require sincerity in the enterprise and commitment to the process, would be a participant in a religious activity. So also is the case of Christians seeking to understand Theravāda Buddhists, with the obvious implication that such is also involved when Buddhists seek to understand Christians, which could be extended to all attempts, honestly, seriously and rigorously, in inter-religious colloquia leading to understanding. Although this brief inquiry is written somewhat broadly without tradition-specific analyses, the general context from which the concern of the chapter has arisen is primarily Buddhist-Christian colloquia, more specifically Theravāda Buddhist and Christian academic.

I

When we consider what might be involved in the human activity of understanding persons participating in religious traditions, important issues arise. We have found that this activity is sufficiently comprehensive that some of us in the academic arena have instituted distinct disciplines as separate modes of knowing whereby we can handle, it is assumed, facets of our more comprehensive subject, namely the human being, *homo religiosus*, humankind in its religiousness. But one wonders whether modes of understanding, disciplines yielding "ways of knowing," will ever satisfy an intellectual's search for understanding, a search ever more inclusive, comprehensive, integrative, converging. And when we turn our attention to an attempt to understand others in the most value-centered core of their lives, the dimension which gives meaning to life and that beyond life, understanding is, I am becoming more and more persuaded, a religious activity. For example, for a Christian or a secular Western scholar to understand *dāna* or the heart of Buddhist meditation, or the meaning of *dhamma* requires the acquisition of knowledge, rigorously so. Understanding demands more than this, requiring a discernment of the cohesive supportiveness that these concepts, practices, notions, and religious symbols provide for other human beings, and in so gaining this one's own humanness will have been thereby enhanced. This is a suggestion that will hardly be readily endorsed today by students of humankind's religiousness. But the suggestion should be taken seriously and, in time, I would argue were length of no concern, will become more central as a subject for further investigation in considerations of our one global human religious history: past, present, and future.

There are studies, for example, dealing with the task of *understanding Religion*, as the task and subject have been worded. Initially the approach to understanding Religion was one of "origin and development," with the customary cultural assumptions of the 19th century out in front of the investigator, as it were. Regularly, and more recently, studies have attempted to define *religion*, occasionally have offered lengthy and cumbersome definitions or characteristics of the concept *religion*, and then have continued with the word and presupposed notion itself. We have learned a great deal from such studies by patient and committed scholars. But we have tended, now, to move beyond this approach.[3]

More recently one notes attempts at understanding the *Study of Religion*. Here, the task has been to demarcate an area of intellectual inquiry called the "Study of Religion," proposing acceptable hermeneutical approaches, particular definitional categories, technical terms of and for analysis—myth, pilgrimage, ritual, purity, sacred space, and the like—composing an accepted vocabulary and a disciplinary canon of received scholarly texts almost all of which have been written by Western investigators (often drawn from several separate disciplines, leading to a kind of premature celebration of an unintegrated interdisciplinary scholarship in this study). Important as this has been, and one applauds the commitment of scholars working in this manner, an intellectual seeking to understand tends to press this procedure asking whether it takes one far enough, or, rather, whether, in reality, it only parries one's inquiry into the primary source for understanding, from human beings to constructed systems, from the *subject* of the inquiry to the *way* legitimate inquiries are to be conducted. It is one thing to understand a particular discipline with its demarcated nomenclature, with analyses appropriate to religious studies or sociology or anthropology or political science, and quite another—and much more—to understand another human being.

Along with the scholarly involvement in studying *Religion* (a human activity) and, more recently, the study of a "field [*NB*] of study," i.e., the *Study of Religion* (also a human activity), has come a consideration of how to interpret religiously the presence of *Religions*. Scholars, particularly engaged Christian theologians, currently speak of interpretive positions as "exclusivism," "inclusivism," and "pluralism." One readily discerns a pattern of designation whereby positions are given their labels from a preferred, distinctive, and distinguishing point of view, much like the categorization of the so-called "worlds:" "first world," "third world," and "second world." "First worlders," of course, coined the phrasing so to speak of others. And, today, although we have more or less lost the "second world," persons continue to speak of "the third world," and persons have adopted this label to refer to themselves, alas, as persons "living in the third world." Our world is and has been one throughout human history, for better or worse, in sickness and in health, too.

"Exclusivism," in Christian interpretations of the presence of other religious men and women, has been around for quite some time. "Radical discontinuity" was a phrase often heard about a half-century ago, and also "Christian absolutism." Often scriptural bases for this position were found in those Biblical passages reflecting a growing particularity of "peoplehood" and the covenantal acts of God recorded in the Old Testament together with the early Christian community's attempt to discern self-definition, adjusting to a new self-consciousness as a confessional community with membership formed by adult affirmations and acceptance *vis-à-vis* a fluid but relatively cohesive Jewish community, under Roman political hegemony, within Hellenistic culture, as reflected in the New Testament. Surely, an exclusivistic syllogism in this case would be consistent with the heritage stemming from the times.[4]

"Inclusivism" has been taken to refer to an interpretation of other religious traditions that incorporates their presence within the doctrinal frame of reference of the interpreter's religious world-view, quite apart, on occasion, from whether or not persons participating in the other religious traditions endorse such interpretations or find them relevant to their self-understanding. In short, this position is said to represent those attempts that *include* within one's own doctrinal scheme the doctrinal schemes and practices of persons of other religious traditions. And, indeed, Biblical passages are found to provide a basis for this interpretation, too, particularly those that reflect the early Christian community's sense of giving expression to God's redemptive act of reconciling the world in Christ.

"Pluralism," apparently the home position for the label-makers in these recent categorizations, admirably recognizes the reality of faith on earth, its variety of manifestations, and the unquestionable facticity of the historical record that we men and women have expressed our religiousness variously through the centuries and magnificently so in numerous ways in great traditions. Pluralism, therefore, recognizes both a validity in the faith of religious men and women around the globe and also the abiding presence of transcendence in light of which, in an engagement with which, persons have discovered, or have been enabled to find, the ability to live life authentically as human beings, to live life religiously. This position, taking full notice of a global religious history unknown to the Biblical writers, has been called, consequently, "liberal," no doubt because of attempts to construct a Christian theology appropriate for the fact of human faith as it can be discerned or inferred around the world in different religious traditions throughout our human history.

One, in the search for understanding religiousness, seeks to understand also the persons who are "exclusivistic," "inclusivistic," and "pluralistic," otherwise the search is incomplete, certainly biased. And one recognizes quickly that in this attempt these categories, although providing topics of conversation, even, perhaps, broad and imprecise analyses, are not particularly helpful. To understand an "exclusivist," for example, one would do well to consider, as thoroughly as one's wits allow, the vibrant relevance of that person's relationship with God, the particularity of the revelatory moment, the singularity of the Christ-event, the reliability through history of the testimony of the Church regarding thought and practice in integrating one's human life in a changing world, whether in the 14th century in southern France or eighteenth century London, or twenty-first century America.

Regarding the "inclusivist," there might well be significant movements yet to be launched in one's utilization of received doctrinal formulations in an attempt to understand others participating in the religious traditions of the world. Whether a Hindu might see himself or herself within categories developed through Christian reflections over the centuries in Europe, say, is an important matter. But one wonders whether inclusivist moves and methods have been written off too quickly as being inappropriate, with a sense that somehow conversation can not take place between persons participating in different religious traditions, that somehow systems must be constructed in isolation, in books, for the intellectual enterprise to be legitimate, expressed on panels at conferences, without recognizing what has always been the case—that persons of different religious traditions can talk among themselves and seek understanding. For example, an inclusivist in considering, say, the case of Islam, might speak of the activity of the Holy Spirit and of General Revelation through history and around the world. Such inclusivist would be advised not to give up too quickly in probing what he or she means by these terms and, for that matter, a Muslim would do well not to react too quickly to that Christian's attempt to give expression to these notions in a multifaceted religious context. In responding constructively to those notions a Muslim might assist a Christian inclusivist to discern new depth of meaning in those cherished ideas.

A pluralist recognizes the fact of the variety of religious expressions, the differing forms of religious institutions, the numerous religious traditions, faith among men and women, and seeks to interpret this reality in an innovative mode, trusting both the value of the religious life clearly manifested around the globe and the abiding quality of transcendence an engagement with which gives rise to that religious life.

But the categories tend to become blurred. One can be a pluralist in this sense while being an exclusivist in recognizing the uniqueness of the Christ-event in one's life and in human history, while being an inclusivist in discerning in that event a manifestation of the integrative, reconciling reality of transcendence to which persons refer as "God." When we seek to understand another, our categories of "exclusivist," "inclusivist," and "pluralist" do not take us far enough.

We should understand what is being stated by these terms, but be aware that the scope of inquiry is not adequately framed by them.

II

The search for understanding has long been a part of our human record, and we note its distinguished presence in the Western intellectual heritage, indicating an inquisitiveness to grasp why things happen, how things occur, a puzzlement encountered in our attempts to come to grips with our surroundings, including others and ourselves, too. We have sought to understand how things, bricks, microbes, quarks, *stūpas* (Pāli *thūpas*), *pirit* (*paritta*), and symbols, have come to be (compare the insightful Buddhist phrase, *yathābhūtam*, "as it has come to be" which term communicates a fundamental affirmation about human understanding, that one becomes free of ego ensnaring projected volitional impositions when one recognizes the causal sequentiality that has given rise to the thing before one's senses or idea in one's thinking).

For Aristotle, who has cast a long shadow through Western intellectual history, including, of course, its religious history, understanding is an authentically human activity. In a splendid book, *Aristotle: The Desire to Understand*, Jonathan Lear provides an insightful observation,

> We want to know *why* the heavens move that way, *why* the phenomena are as they are. We are after more than knowledge, we are after understanding. Aristotle was, I believe, aware of this. Although 'to know' is an adequate translation of the Greek '*eidenai*,' Aristotle used this term generically to cover various species of knowing. One of the species is '*epistasthai*' (literally, to be in a state of having *epistēmē*) which has often been translated as 'to know' or 'to have scientific knowledge,' but which ought to be translated as 'to understand.'[5]

Systematic inquiry, inquisitiveness and continuing explorations into everything around one are natural activities in being human that involve *epistēmē*, which, Lear stresses, "*is by its nature reflective: one cannot understand the world unless one understands the place of understanding within it*."[6] In this process of understanding one's understanding, one also understands the desire to understand, leading to the understanding of "first principles," which reflective process of understanding is participating in Mind (*nous/νοῦς*), and, for Aristotle, this activity is participating in the Divine. Lear puts it succinctly;

> when man acquires this understanding, he is not acquiring understanding of a distinct object which, as it turns out, is divine [as one might consider God as a first principle]: the understanding is itself divine. Thus in the acquisition of this understanding, in philosophical activity, man partially transcends his own nature.[7]

I would add to Lear's observation "in philosophical activity," the point that such philosophical activity is also, at the same time, religious activity. I would also want to indicate that the point at issue is not that "man partially transcends his own nature," as Lear puts it, but that in this way men and women achieve their true nature, that they can become, authentically, genuinely human.

"Aristotle believed," Lear makes clear, "that to understand ourselves we must understand the world" and continues, "his insistence that understanding and self-understanding are each dependent on the other is . . . a truth whose depth we have only begun to appreciate."[8] And Lear provides a summation:

> Such investigation and understanding, the complete satisfaction of the desire to understand, ultimately constitute the highest form of self-understanding. That is, once we have penetrated deeply into the world's intelligible structure, we come to understand God, or, equivalently, God's understanding. But divine understanding simply *is* the intelligible ground of the world. And so we discover that what we have been thinking (in our investigation of the world) simply *is* Mind. At this point, our thinking

> is imitating and re-enacting God's thinking. It is in this re-enactment that man comes to understand the world and to understand God, but he also comes to understand himself.[9]

Lear's interpretation of Aristotle demonstrates his apprehension of the integrated reality of an intelligible world, of one's capacity to discern intelligibility, of one's fulfilling oneself as a human being in the activity of understanding—which activity participates in a divine order which depends upon the activity of that which Aristotle perceived to be God. Aristotle's world-view is hardly the one shared today. However it is remarkably instructive to learn that he found the activity of understanding to be uniquely human, that one becomes fully human, rises to what is best in being human, in the activity of understanding the world (bones, bushes, birds and neighbors) which process involves self-understanding and is nothing other than participating in the divine. Understanding, for Aristotle, is hardly limited to control of information, handling data, or systems analysis. Insofar as understanding involves participating in the divine intelligibility of the world in which one finds oneself, engaging in an activity that is both distinctly human and at the same time enables one to become genuinely human, fully human, the best that it is humanly possible to become, *that activity is religious*, enabling one, as it does, to live with meaning in life, to relate with things and with persons in an orderly and responsible manner, a way that is both moral and consistent with the order of the universe.

Twenty-four centuries after Aristotle lived and thought and died, one of the greatest Christian theologians in recent times, H. Richard Niebuhr, observed, about the reflective method, which we have seen was stressed in Lear's interpretation of *epistēmē*, that it

> is not solipsistic. We can carry on our effort to understand ourselves only in the company of other selves whom we are trying to understand and who are trying to understand themselves and us. The reflective method is always

> interpersonal, dependent on communication, seeking verification, correction, guidance from the reflections of others as these are mediated through statements about faith and definitions of the idea of faith. We do not even seem to know ourselves as selves in isolation but only in interpersonal society, in which we communicate with each other about common objects, whether these be the objects of perception or of reflection.[10]

One of H. Richard Niebuhr's major contributions to our thinking is his thematic stress and structural clarification of the social context of human valuations and the degree to which faith, as trust and responsibility among persons, lies at the heart of human attempts to understand. Although Niebuhr is fully conversant with Aristotle's thinking, and although he acknowledges his ethical position, presented succinctly in one of his chapters, "The Center of Value," is more indebted to G. H. Mead than to Aristotle,[11] had Lear's interpretation been available for Niebuhr one might well conjecture he would have found himself standing to a considerable degree in agreement with Aristotle, man of the *polis*. Niebuhr instructs us, in a chapter, entitled "The Reconstruction of Faith,"

> Without acknowledgment in trust of other persons who have bound themselves to us in loyalty and without a covenanting binding of ourselves to them as well as to causes that unite us, we do not exist as selves; we cannot think, we cannot communicate with objects or with one another. Without interpersonal relationship in faith, in the great triadic interaction of self, companions and cause, we might perceive the data offered to our senses but it is questionable whether we would possess concepts.[12]

But, as Niebuhr stresses, "Our human dilemma is this: we live as selves by faith but our faith is perverted and we with it."[13] "This is our anxiety," he writes, "a result not of our finiteness but of our dependence on an infinite and on finites which have the freedom to deceive us. There is no escape from this dilemma."[14] Niebuhr, the faithful Christian theologian, points out that there is a promise of healing of what he calls this "diseased faith," namely, "the New Covenant."[15]

The interpersonal basis of understanding runs throughout Niebuhr's writings, highlighting his triadic sense: of person and person(s) and object, which object, ultimately, for Niebuhr, is "the nameless, ultimate Transcendent and Circumambient."[16] This triadic structure of faith is entirely relevant and operable in seeking understanding of humankind's religiousness: oneself, the other religious person(s) and the ultimate Transcendent and Circumambient. It is largely due to one's having discerned wherein one is dependent on, is responsible to, other human beings while ascertaining a ground upon which those human relations can be discerned as fitting, as being supported by a moral order, and to one's becoming engaged with a transcendent reference made available to human apperception and memory, that one can begin to have a glimpse of the profound significance of *dhamma* in the lives of Buddhist men and women. Although Niebuhr would have moved to this notion of "the nameless, ultimate Transcendent and Circumambient" through an apprehension of a personal deity, which, in the grammar of his religious language he would refer to as God, Theravāda Buddhists would find his phrase helpful in pointing to *dhamma* in the highest sense of salvific truth, that truth which is transcendent and also circumambient, that surrounds us and is not apart from us.

III

The search for understanding is familiar to us all, and Aristotle, surely, endorsed its centrality in a quest to become fully human. In considering issues of religious pluralism, efforts to seek understanding of others, giving rise to a concomitant process of self-understanding, might well provide a category of religious thought more promising for further inquiry than we, perhaps, might have previously thought. Understanding requires knowledge, of course, but knowledge alone does not necessarily include understanding. Understanding, rather, is a supplement of knowledge, and by adding to it understanding completes it. Wilfred Cantwell Smith puts it this way:

> In the study of human affairs, 'to know and to understand' must be the twin objectives of intellectual inquiry. It is easy for a person to be ignorant of the data of human history, in general or for a particular sub-process; it requires much effort to come to know, even in small part. Yet to know but not to understand (to know what human beings have done or do, but not to understand them or it) is in its turn all too possible. It is, also, manifestly inadequate intellectually. This is conspicuously so in the history of religion, where knowledge without understanding has been common, and continues into our day. The category of understanding could, I suggest, become of potentially much greater significance than that of believing. It could prove more helpful, more illuminating, even decisive.[17]

Of course, what Aristotle meant by Mind (*nous*) or by God is not the same as what a Christian theologian might mean by God, nor would it be what a Theravāda Buddhist might mean by God. The movement in understanding that is involved, the activity of seeing the point, is not that of incorporating into one's own world-view a notion taken from another world-view and inserted into a paradigmatic complex circumscribed, defined, by a pattern of meanings with which one is already familiar, but to understand *as others have understood.*[18] Smith states it succinctly,

> By 'understanding' here I intend his [a Theravāda Buddhist's] apprehending not what the term 'God' means in his own world-view, where it refers to something that perhaps does not exist or is unworthy, but rather what it has meant to those who have used it to denote and to connote a great range of their life in the world, and the universally human reaching beyond the world: their perception both of empiricals and of ultimates."[19]

This orientation toward understanding of the world, of persons and the centers of value in terms of which they, themselves, find personal integration, responsible relationships with others, and orientation to the world, can move us beyond the inadequate fixation on belief systems, syllogistic arguments and theoretical models like "exclusive," "inclusive," and "pluralistic," with associated cudgel-like categories of "true" and "false" disconcertingly applied to something simultaneously more engaging and more productive of convergence: seeking to become ever more true to the truth one has been enabled to discern, on the one hand, and, on the other, seeking to deepen one's understanding of the apprehensions of transcendence to which others bear witness.

Primary focus need not remain on what *Religion* is or on what has been written and discussed in the *Study of Religion*, or on what all *Religions* might have or not have in common. Utmost importance need no longer be placed on whether one is an "exclusivist" or an "inclusivist" or a "pluralist" as one attempts to sort out a position among positions within current Christian reflection. One can place aside the patterns of judging religions as being true or false—a really surprising practice in light of the overwhelming and variegated movements and dimensions of the religious traditions through many cultures over the centuries. How is one to "freeze frame" the dynamic and cumulative global process in order to set up mutually agreed upon syllogistic formulae by means of which to judge this or that religious tradition as true or false? And, further, grappling with the particulars of a religious tradition, the facts of the case, checking them, testing them rigorously as serious inquirers, would not require that one maintain an impersonal distance, a kind of so-called objectivity, a matter-of-fact lack of involvement face to face with magnificent human concerns. Understanding leads beyond all of this, is required of us and in it we discover, refreshingly, a genuinely human activity. As Smith says, "The requirement that one's own ideas be true is a moral demand; the requirement that others' be understood is a moral demand also."[20] This search for understanding is not restricted to the acquisition of facts and assimilation of information, nor is it mere speculation, an abstract arm-chair activity. This search for inter-religious understanding requires the discipline of an intellectual, the humane sensitivity of a self-conscious human being, and the commitment to truth that provides both motivation and orientation. This search for understanding is at the heart of what it means to be genuinely human, and the quest to become such is a religious quest.

Notes

1. In the three decades during which it was my good fortune to have known Godwin Samararatne, I have deeply appreciated his quest for understanding. In his inquiry into the activity of the mind, into human relationships, into cross-cultural and inter-religious understanding, Godwin was faithful to a Buddhist principle: "don't get stuck." Ever open to the new, continuingly and creatively receptive of others, never judgmental of theological affirmations, Godwin demonstrated to students at Colgate University and to Colgate students on three occasions at his meditation center at Nilambe, Sri Lanka, the integrative orientation to the truth by which he lived his life and the moral commitment by which he sought to understand others and the world in which we live.

2. One might agree with David Hume that fundamentally cognition is a combination of impressions arising from sensations and reflection on those sensations, yielding simple ideas that can become more complex either as a response to complex sensations or to the activity of the human imagination rearranging those ideas. According to this view, knowledge arises when resemblances between and among ideas are arranged and categorized. (This conceptualization of the process reflects, of course, the system-structuring of categories prevalent in Western scientific procedures.) Whatever might be a process of greater abstraction beyond these restructuring of resemblances of ideas, as this particular interpretation puts it, is due to habit or custom, a frequency of recurring usages only, not at all demonstrable from the empirically given. It is this habit or custom that leads one to propose a similarity in causes yielding particular effects, but such cannot either be inferred with reliability or demonstrated with precision. (One would want to recall some of the points about habit or custom in the foundation of morals suggested by Hume's contemporary, Edmund Burke, 1729-1797.) If it were not to appear arrogant or flippant, one would want to say in response to Hume and of this line of inquiry, "Well, of course." We are, indeed, so constituted that sense perception and sense impressions are fundamental, without question, as building blocks with which our distinctive

reflection, even imagination, set about to structure experiences upon which the mind can reflect in its cognitive processes, which are primary, without, of course, denying other forms of human experience. One recalls the words of the *Dhammapada*,

> Preceded by perception are mental states,
> For them is perception supreme,
> From perception have they sprung . . . .

See the opening two verses of "The Pairs" (*Yamaka-vaggo*) of the *Dhammapada*. The Pāli reads, *manopubbaṅgamā dhammā manoseṭṭhā manomayā.* John Ross Carter and Mahinda Pālihawadana, *The Dhammapada: A New English Translation with the Pāli Text and the First English Translation of the Commentary's Explanation of the Verses with Notes Translated from Sinhala Sources and Critical Textual Comments* (New York: Oxford University Press, 1987): 89.

3. The case has been made, convincingly, by Wilfred Cantwell Smith in his now classic work, *The Meaning and End of Religion* (Minneapolis: Fortress Press, 1991) (of the work republished often since 1962).

4. Occasionally in considering the "exclusivistic case" expressions like "my Jesus," or "my God," are written off as a kind of *genitive of possession*, suggesting an inadequate theological awareness that one is attempting to possess Jesus, God, in one's own conceptualization. But could not this be interpreted as a *genitive of engagement or relevance* whereby one is giving testimony to the abiding presence of God in Christ in one's life?

5. Jonathan Lear, *Aristotle: The Desire to Understand* (Cambridge: Cambridge University Press, 1999): 6. Twin strands that have shaped mightily the religious heritage of the West, as often noted stemming from Palestinian and Greco-Roman complexes, have largely, though not exclusively, developed from the Greek language. The writers of the *koinē* Greek New Testament demonstrate a clear preference for two Greek terms, and their derivatives, to communicate knowledge/understanding: *oida* (οἶδα) and *ginōsko* (γινώσκω, a later form of γιγνώσκω), with much less predilection for the Greek word from which has derived the much more popular key term in philosophical discourse today: *epistēmē* (ἐπιστήμη). One finds *epistamai* "understand something, know," or "be acquainted with," prevalent in Acts, particularly in indirect discourse, and as participle in I Timothy and Mark and *epistēmon*, "expert, learned, understanding," as noted in James. In fact, *epistēmē* itself appears only as a variant reading at Philippians 4:8.

6. Ibid., p. 8.

7. Ibid., p. 9.

8. Ibid., p. 14.

9. Ibid., pp. 316-317.
10. H. Richard Niebuhr, *Faith on Earth: An Inquiry into the Structure of Human Faith*, ed. Richard R. Niebuhr (New Haven: Yale University Press, 1989): 24.
11. H. Richard Niebuhr, *Radical Monotheism and Western Culture, with Supplementary Essays*, (New York: Harper & Row, 1960): 105, n. 1.
12. Niebuhr, *Faith on Earth*, p. 83.
13. Ibid.
14. Ibid., p. 84.
15. Ibid., p. 85.
16. Ibid., p. 84.
17. Wilfred Cantwell Smith, *Faith and Belief* (Princeton, New Jersey: Princeton University Press, 1979): 146.
18. This would suggest that one not stop one's inquiry by arguing for a kind of "comparative theology" in which one takes similarities found in another tradition and uses them to draw attention to fresh currents of thought and practice in one's own religious tradition or to take ideas in one's own religious heritage and utilize them in interpreting the religious insights of others. These hermeneutical moves can be helpful, but one would want to be rigorous in application and also mindful of a kind of reified conceptual divide between systems of thought possibly leading to an inadequate appreciation for novelty in expressing engagement with transcendence and the life of persons responding to transcendence.
19. Smith, *Faith and Belief*, p. 147.
20. Ibid., p. 170.

Part Two

Ritual and Cosmology

In the Presence of the Buddha

Donald K. Swearer

I first met Godwin Samararatne when he conducted a week's meditation workshop at Swarthmore College over twenty years ago. My memory of the precise date is vague. I believe it was in the spring of 1979; I can't be sure. But the picture of Godwin instructing a group of thirty students in *vipassanā* meditation in the gothic ambience of Bond Hall on our lower campus remains almost as vivid as the week he was actually there. On the last day of the workshop Godwin led us in *mettā bhāvanā*. As we extended loving-kindness in ever widening circles—from those near and dear to those distant in time, space, and affection—a miraculous sense of com-union occurred. Was it the feelings of goodwill that Godwin had engendered in us during the hours we had spent together? Or was it a brief transformation of ordinary, individuated consciousness, as even now my attentive recollection of a warm spring afternoon in Bond Hall makes Godwin palpably present through the memory of his person and his teaching.

Memory, remembrance, recollection, mindfulness, mnemic awareness are among the most important concepts in Buddhist philosophy, psychology, meditation, and ritual practice. Remembrance of past lives is one of the powers associated with the achievement of advanced states of consciousness; recollection plays an important role in the development of concentration in Buddhaghosa's *Visuddhimagga*; and remembering the lives of saints and their virtues provides moral and spiritual guidance for devotees.[1] Of the various uses of memory in the Theravāda tradition, recollecting the Buddha has been and continues to be of supreme importance. In this essay in remembrance of Godwin Samararatne I shall briefly examine recollective strategies by which the Buddha is made present to Buddhist practitioners. All occur within the context of the northern Thai Buddha image consecration ritual or, as it is called, the eye-opening ceremony.[2]

Opening the Eyes of the Buddha

In northern Thailand the ritual to consecrate new Buddha images reenacts the night of the Buddha's enlightenment. Ordinarily the ceremony will take place in the main hall of a monastery in a specially constructed space that replicates the *bodhimaṇḍa*, the site of the Buddha's enlightenment. The ceremony begins in the early evening and continues until sunrise. After an opening *paritta* recitation, the evening's main activities include monastic chant unique to the *buddhābhiseka,* the preaching of sermons describing the Buddha's journey to enlightenment, and extended periods of meditation. These activities take place around the *bodhimaṇḍa,* a sacred space encircled by a protective fence *(rājavati)* over which extends a web of consecrated string (Thai, *sai siñcana*) arranged into 108 squares, the sum of the powerful and radiant qualities *(guṇa)* of the Buddha, the *dhamma*, and the *saṅgha*. Following a reenactment of Sujātā's offering of sweetened milk-rice to the future Buddha, as the morning sun breaks over the horizon, the monk ritualists preach the *Dhammacakkappavattana Sutta* symbolizing the Buddha's enlightenment and first teaching on the cause and cessation of suffering. Meanwhile, white cloth head coverings that had shrouded the Buddha images throughout the evening are removed, marking the successful completion of the enlivening empowerment of the image.[3]

The consecrated image is now the Buddha's real presence. The northern Thai *buddhābhiseka* ceremony, like eye-opening rituals in other Buddhist cultures, makes the Buddha present in the image. To be sure, the precise meaning of the claim that the *parinibbāned* Buddha is present in any material form has been debated throughout the history of Buddhism up to the present. It can be seen, for example, in the *Mahāparinibbāna Sutta* and what appears to reflect a dispute over the nature of the Buddha. After his death will the Buddha simply be absent from historical existence or will the Buddha somehow be present? Will the Buddha be present in the *dhamma*, in his bodily relics, in both, or in neither? These questions—as well as the proto-Mahāyāna cosmic-Buddhological issue of seeming omnipresence of previous Buddhas in past aeons—pose a contentious problem for Buddhist philosophy and for Buddhist ritual practice. It is well and good to argue that whoever sees the universal law of *paṭicca-samuppāda* sees the Buddha, but to his followers the Buddha was not an abstract principle of dependent co-arising. The Buddha is teacher, moral exemplar, powerful conqueror of men and gods, the Thus-Gone One *(tathāgata)* and Blessed Lord *(bhagavant)*. The devotee's desire is to be in the presence of this very person.

The *buddhābhiseka* ritual suggests practical ways in which this happens. As a mimetic reenactment of the night of the Buddha's enlightenment, the ritual brings into time a timeless truth. As the abstract, eternal *dhamma* is hypostasized by Gotama Buddha, the *buddhābhiseka* instantiates the universal Buddha paradigm in a particular time and place. The skillful means by which this takes place are chant-recitation, sermon-story, and focused recollection.[4] Each of these strategies has a performative function within the context of the ritual; hence, their power and affective meaning can only be partially understood if one has not experienced the event itself. Yet, each strategy has a cognitive content that contributes to its total meaning, and it is to this we turn to describe the Buddha whose presence is evoked in the Buddha image consecration ritual.

The Image As Buddha Surrogate

The story of the making of the first Buddha image clearly indicates that the statue was intended to be a surrogate for the living Buddha. Versions of the root story vary in detail but they all share a similar structure. A retinue of the faithful travel to pay respects to the Buddha but the Buddha is absent. The disappointed visitors request that an image be made as a stand-in for the Buddha whenever he is away. Although in these tales the Buddha is physically not present for such reasons as preaching the *Abhidhamma* to his mother in Tāvatiṃsa Heaven or being away on a teaching mission, they can be read as justifying the making and use of Buddha images after the Blessed One's *parinibbāna*. While the stories serve as etiological myths in which the Buddha, himself, authenticates the fabrication of an image, what the stories reveal about being in the presence of the Buddha is of even greater interest. I shall summarize a Pāli version of this story, the introduction to the *Vaṭṭaṅgulirāja Jātaka*, included in a collection of fifty *jātaka*s *(Paññāsa Jātaka)* written in Chiang Mai, Thailand in the 13th or 14th century, rather than using the more widely known legend of the making of the sandalwood image recounted by the Chinese pilgrims Faxian (fifth century) and Xuanzang (seventh century).[5]

> Once upon a time the Lord journeyed from Sāvatthi to a distant place to preach the Law. At that time King Pasenadi of Kosala, surrounded by a great number of people carrying perfume, garlands, and other means of worship went to the great monastery in Jetavana. Not seeing the Enlightened One, the king was filled with disappointment and saying, "Alas, alas, this Jetavana is empty without the Lord," he returned home greatly dejected. The citizens, filled with agitation, said to each other, "Alas, O sirs, this world without the Enlightened One, is indeed empty, without a refuge and without a protector." After some time, the Lord returned to Jetavana. Hearing the news, the king returned with the citizens to pay his respects to the Buddha. Having worshipped the Master he said, "O Lord, even while you

> are still alive, whenever you go away and people can't see your form they become full of misery, (thinking) they have no protector. How could they ever be happy and not feel bereaved when you will have entered *parinibbāna*? Therefore, O Lord, please allow me to make an image of you to be worshipped by both men and gods." Hearing the king's words, the teacher, perceiving that it would bring welfare to the entire world, and to ensure that his teaching endure forever, gave permission to the king to make an image.[6]

Subsequently the Buddha, the narrator of the *jātaka*, tells the story of king Vaṭṭaṅgulirāja, he then returns to the frame story of King Pasenadi, the building of the Buddha image, and the rewards for such a meritorious act.

> Having heard this story, King Pasenadi returned to his residence and selecting a sandalwood tree had a beautiful image of the Buddha made from it. Covering the image with a set of divine robes, he placed it on an elevated seat in his palace. The king and his assembly saw the Buddha image seated there shining as though endowed with life. The king, contemplating the Buddha image, was filled with joy. He then went to Jetavana and invited the Buddha to see the image. "O sir, I have made your image as you permitted me. That image shines with light, as if it were alive. Please come in order to perceive your own form." The next morning the Lord and his chief disciples entered the great pavilion in the palace of the king in order to see the Buddha image. At that very moment, the sandalwood image, immediately upon seeing the Buddha, became animated, as if by the power of the Buddha, and thought thus: "When the great Buddha is alive and comes here, it is not proper that I should be seated here on this high seat. Let me pay my respects to him." Thinking thus, the image lifted one foot from the pedestal in order to rise and welcome the Buddha. Observing this, the Lord raised his right hand and said, "Be seated, O noble one. I shall be entering into *parinibbāna* soon. May you sustain my *sāsana* for five thousand years to come.[7]

In these selections from the *Vaṭṭaṅgulirāja Jātaka*, the

image represents the Buddha's presence in several different ways: 1) it is animated by the power of the Buddha, himself; 2) being in the presence of the Buddha or the image as the Buddha's double has an affective import, evoking joy at the Buddha's presence and disappointed agitation when the Buddha is absent; 3) a monastery is "empty" without the Buddha's presence, and, in a like manner, the presence of the Blessed One or the Buddha's surrogate guarantees the continuance of the *sāsana*; and, 4) the efficacy of merit-making rituals is guaranteed by the presence of the Buddha and jeopardized by his absence. The text expands effusively on the various rewards earned by sponsoring the construction of Buddha images, so much so, in fact, that the *Vaṭṭaṅgulirāja Jātaka* could be classified as an *ānisaṃsa* or merit-making text.

To be in the presence of the Buddha also means to be in the presence of the *dhamma*. The relationship between the Buddha and the *dhamma/dharma* posed one of the most contested Buddhological problems in the history of Buddhist thought, and this problem became central to philosophical distinctions among different Buddhist schools. In the context of the northern Thai, Lao, and Khmer *buddhābhiseka* ritual, however, the body of the Buddha, or to be precise, the body of the Buddha image, gives visual form to the *dhamma*. This identification between the body of the Buddha (*rūpakāya)* and the body of the *dhamma* is delineated via a dhammic template programmed into the body of the image by means of a *dhāraṇic—mantric* strategy performed by a monk ritualist who touches parts of the image while reciting particular doctrinal teaching. Implanting these 'auspicious signs' makes the image a cult icon worthy of veneration: "The body parts correspond to doctrinal concepts so that the statue whose shape forms an image of the Buddha's body will also be the body of the *dhamma*."[8] The following selections serve to illustrate how the Buddha through the surrogacy of the image represents the *dhamma* in a visual, material sense.

Rūpakāya	Dhammakāya
The Head of the Image	*sabbaññutāñāṇa* (supreme Omniscience)
The Noble Forehead	*catutthajjhāna* (the fourth *jhāna*)
Two Noble Eyes	*dibbacakkhu paññācakkhu buddhacakkhu dhammacakkhu* (divine eye, wisdom eye…)
Two Noble Ears	*dibbasota ṭāṇa* (divine wisdom ears)
Two Noble Lips	*lokiya/lokuttaraṃ ñāṇa* (mundane and transmundane wisdom)
The Noble Tongue	*catusacca ñāṇa* (knowledge of the four noble truths)[9]

Such ritual strategies, seemingly at odds with the conventional view of the Buddha image in Theravāda Buddhism as a symbol or mere reminder of the Blessed One, give locative form to the *dhamma* as a universal principle and its 84,000 particular elements. Through a similar strategy the image is also infused with the Buddha's perfections *(pāramī)*:

> The ten forces of knowledge that should be known,
> The ten perfections *(pāramī)* ... the preaching of the noble *dhamma* to save the lives of countless beings in all regions and cities who have taken refuge [in the Buddha],
> I invite all the *dhamma*s of the Jinas to come together and immediately to enter the statue.[10]

Yantric strategies may be employed, as well. A collection of northern Thai Buddha image consecration texts includes a scheme of eleven acrostic type grids inscribed with Pāli letters that extol the power of the Buddha, the *dhamma*, and the *saṅgha*. Their meaning, hidden to those without the key to decipher the sequence of letters, is inscribed onto the image by applying the grids to its various bodily parts.[11]

Buddha Story and Buddha Presence

There is much truth in the saying, "We are our stories." When we contemplate the question, "Who am I?", we are apt to think in autobiographical terms rather than of an essential self that defines us through time and space. While Gotama's *nibbāna* was the defining moment of his Buddhahood, it was also the culmination of a six-year quest to discover the cause and cessation of suffering. Furthermore, the Buddha's life was preceded by many prior *bodhisatta* lives of moral and spiritual preparation recounted in the Pāli *Jātaka.* During the *buddhābhiseka* ritual the Blessed One is made present through the Buddha story recounted in sermons and recited in chant lasting through much of the night. Murals depicting the story of Gotama Buddha's life and the ten *bodhisatta* existences immediately preceding it also adorn the temple walls, thereby enabling the ritual participants to experience the Buddha's presence through his story on multiple levels—aurally, visually, and performatively. In effect, through a mimetic reenactment of the night of the *bodhisatta*'s journey to and achievement of enlightenment, they enter into the presence of the Buddha, becoming actors on the stage of a sacred history.

The biographical texts recited during the *buddhābhiseka* ritual include the *Paṭhama Sambodhi* and the *Buddha Abhiseka Gāthā.* A 1671 C.E. palm leaf manuscript copy of the latter states that the text was written by a monk from Jayasenapura (modern Chiang Saen) in 1591 C. E.[12] The narrative shares much in common with the structure of the story of the Buddha recounted in the introduction to the *Jātaka* commentary. It begins with an abbreviated account of previous Buddhas, and then proceeds to describe the Buddha's thirty perfections, the future Buddha's rebirth in Tusita Heaven, the five prognostications and the Buddha's birth, the four sights, the renunciation, the future Buddha's encounter with King Bimbisāra, the search for a teacher, the *bodhisatta*'s extreme efforts together with the five ascetics, the future Buddha's five visions, Sujātā's offering of sweetened milk-rice, Sotthiya's offering of *kusa* grass that becomes the throne of enlightenment, the enlightenment event, the Buddha's qualifications, the seven week period after the Buddha's enlightenment, the encounter with Sahaṃpatibrahmā and the Buddha's decision to teach the *dhamma*, the first discourse, and several events leading up to the Buddha's *parinibbāna*. This text and other versions similar to it conclude with a recitation infusing the qualities of the Buddha's life into the image:

> The Buddha, filled with boundless compassion, practiced the thirty perfections for many eons, finally reaching enlightenment. May all his qualities be invested in this image.
>
> May the Buddha's boundless omniscience be invested in this image until the *sāsana* ceases to exist.
>
> May the Buddha's boundless virtue acquired during his activities immediately after his enlightenment be stored in this image forever.
>
> May the knowledge contained in the seven books of the *Abhidhamma* perceived by the Buddha in the seven weeks after his enlightenment be consecrated in this image for the remainder of the life of the *sāsana*.
>
> May the power acquired by the Buddha during the seven days under the Ajapāla tree, the seven days at the Mucalinda pond, etc., be invested in this Buddha image for 5,000 rain-retreats. The Buddha then returned to the Ajapālanigrodha where he preached the 84,000 verses of the *dhamma*. May they also be stored in this Buddha image....[13]

Rehearsing the Buddha's biography provides an opportunity for the congregants to review the salient events of the narrative that represents the Buddha. Moreover, by means of this narrative construction, the image becomes not only the *dhamma* ritually programmed into the image as auspicious signs, but it also becomes the Buddha's life story. When the congregates gaze on the form of the Buddha, his *rūpa-kāya*, they see not only the *dhamma-kāya* but an exemplary figure whose life monks strive to emulate and lay persons, as well, when they give generously, act compassionately, and seek to lead lives of mindful awareness.

Commemorative Visualization

I spent the 1967-68 academic year on sabbatical leave in Sri Lanka, Thailand, and Japan. In each of these settings I sought out meditation teachers in order to understand better questions of Buddhist epistemology with which I had struggled in my doctoral dissertation. My teacher in Bangkok, whom I later invited to conduct a January term meditation workshop at Oberlin College, was Sobhana Dhammasudhi, better known as Dhiravamsa.[14] His account of his early meditation experiences represent what Paul Harrison has characterized within a ritual context as "commemmorative visualization."[15] As a young novice monk, Dhiravamsa would often spend long hours during the night in his monastery's main image hall. Focusing his attention on the face of the large, candle-lit Buddha image, he would then close his eyes and visualize the image while concentrating on in and out breaths until he became suffused with the presence of the Buddha. Participants in the Buddha image consecration ritual report having a similar experience engendered by its overall ambience, the aural and visual effects, but primarily by an intensified mindfulness (*anussati)* of the Buddha so multifacetedly present in the ceremony. This act of concentrated attention brings into sharp focus what it means to be in the presence of the Buddha during the *buddhābhiseka* ceremony but at all other times, as well. Being in the presence of the Buddha is not merely a vague memory or casual recollection but, like Dhiravamsa as a young novice monk or the consecrated Buddha image, being infused with the very person of the Buddha.

The qualities that constitute the Buddha's personhood are recited during the Buddha image consecration ritual and are also the focus of intense meditation, at least by some of the participants. Buddhaghosa enumerates these qualities systematically in the seventh chapter of the *Visuddhimagga* on the six types of intense mindfulness. In the text they appear almost as a list of titles. The Buddha is accomplished (*arahanta)*, fully enlightened (*sammāsambuddha*), endowed with clear vision and virtuous conduct (*vijjācaraṇasampanno)*, sublime (*sugata*), knower of worlds (*lokavidū*), incomparable leader of men to be tamed (*purisadammasārathi*), teacher of gods and men (*satthā)*, blessed (*bhagavant*).[16] Buddhaghosa provides elaborate descriptions of each of the Buddha's qualities often using an exegetical method based on intricate word play. For example, the Buddha is accomplished (*arahanta*) because of his remoteness (*āraka*) from defilements; because his enemies (*ari*), the spokes (*ara*) of the wheel of becoming made by ignorance and craving, have been destroyed (*hata*) (vii. 4-7). He is sublime (*sugata*) because of having gone to an excellent place (*sundaraṃ ṭhānaṃ gatattā*) (vii.33), and blessed (*bhagavā*) because he has achieved the end of becoming (*bhavantago*) (vii. 56). In their ritual use these epithets or attributes become a formula of transformative empowerment—*iti pi so bhagavā arahaṃ sammāsambuddho*...: This Lord is indeed the *Arahant*, the fully awakened one, perfected in knowledge and conduct, the well-gone one, the knower of the world, the supreme one, the trainer of men, the teacher of gods and humankind, the Buddha, the Lord.[17] By concentrated attention to and repetition of these sublime qualities of the Buddha, the three poisons of lust, hatred, and delusion are displaced; one overcomes the five hindrances of sensual desire, ill-will, sloth and torpor, excitation and guilt, and doubt; and achieves the rapture that leads to tranquility.[18] Buddhaghosa extols being in the presence of the Buddha through intense mindfulness as follows:

> And the monk who is devoted to this recollection of the Buddha is respected and reverent to the Teacher; reaches an abundance of faith, mindfulness, wisdom and merit; is always full of zest and joy; overcomes fear and dread;

> is able to bear pain; obtains a sense of intimacy with the Teacher; and his body which has embodied this recollection of the Buddha is, like a shrine, worthy of worship; his mind steers in the direction of Buddhahood.[19]

Paul Harrison finds in *anusmṛti/anussati* a power not only to bring about the kind of personal transformation Buddhaghosa eulogizes but, as a commemorative act, an instrument of communion and co-participation. So often meditation—whether insight training (*vipassanā*), focusing on the repetition of *Buddho, Buddho* associated with Thailand's northeastern forest tradition, or forms of *samatha* concentration promoted by Phra Aajān Thong at Wat Muang Man in Chiang Mai—are thought of solely as an individual pursuit. But, while meditation demands individual discipline and practice, it leads to expansive states of consciousness and deeper levels of awareness of self, others, and one's surroundings.

I believe that on a warm Spring afternoon on the campus of Swarthmore College over twenty years ago Godwin Samararatne evoked in us a "commemorative visualization of mourning, gratitude, and responsibility" not only for those of us gathered there but for all sentient beings with whom we share this planet earth.[20]

Notes

1. See Janet Gyatso, ed. *In the Mirror of Memory: Reflections on Mindfulness and Remembrance in Indian and Tibetan Buddhism* (Albany: State University of New York Press, 1992). Gyatso points out that one of the thematic tensions in the various uses of memory and related terms is between recollective memory of past experiences and mnemic awareness.
2. For a more detailed description and analysis of the northern Thai Buddha image consecration ritual see Donald K. Swearer, "Hypostasizing the Buddha: Buddha Image Consecration in Northern Thailand," *History of Religions* 34, no. 3 (February, 1995): 263-280. See also Stanley J. Tambiah, *The Buddhist Saints of the Forest and the Cult of Amulets* (Cambridge: Cambridge University Press, 1984): chap. 17, and Donald K. Swearer, *Becoming the Buddha: Image Consecration in Northern Thailand: Sources and Interpretation* (Forthcoming).

3. "Because they [Buddha images] are, in a sense, alive, and not simply dead representations, these icons are images of power" (Bernard Faure, "The Buddhist Icon and the Modern Gaze," *Critical Inquiry* 24, no. 3 (Spring, 1998): 768).

4. I have in mind here the Mahāyāna notion of *upāya*, especially the stratagem of the father in the Parable of the Burning House in the Lotus Sutra.

5. I.B. Horner and Padmanabh S. Jaini, trans., *Apocryphal Birth Stories (Paññāsa Jātaka)*, vol. 2., bk.38 of *Sacred Books of the Buddhists* (London: Pāli Text Society, 1985), and Padmanabh S. Jaini, "On the Buddha Image," *Studies in Pāli Buddhism*, ed. A. K. Narain (Delhi: B. R. Publishing Corp., 1979): 183-187. The *Kosala-Bimba-Vaṇṇanā*, a thirteenth or fourteenth century Pāli text from Sri Lanka, differs from the introduction to the *Vaṭṭaṅgulirāja Jātaka* only in minor details. See Richard F. Gombrich, "Kosala-Bimba-Vaṇṇanā," *Buddhism in Ceylon and Studies on Religious Syncretism in Buddhist Countries* (Symposium zur Buddhismusforschung, I), ed. Heinz Bechert, (Göttingen: Abhandlungen der Akademic der Wissenschaften, 1978): 304-34.

6. Adapted from *Apocryphal Birth-Stories*, 103-104, and Jaini, "On the Buddha Image," 185.

7. Adapted from *Apocryphal Birth-Stories*, 114-115, and Jaini, "On the Buddha Image," 185-186.

8. François Bizot, "La consécration des statues et le culte des morts," *Recherches nouvelles sur le Cambodge*, ed. François Bizot (Paris: École française d'Extrême-Orient, 1994): 110.

9. Excerpted from my forthcoming book, *Becoming the Buddha*, chap. 3. See also, François Bizot, *Le Chemin de Lanka* (Paris: École Française d'Extrême-Orient, 1992): 293-299; also, George Coedès, "*Dhammakāya,*" *Adyar Library Bulletin* 20 (1956): 239-286.

10. Bizot, "La Consécration," 114.

11. Swearer, *Becoming the Buddha*, chap. 3

12. References to this manuscript are from a draft translation by the late Bumphen Rawin, Faculty of the Humanities, Chiang Mai University, made in 1997.

13. Slightly adapted from Donald K. Swearer, (1995) *op. cit*.," 278.

14. An account of this workshop is included in Donald K. Swearer, *Secrets of the Lotus: Studies in Buddhist Meditation*, 2nd edition (Delhi: Sunil Gupta, 1995).

15. Paul Harrison, "Commemoration and Identification in Buddhānusmṛti," *In the Mirror of Memory: Reflections on Mindfulness and Remembrance in Indian and Tibetan Buddhism*, ed. Janet Gyatso (Albany: State University of New York Press, 1992): 215-238.

16. Vism vii.1-76.
17. For a study of the *mantric* use of the *iti pi so* formula see, F. Bizot and O. von Hinüber, *La Guirlande de Joyaux* (Paris: École Française d'Extrême-Orient, 1994).
18. Harrison, "Commemoration and Identification...", 217-218.
19. Ibid., 218.
20. See ibid., 230.

Establishing the Basis of the Sāsana:

Social Service and Ritual Performance in Contemporary Sri Lankan Monastic Training[1]

Jeffrey Samuels

In the commentary on the Gradual Discourses (*Aṅguttara Nikāya*) there is a story about a debate that took place during the first century BCE in a temple called *Maṇḍalārāmavihāra*. The subject of the debate centered around the question of what constituted the foundation or basis of the Buddhist religion (*sāsana*).[2] While certain rag-clothed (ascetic?) monks (*paṃsukūlikatherā*) argued that the basis of the *sāsana* was practice (*paṭipatti*), the *dhamma*-preaching monks (*dhammakathikātherā*) argued that the basis was learning (*pariyatti*). The commentary, attributed to the famous *dhamma*-preaching monk and synthesizer Buddhaghosa, further reveals (not surprisingly) that the *dhammakathikātherā* won the debate, thereby establishing study—or 'the burden of the book' (*ganthadhura*)—as the basis of the *sāsana* over the path of practice, or 'the burden of meditation' (*vipassanādhura*). In the conclusion of the description of this debate, Buddhaghosa justifies the primacy of studying by explaining that learning preserves the *sāsana*: "Even if a hundred or a thousand monks are proficient in *vipassanā*, if there are no monks with learning, there would cease to be realization (or knowledge) of the noble path."[3]

Whether apocryphal or not, this story reveals an important debate within Theravāda Buddhist history. Despite the supposed resolution of the debate in the first century BCE, the discussion about what constitutes the foundation of the *sāsana* has been ongoing. Through examining a new monastic training institution established in Sri Lanka in the early 1990s, the *sāmaṇera* training center, this article will add yet another voice to this omnipresent debate.

By placing the founders' and head monks' ideas about the *sāmaṇera* training centers and ritual performance within larger discourses of decline and revival, this article will consider how these leading figures implicitly argue for a different basis of the *sāsana*—ritual performance—and how that basis, like other bases before it, becomes seen as the principal factor contributing to the continuation of the Buddhist religion on the island.

Sāmaṇera Training Centers: Visions of Decline and Revival

The impetus behind the establishment of *sāmaṇera* training centers in Sri Lanka came in the wake of a perceived decline of Buddhism on the island. Despite the absence of any census figures showing actual declines in the number of Buddhist monks or lay people, the sentiment that the *saṅgha* is in a state of decline—which has been, and still is, a very powerful motivator for monastic change—is quite prevalent among segments of the lay and monastic populations. It was among such a group of lay people and monks that the idea of creating a monastic institution directed to the training of young novice monks first arose.

In 1992, prior to the 2300 year celebration of the introduction of Buddhism to Sri Lanka by the *arahant* Mahinda (*Mahindu Jayanti*), a meeting was held in Colombo to evaluate the place of the *saṅgha* in Sri Lanka and the directions that should be taken by the Ministry of Buddhist Affairs

(*Buddha Sāsana Amātyāmśaya*). One of the chairs of the committee, Venerable Vaelamiṭiyāvē Kusaladhamma, principal of Vidyālaṃkāra Piriveṇa and chancellor of Kelaniya University explained:

> In 1992, a conference was held at the Bandaranaike Memorial International Conference Hall in Colombo.... At that conference, many committees were set up to discuss the present state of Buddhism in Sri Lanka. One of them, for which I was the chairman, was devoted to the issue of monastic training.
>
> There were around sixty people, both lay people and monks, from various fields and areas. As we met, they began to criticize the growing impropriety of monks, especially young monks. They also criticized the monks' growing inability to fulfill the religious requirements of the devotees. I replied to those people that the accusations directed toward young monks were pointless without having a proper place where they could be trained.... I proposed to them that we implement some kind of solution under the new ministry. This was how the idea of *sāmaṇera* training centers was started.[4]

According to Kusaladhamma and other elder monks with whom I spoke, prior to the 1960s prospective, *sāmaṇera*s in Sri Lanka were informally trained through an apprenticeship period of two to four years in the temple (*vihāra*) where they were seeking ordination as novices. During that time, the boys learned to perform common religious rituals, gained a knowledge of basic Buddhist doctrines, and began establishing relationships with the lay donors of the temple. Only after completing this long initiatory period were the boys granted admission into the *saṅgha* as *sāmaṇera*s and only after that point were they permitted to pursue a formal course of study in a monastic school (*piriveṇa*).

According to the founders and head monks associated with these new centers, however, this traditional method of training prospective *sāmaṇera*s through an initiatory period of several years has gradually given way to the novices having little or no initiatory period. Instead, boys seeking entrance into the monkhood are ordained as *sāmaṇeras* without delay, after which they are almost immediately sent off to monastic schools (*piriveṇas*) where, as boarders, they are taught Buddhist texts, stories, and doctrine. Despite acquiring sufficient knowledge during their formal monastic education in the *piriveṇas,* the absence of a pre-ordination initiatory stage is thought to leave them disconnected from everyday monastic life, including the lives and concerns of the laity. As a result, it is believed that novices remain unqualified and even unable to fulfill the laity's basic religious needs, such as performing Buddhist rituals and teaching the *dhamma*.

In one way, the criticism voiced in 1992 toward the *saṅgha* was not unique. Many prior attempts at reforming the *saṅgha*, both from within and without, have focused on the impropriety of monks.[5] An important difference between the 1992 meeting and other *vinaya*-oriented reforms, however, is the second reason for the decline of Buddhism on the island: *the monks' inability to fulfill the religious needs of the laity*. As a result of this, a different method for ameliorating the problem was put forth: rather than altering the monastic college (*piriveṇa*) curriculum or establishing post-*piriveṇa* training institutions where monks could be trained in providing social service and engaging in missionary work, the government, in an unprecedented move, approved the establishment of training centers dedicated solely to novices. In these centers, the novices, following their entrance into the monkhood, are trained in monastic deportment and especially in ritual performance. To be able to appreciate the uniqueness of these institutions and the different ways that they implicitly establish a different basis of the *sāsana*, I will turn to the features of the centers' training course and curriculum.

The Training Program for Novice Monks: The Monastic Curriculum

Earlier discussions of ideal monastic service and roles have often centered on such activities as practicing meditation, studying, teaching, strictly following the monastic discipline or *vinaya* and so on. For the founders of the *sāmaṇera* training centers, however, ideal monastic service is primarily based on pleasing the laity by the proper performance of rituals. Although the charter mentions several important rituals that the novices *must* learn, an examination of the training curriculum points to a wider range of rituals that are taught to the novices during their first two years in the centers.

One ritual that *sāmaṇera*s are taught almost immediately following their entrance into the monkhood is the administration of the five precepts to the laity. As administering the five precepts often occurs in a ritual in which the laity are performing an act of merit, the novices must also memorize and learn to recite properly the verses that extol the merit (*piṅvākya*) that lay people receive by doing acts of charity. Within the first months of their entrance into the *saṅgha*, the novices are also taught the verses to be recited when worshipping the Buddha in the morning, afternoon, and evening. Along with learning to recite the precepts, the *pivākya*, and the verses when worshipping the Buddha, the novices are instructed in receiving alms (*dāna*), especially during death anniversary rituals when the novices would recite a number of verses of benediction or thanks (*anumodana*).[6]

The charter for the establishment of the *sāmaṇera* institution also mentions the need for novices to become proficient in the performance of two other important rituals: a ritual venerating the twenty-four or twenty-eight previous Buddhas (*suvisi bodhipūjā* or *aṭavisi bodhipūjā* respectively) and protection or *pirit* ceremonies. Learning to perform the *bodhipūjā* ritual, which has increased dramatically in popularity during the last three decades,[7] involves memorizing numerous Sinhala and some Pāli verses. Unlike the drone chanting accompanying most protection ceremonies, the verses recited in the *bodhipūjā* ritual are sung; thus, in their training, the novices learn to chant the verses in a melodious and aesthetically appealing manner. The novices are also taught to give short sermons, most often on the subject of cultivating compassion and loving-kindness, which usually conclude the *bodhipūjā* ritual.

The rituals that require the longest and most involved training during the two year in-house training course at the *sāmaṇera* centers are the protection ceremonies. Protection rituals, which play a key role in Sinhala society, consist of monks chanting a wide array of discourses and protective verses. Though less training is needed for monks to become proficient in performing shorter *pirit* ceremonies (which last anywhere from ten minutes to an hour), novices must memorize a host of Pāli discourses (*sutta*s) and protection verses (*paritta*) before performing the longer ceremonies, which may last all night or even several days. Of particular importance to the novices' training in this ritual is the triple-discourse (Sinhala: *tun-sūtraya*): the *Mahāmaṇgala*, *Ratana*, and *Karaṇīyametta sutta*s. These three *sutta*s—which pivot around important doctrinal themes such as what is auspicious (*Mahāmaṇgala Sutta*), the blessings derived from the power of the Buddha, *dhamma*, and *saṅgha* (*Ratana Sutta*), and the role and importance of benevolence (*Karaṇīyamettā Sutta*)—are of central importance, since they are, as Lily de Silva notes, "invariably recited in all *paritta* rituals."[8] Beyond the triple-discourse, the *sāmaṇera* training center charter mentions the need for novices to learn the appointed sections of the *Sāmaṇera Baṇadaham Pota* which, according to the head monks of several centers, include such texts as the *Dasadhamma Sutta*, *Mettā Sutta*, *Aṭavisiparitta*, *Jayaparitta*, *Abhayaparitta*, *Jayamaṇgalagāthā*, *Āṭānāṭiya Sutta*, *Aṇgulimālaparitta*.

The attention and importance given to training novices in the proper performance of a wide range of Buddhist rituals is further borne out in the daily schedule that regulates the novices' lives in the training centers. In the typical daily schedule of the centers, for instance, a significant amount of time each day is devoted to the novices learning texts and becoming proficient in ritual performance. Discussing the schedule for the *sāmaṇera*s at the Jemsen Training Center, the head monk explained:

> Here, we wake up at four o'clock. The monks wash their faces and worship the Buddha. The monks then start their memorization work (*kaṭapādaṅ*) and do temple activities. After that, the monks test each other on the lessons that they were supposed to learn by heart and that is followed by more studies. Then they wash their robes and have a bath after which the monks take their noon meal. After cleaning the alms hall, the monks worship the Buddha while we recite and study the *Dasadhamma Sutta*. That is followed by more school (*abhyāsa*) work, including learning languages and letters. In the late afternoon, there is more time allotted for temple activities which is followed, again, by worshipping the Buddha. Then there is time for *vat baṇa* (preaching practiced between monks) and *vat pirit* (protection ceremonies practiced between monks). There is also some short time for meditation.

According to the head monk of that center, over eight hours each day is dedicated to the novices learning a multitude of verses (*gāthā*), discourses (*sutta*s), and protective texts (*paritta*s) that are relevant to various types of rituals. The novices' memorization work (*kaṭapādaṅ*), moreover, is further reinforced by periods within the daily schedule devoted to the novices practicing the ceremonies and rituals amongst themselves. Unlike the text-centered education that they might receive in a monastic school or *piriveṇa*, novices in the training centers learn by continually doing and perfecting the rituals.

Once the novices become proficient in the rituals, they

may be called upon to perform the rituals for the laity. Indeed, many of the young monks living in the centers were "strongly encouraged" to perform the rituals for the laity, and the head monks from the Hantana, Hal Oluwa, and Jemsen training centers pointed out that many of the nine and ten year old novices had already performed several types of rituals for the laity. The head monks further believed that through this "forced" interaction with the laity, the novices would become very comfortable in facing the laity and, as a result, would begin building close social and emotional ties with them.[9]

Ritual Performance as Social Service: A Reinterpretation

What is perhaps most innovative about the *sāmaṇera* training centers is how the head monks and novices have come to interpret ritual performance as a form of social service (*samāja sevāya*). For instance, in discussing the role of monks in the 21st century and the need for monks to perform social service, the head monk from the Jemsen Training Center remarked:

> We provide social service (*samāja sevāya*). We learn these particular things because they are needed by the laity. We must fulfill their requirements. Recently, one donor wanted a monk for *baṇa*. The monk went to his house and recited *baṇa* for forty-five minutes. He was only twelve years old. They were really impressed with him.

When I asked the head monk at the Jemsen Training Center to comment further about what he understood as social service, he succinctly remarked: "Basically, it is training monks in *baṇa* (preaching), *pirit* (protection rituals), *anuśāsanava* (lit. advice or guidance given to the laity), and especially *bodhipūjā* (worship of the twenty-four or twenty-eight previous Buddhas). Those are the special activities that the donors need. The monks here are trained in those activities during this period."

Although the concept of social service is not new to Buddhism, defining it as ritual performance goes against many late nineteenth- and early twentieth-century understandings of the term. For instance, for the great Buddhist reviver Anagārika Dharmapāla, social service largely precludes ritual performance. Born in Colombo in 1864, Dharmapāla sought to return Buddhism to the old, glorious position it once had in Sri Lanka by arguing for a more engaged role for monks in society. Despite his continued belief that monks should maintain a renunciatory attitude, Dharmapāla believed that they should serve society in economic and nationalistic ways: by working toward the economic well-being and self-sufficiency of the people as well as by creating a Sinhala Buddhist nation-state.

Of even greater importance for our purposes here is the disdain that Dharmapāla shows toward a wide range of "superstitious" rituals. In his call for the Sinhalese Buddhist monks and laity to return to righteousness, Dharmapāla belittles the ritualism of peasant Buddhism: "The ignorant Burmese, like the ignorant Sinhalese, propitiates these harmless ceremonies; but the enlightened Buddhist only laughs at them."[10] Dharmapāla further argues that the Buddha "denounced every form of belief that destroyed individual activity" and destroyed one's own self reliance.[11] In a seeming disregard for sections of the *Mahāparinibbāna Sutta* (such as D II 142) in which the Buddha discusses the benefits that ensue from worshipping his relics, Dharmapāla points out that "when the *Bhikkus* [*sic*] assembled to hear the final words of their loved Teacher, He exhorted them not to be engaged in paying homage and worship to His memory and to his Relics, but that they should qualify themselves by strenuous effort and to become the heirs of a greater inheritance than the joys of heaven."[12]

This economic-*cum*-political understanding of social service did not vanish in 1933 when Dharmapāla died; rather, it continued in several stands of Buddhist monasticism in Sri Lanka. As H.L. Seneviratne has documented in his recent publication on Buddhist modernism, Dharmapāla's two-fold understanding of social service became bifurcated in the two major Colombo-based centers of learning: Vidyodaya, which followed the economic forms of social service, and Vidyālaṃkāra, which interpreted social service along more political lines. Though a number of the leaders of the two *piriveṇa*s drew on different facets of Dharmapāla's conception of social service, many of them shared Dharmapāla's move to omit ritual performance from their understanding of the concept. Discussing some of the principal leaders of Vidyodaya Piriveṇa, for instance, Seneviratne remarks how the leaders relegated to the background "the ritual services of *dana* (accepting alms), *bana* (delivering sermons), and *pirit* (chanting texts for magical purposes) which have not done much to give them [i.e., the monks] status in a changing society."[13]

At Vidyālaṅkāra Piriveṇa, we find a similar move to preclude ritual performance from social service in the writings of the great Buddhist pundit, Walpola Rahula. In his discussion of the true heritage of the monk or *bhikkhu*, Rahula does not mention ritual performance; instead, he speaks about the need for monks, especially more educated monks, to take up a wide range of activities for the betterment of society. In *The Heritage of a Bhikkhu*, for instance, he states:

> More and more young *bhikkhu*s received higher education and were increasingly engaged in educational and social activities. They were not content only with looking after their temples and performing religious rites and ceremonies. Some of them, for example, organized in rural areas *śrāma-dāna* (gift of labor) groups, i.e., groups of people voluntarily helping the villagers by building their roads, digging their wells, erecting their houses, repairing their dilapidated old irrigation reservoirs, etc. Those who received appointments as teachers in schools were traditionally devoted to the instruction of children and improving schools (1974:108).[14]

For Rahula, the ideal monk is not someone who remains on the periphery performing Buddhist rituals; he is, as Seneviratne points out, in the center working for what he sees as the benefit of the people.

According to Rahula, the social service/political role that is the true heritage of the *bhikkhu* is not new. Even though monks have "always" played a political/social role in society (which Rahula argues based on his reading of the early Sinhalese chronicles such as the *Mahāvaṃsa*), their function in society became narrowed down when the state of monastic education and the status of the monks themselves began to deteriorate:

> With the missionaries asserting their power under the Christians, the position of the *bhikkhu* began to deteriorate. As the Buddhists monks could not adapt themselves to suit the changed political, economic, and social situation, they were rendered useless to society.... thus the *bhikkhu*, circumscribed both with regard to personality and education, was by force of circumstances driven to limit his activities to the recitation of the *Suttas* (*Pirit* chanting), preaching a sermon, attendance at funeral rites and alms-givings in memory of the departed, and to an idle, cloistered life in the temple.[15]

Despite using the same term, social service (or *samāja sevāya*), to describe their activities, the head monks and novices of the *sāmaṇera* training centers had a very different idea of monastic service in mind than economic (Vidyodaya) and political (Vidyālaṃkāra) activities. For them, serving society is primarily defined as fulfilling the religious needs of the laity; when it comes to important events such as death, illness, and moving into a new house, it is crucial to have an able body of monks who are willing and able to perform the appropriate rites. According to the head monk from the Hal Oluwa Training Center, for instance, the duty of monks is to care for their donors, especially in times of trouble or uncertainty:

> Those who are coming from this institute have developed their ability to do social service (*samāja sevāya*), to work with the people. After leaving here, they usually go to an ordinary temple (*vihāra*) to do their social service. They

> have the training to do so. Right away they can start working with the people. Here we train them to visit devotees during wakes. Yesterday I went to a wake. I took one monk with me. In that way, I provide my students with the knowledge about how to visit wakes and funerals of the devotees and how to treat the devotees as friends. As far as I know, in ordinary temples no one visits their own devotees' wakes before the funeral (*paṃsakula*) ceremony. Whether we are invited or not for *paṃsukula*, we visit the laity's houses as a responsibility. Also, if they experience other types of problems, we visit them. When they are in trouble, we must visit them and see what we could do. That is our social responsibility.

For the head monks from the centers, social service is not defined as improving the economic standards of a village through development projects (*grāma saṃvardhana*); rather, social service is accomplished by visiting the laity when they are ill or suffering and especially by performing the necessary religious rituals when requested. Social service implies being available to the laity and being ready to be called upon when the time comes to serve their religious and spiritual needs, especially in trying times. Conceived of in this manner, the needs of the laity are foregrounded *vis à vis* the *saṅgha*'s own requirements. Discussing this understanding of social service, the deputy head monk (*anunāyaka*) from the Hal Oluwa temple explained: "To do a service as a monk, you should have connections with the village. The *Sāmaṇera* training centers work to develop that relationship so that the monk can do his social service."

Social Service: Reconfiguring Ritual Performance as the Basis of the Sāsana

Closely related to head monks' redefinition of social service as ritual performance is their reinterpretation of the factors that have led to the decline of Buddhism in Sri Lanka as well as the factors that would contribute to the prolongation of the *sāsana* on the island. A number of late nineteenth- and twentieth-century movements directed toward prolonging the life of the *sāsana* have focused on "reviving" the forest tradition,[16] compelling monks to adhere strictly to the monastic disciplinary code,[17] improving the post-*piriveṇa* training for monks,[18] or even, as we saw above, having monks work toward raising the living standards of Sri Lankans through non-religiously-oriented activities such as political activism and economic uplift programs. For the head monks and novices of the training centers, the basis for the continuation of the *sāsana* was not directly correlated to studying or meditating; for them, it is through fulfilling the religious needs of the laity that the continuation of the *sāsana* could be ensured. For example, in one conversation the head monk from Hal Oluwa mentioned a temple where the monks refused to involve themselves with social service and the possible outcome of their refusal to do so:

> In Harispattuwa, I received letters from monks who were organizing a protest of the building of a new church. Later I met that group of monks and the one who sent me the letter. I realized, though, that we cannot blame the Christians for coming into the villages and starting their activities. The fault should be placed on the monks. I found out that from the temple where the complaints were sent, no social service was being provided by the monks. The monks have enough money and a good life. They are not concerned about the devotees' religious requirements. As a result, the devotees might have felt fed up with the temple. The only option for them was to go to the next temple and ask them to fulfill their (i.e., laity's) religious needs. If they go to the next temple to invite monks for, say, a *paṃsukula,* the monks in that temple will be blamed by the monks in the first temple who are not providing the social service to begin with. What would happen to the people then? They will be in trouble as they have no other solutions after the monks in the second temple refuse. So, if the people need monks for a funeral and the monks in the first temple do not come and the monks in the second temple do not come out of a fear of being rebuked by the monks in the first

> temple, what can the laity do? They would go to the church. If people have nowhere to go, they will look to other possibilities such as the church.

For him and the other head monks associated with the training centers, protecting society is not necessarily accomplished through economic or political activities undertaken by members of the *saṅgha* or through meditating in the forest or following the *vinaya* rules very strictly; rather, it is through serving the laity by fulfilling their religious needs that society and Buddhism in Sri Lanka can be protected. The head monk from Hal Oluwa further explained how monks who devote their time and energy to fulfilling the religious needs of the laity play a vital role in protecting society:

> I think that a monk is like a soldier who protects society. He should be ready to go at any time no matter if it is midnight, rainy, or hot. If people come and say, "*hāmuduruwo*, there is a patient who needs some *pirit*," he should be ready to go with them even if it is midnight. You cannot say, "I have a lot of work to do. I have my studies." Those excuses are completely irrelevant. You should go. That is why I always tell my students that the person who is willing to be a monk should be ready to take that challenge: to work for the devotees without being concerned whether it is day or night, whether they are hungry or full. I told my students: "You should be ready at any time. You should sacrifice everything for the devotees. You should sacrifice all your private comforts. That is called the burden of social service (*samāja dhura*)."

For this head monk and head monks from other *sāmaṇera* training centers, the revival of Buddhism is not accomplished by freeing Buddhism from its superstitious elements but by engaging in a form of social service that is oriented toward the performance of Buddhist rituals.

Ritual Performance and Social Service: An Innovation of Tradition?

The *sāmaṇera* training institution, with its focus on ritual performance, its reinterpretation of social service, and its understandings of the factors leading to the decline and the revival of the Theravādin tradition, represents an important break from other late nineteenth- and twentieth-century Buddhist reform movements. Even though the idea of establishing monastic training institutions where ritualists are trained represents a very important innovation from within the Theravādin tradition, the head monks and founders of the institutions, like many of the founders of other reform movements, do not see the training centers as that innovative. For them, rather, the *sāmaṇera* centers represent more of a return to traditional Buddhist training than a departure from it. According to Reverend Kusaladhamma, for instance, the *sāmaṇera* training centers are a way of returning to the religious training that was given to young boys prior to entering the monkhood:

> In Christianity, a father, before he becomes clergy, needs six years of training in a seminary. For us we don't have that basic training. Earlier, that kind of training was given. When boys came to temple, they had to be there before being ordained for a year or two and learn the basic religious things needed for *sāmaṇeras*. Only then would they be ordained.
>
> Now, that method is no longer followed. Now they bring boys to temples, keep them for one month, ordain them, and send them to *piriveṇa* after one month. At the *piriveṇa*, priority is given to language learning and other syllabus work. They check their knowledge of language and doctrine and after that they put them into a particular class. They don't teach them about the life of a monk. *Sāmaṇera* training centers are institutes where they are taught about that. For two years, that training has to be received. Only then can they be directed to formal education in *piriveṇa*.

In a similar manner, the head monk from the Jemsen

Training Center remarked:

> In the past when boys came to the temples, they received at least three years of apprenticeship in the temple prior to entering the *saṅgha*. Nowadays, it is very rare.... I also stayed here more than three years as an acolyte. More recently, however, parents expect that their sons will become monks soon after they come to a temple. Even the boy himself expects to become a monk quickly.... After the ordination, the parents also want to send them to *piriveṇa* quickly. In *piriveṇa*, they receive some scholastic education. Following such a course, the novice monks miss so many things that *sāmaṇera*s learned during the pre-ordination period earlier. That is *baṇa* and *vat piḷivet*.[19] To receive this apprenticeship, the constitution of the *sāmaṇera* training centers mentions having a training period for two years. After that, they are sent to *piriveṇa*. They need to learn *vat pilivet*, *baṇa*, *pirit*, *bodhipūjā*. They also need to know how to advise the donors.

Closely related to the head monks' and founders' views regarding how the *sāmaṇera* training centers are a return to a more traditional system of learning is their belief that the social service/ritual performance function of Buddhist monastics is not new. Unlike Rahula, who argued, as indicated above, that the ritual role of monks is relatively new, the head monks of the centers all spoke about how monks have always played this important function in society. Discussing further the role that rituals have played in the lives of lay Buddhists, the head monk from Hal Oluwa explained:

> In the early history of Sri Lanka, the *brahmins* were the ones who calculated the auspicious times, who produced protection threads for sick people, and who chanted some kind of *mantras* for helping people. When the monks went to those areas, the *brahmins* left; however, the needs of the people remained the same. As a result, it was the monk who adopted those responsibilities and fulfilled those needs. When children were born, people came to the monks and informed them so that they may chant *pirit*. The monks tied protection threads. The place of the *brahmins* was taken

over by the monks.

For the head monks and founders of the training centers, the *sāmaṇera* institution does not represent such a great departure from more "traditional" forms of monastic training and "traditional" conceptions of ideal monastic service. Like the monks who first came to Sri Lanka in the first two centuries BCE, the monks of today must fulfill the religious needs of the laity by chanting protection verses, tying protection strings, and helping the people.

Despite the head monks' claim regarding the relationship between the *sāmaṇera* training centers and other earlier forms of Theravāda monasticism in Sri Lanka, the training institution is innovative in its concern for specific institutional systems through which ritualists are trained. Through the establishment of a training program based on fulfilling the ritual needs of the laity, the ritual-performance role of monks and novices becomes brought to the fore and understood as one of the defining features not only of social service but of the ideal monastic role. In this process of foregrounding a role that might have always implicitly been there as one of the many duties of a Theravāda Buddhist monk, the image of a monk as ritualist becomes concretized and, in the process, other bases of the *buddhasāsana* (such as study and meditation) become relegated to a less prominent place. For the head monks and novices living in the centers, then, it is not so much that there would cease to be realization of the noble path without learning (*pariyatti*), but that without monks willing and able to take up the important monastic vocation of ritual performance, the numbers of Buddhist monks and lay people on the island would decline to such a degree that the survival of the Buddhist religion would be called into question.

Notes

1. The research on which this article is based was completed from 1998 to 2000. Though Godwin Samararatne died before the research for this project was completed, he played a very important role in the formation of my initial premises and questions. Despite the fact that this article does not focus on the meditative tradition of Sri Lanka, it does examine the various facets of the Buddhist tradition which, I believe, Godwin would have appreciated.

2. *Pariyatti nu kho sāsanassa mūlaṃ, udāhu paṭipatti* (Mp I.92).

3. *Evamevaṃ āraddhavipassakānaṃ bhikkhūnaṃ satepi sahassepi saṃvijjamāne pariyattiyā asati ariyamaggapaṭivedho nāma na hoti* (Mp I.93). The same idea is present in the commentaries to other sections of the Pāli canon such as Sv III.898; this same phrase is repeated in Ps IV.115.

4. Personal communication from an interview in December, 1999.

5. The concern about monastic discipline is part of the impulse behind the Vinaya Vardena Society, the *tāpasa* movement, the forest tradition, and the segmentation of the *saṅgha*.

6. Richard Gombrich describes this ritual in detail in his article on merit transference: "'Merit Transference' in Sinhalese Buddhism: A Case Study of the Interaction between Doctrine and Practice." *History of Religions* II, *no. 2: 203-219.*

7. Gombrich (1981) and Seneviratne and Wickermeratne "Bodhipuja: Collective Representations of Sri Lankan Youth." *American Ethnologist* 7, no. 4 (1980): 734-43.

8. Lily de Silva "Paritta: A Historical and Religious Study of the Buddhist Ceremony for Peace and Prosperity in Sri Lanka," *Spolia Zeylanica* vol. 36, ed. P.H.D.H. de Silva. (Colombo: Department of Government Printing, 1981).

9. In section five of the *sāmaṇera* training center charter, for instance, we read how the centers should be a place where the laity may turn for their religious needs: "It is a duty of devotees to supply meals for *sāmaṇera*s. They should make arrangements to implement programs which can help develop the relationship between the *sāmaṇera*s and devotees. At the same time, they should make use of the center to fulfill their own religious requirements" (V. Kussaladhamma, *Aramuṇu Kondēsi Hā Pāḍamālāvē Svarūpaya* [Aims, Terms, and the Nature of the Training Course], Ministry of Buddha Sasana Letter, 1994).

10. A. Dharmapāla, *Return to Righteousness: A Collection of Speeches, Essays and Letters of the Anagārika Dharmapāla*, ed. Ānanda Guruge (Ceylon: The Anagarika Dharmapala Birth Centenary Committee, 1965): 638.

11. Ibid., 194.

12. Ibid., 395.

13. Ibid., 73. According to one of the leaders of Vidyodaya, Kalukondayāve Paññāsekhara, for instance, the path of heaven is not one that is based on ritual performance but on good works:

    Heaven is ensured not by ritual activity [but] by a good life here and now, which can be done with honest and hard work. This goes against much of traditional rural Buddhism, in which heaven is the reward for ritualized good works. Since prosperity in this life is the basis for heaven in the hereafter, there is in this theory an encouragement of rational economic behavior, such as hard work, saving, and reinvesting (H.L. Seneviratne *The Work of Kings: The New Buddhism in Sri Lanka*. (Chicago: University of Chicago Press, 1999: 82).

14. Walpola Rahula, *The Heritage of the Bhikkhu: A Short History of the Bhikkhu in Educational, Cultural, Social, and Political Life*. (New York: Grove Press, 1974): 108. In another section of his *Heritage,* Rahula writes:

    > A *bhikkhu* with such a knowledge of the modern world, and of the ancient heritage of his country, aware of the problems of the day, if he is energetic and enterprising, would not like to sit idle, satiated with the sanctity afforded him within the temple precincts, devoting his life only to receive alms, chant *pirit*, perform funeral rites, and deliver the usual sermons when the country, the nation, and the religion are declining (Ibid., 96f).

15. Ibid., 91. Rahula's retelling of the recent history of Sri Lanka is remarkable as it fails to account why in Thailand, which was never colonized and overcome with missionaries, monks fulfill the same ritual functions—*Pirit* chanting, preaching sermons, and attending funeral rites and alms-givings in memory of the departed—as the monks in Sri Lanka.

16. This has been discussed in Michael Carrithers' works on the forest tradition in Sri Lanka. See especially *The Forest Monks of Sri Lanka: An Anthropological and Historical Study*. (Calcutta: Oxford University Press, 1983) and "The Modern Ascetic of Lanka and the Pattern of Change in Buddhism." *Man: The Journal of the Royal Anthropological Institute* 14, no. 2 (1979): 294-310.

17. This was a solution advocated by the United Society for the Protection of the Vinaya (or the *Eka Abadda Vinaya Vardena Sangamaya*), established in 1932 by the Buddhist layman, G.V.S. Jayasundera. This society bases itself on the assumption that present day monks are no longer living up to the ideals of Buddhist monasticism. To bring the *saṅgha* back to the "true" Buddhist ideals, the society emphasizes the need for monks to abide by all of the 227 *vinaya* rules. For example, the society believes that monks should follow

all of the monastic rules and, thus, should not handle money or use porcelain plates, black umbrellas, shoes, or sandals. The Society emphasizes the need for monks to follow *all of the vinaya rules* because it interprets the *vinaya* as being inseparable from the *dhamma*. For a complete discussion of this society, see S. Kemper. "Buddhism Without Bhikkhus: The Sri Lanka Vinaya Vardena Society." *Religion and Legitimation of Power in Sri Lanka*, ed. Bardwell L. Smith. (Chambersburg: Anima Books, 1978).

18. This was one of the goals advocated in the 1956 report preceding the *Buddha Jayanti* celebrations.

19. *Vat piḷivet* refers to a wide range of temple activities from worshipping the Buddha to cleaning the temple grounds.

Buddhist Non-theism:

Theory and Application[1]

Asanga Tilakaratna

I. Introduction

Two most important points where Buddhism departs from many other religions are its denial of the existence of a creator God and an everlasting soul. In the history of Buddhism it is clear that these two positions have never been contested. Even the Personalists (*pudgalavādins*) who came close to believing in something akin to the soul were, in their self-understanding, *anātmavādins* or holders of a no-soul view. Similarly, no Buddhist tradition, Hīnayāna, Mahāyāna or Vajrayāna, has ever incorporated into its system the belief in a God who is creator and saviour. With the possible exception of certain Mahāyāna traditions of more recent origin no Buddhist tradition has ever held the Buddha to be a creator god or has subscribed to any such similar idea.

Buddhism, nonetheless, is replete with gods. Even the Buddhist texts that are judged as belonging to an early period contain many episodes regarding gods. *Saṃyutta Nikāya* has its very first section devoted to Buddha's interactions with various divine beings. In addition to it, both the *Sutta* and the *Vinaya Piṭaka*s contain many instances where gods have figured in the life of the Buddha and his disciples. These divine beings are depicted as those who experience the beneficial fruits of their good past *karma*s. Their life span is very long but not everlasting. At the termination of the effects of their *karma* they are believed to take birth as human beings. There is also a higher group of divine beings, called '*brahma*' who are believed to occupy a higher place in the Buddhist universe. They are born in the Brahma realm as a result of their attainment of '*jhāna*' (different degrees of mental concentration). Their life-span is even longer than that of divine beings; but still not everlasting.

Of these two kinds of beings, gods are closer to the life of ordinary people, including monks and nuns, than brahmas. Brahmas with their higher spiritual attainments do not seem to have much to do with those lesser beings. However, gods, very often, are depicted as protecting and helping monks and nuns who, for instance, meditated in forests. According to the *Mahāparinibbāna Sutta*, when Sunīdha and Vassakāra, two ministers of king Ajātasatthu, were building a city at Pāṭaligāma, the gods who were residing in that area took up residence in the houses that were being built. The story says that the higher gods began to reside in the houses built for higher officials while the gods of lesser status in the heavens started occupying the houses built for ministers of corresponding medium and lower status. The account is concluded with the following statement: *devatānukampito poso sadā bhadrāni passati*:[2] 'one who receives kindness from gods always enjoys happiness'. In this manner, the divine beings are depicted as having a close relation with and a salutary effect on, human beings.

These divine beings, however, do not pose a problem as regards the basic tenets of the Buddhist philosophy. They are not everlasting and hence they do not contradict the Buddhist understanding of reality as impermanent, unsatisfactory and devoid of substance (*anicca*, *dukkha* and *anattā*). Since none of them is attributed with the power of creating the world, a position which makes such a being independent of dependently co-originated (*paṭicca-samuppanna*) nature of reality, there is no violation of the Buddhist view of the dependent character inherent in reality. The more crucial point is that the presence or the absence of these divine beings has nothing absolutely to do with one's attainment of *nibbāna* which is to make an end of one's suffering by eradicating thirst for pleasure (*tanhā*).

The question, however, is: how valid is this rational picture with regard to the lived reality of the religion of ordinary men and women? In other words, how did ordinary people who are committed to following the Buddha, cope with the denial of God? In the theistic religions God has been understood as having the characteristics of omniscience, omnipotence and kindness. He is credited with the creation of the world and protection of what he created. The main attraction in God is that he is the source of the sense of security which ordinary human beings need badly for their existence. Also God guarantees salvation for those who believe in him. While God's protective function can be accommodated within the Buddhist tradition, the belief in his creation and salvation of the world does not find a place in it.

The purpose of this paper is to examine how Buddhism accommodated the needs of ordinary people for whom realization of *nibbāna* by eradicating all sorts of desire was not the immediate need. I will argue that Buddhism accommodated certain aspects of a traditional theistic concept of God within the Buddhist tradition without doing harm to its unique philosophical and ethical standpoint. The argument will be developed in the following manner: first I will discuss the Buddhist attitude to the concept of God and show that Buddhism clearly and unequivocally denied the concept of God. In the next section I will discuss how Sakka, the king of gods, Yama, the king of the unhappy world—hell—(*apāya*) and Brahma, the embodiment of virtue and goodness, three divine beings occurring in the Pāli canon, together represent three very important aspects attributed to God in theistic religions. In the concluding section I will discuss the religious and philosophical implications of this development.

By way of a note on methodology, it would be useful to mention that what I mean by 'Buddhism' in the present paper is primarily the Buddhist thought and the tradition represented by the Pāli canon. The textual references are usually to these texts in Pāli language. What I refer to as 'early Buddhism' is the system of teachings represented by this literary tradition. I use the term 'Theravāda' to refer to the Buddhist tradition developed in countries such as Sri Lanka, Myanmar and Thailand having the Pāli canon and the commentaries written on it as its doctrinal base. This limitation in scope, however, does not necessarily mean that other traditions of Buddhism are totally different from Theravāda or that the findings of the paper are not relevant to those traditions.

II. Denial of God in Buddhism and the Reasons Behind It

The dominant religious tradition of India by the time of the Buddha was Brahmanism, which at least in its more popular form, was a theistic creationism. The belief in an individual soul (*ātma-vāda*) and the belief in a creator God (*īśvara-nirmāna-vāda*) were the two key aspects of this religion. Most of the *śramaṇa* traditions differed from Brahmanism in rejecting its theory and practice of social division (*varṇa-āśrama-dharma*) although a large number of the former shared with Brahmanism its belief in a soul. Buddhism which was itself a *śramaṇa* tradition differed from most of the other similar traditions in rejecting the soul theory along with the belief in a creator God.

In the Indian religious tradition, it was held without any doubt that Buddhism was a *nāstika-vāda* or a negativism, a system which denied the authority of the Veda and the existence of a soul and God. The Brahmanic religious tradition described itself and others who accepted the reality of a soul and God as *āstika-vādins* or positive view-holders.[3] The contemporaries of the Buddha seem to have been very clear about this. The following criticism which has been made against the Buddha is an example: *venayiko samaṇo gotamo; sato sattassa ucchedam vināsam vibhavam paññapeti*:[4] 'ascetic Gotama is a destructionist; he asserts the annihilation, destruction and non-existence of an existing being'. This statement obviously refers to the *anātmavāda* of the Buddha. The belief in God is not very different from this for the allegedly everlasting and permanent soul is nothing other than the microcosm of the macrocosm that is God. In the Brahmanic tradition this distinction is articulated as *jīva-ātma* (individual soul) and *parama-ātma* (absolute soul). Buddhism rejected both these beliefs. Therefore the general understanding was clear that Buddhism was non-substantialist and non-theistic.[5]

In the Pāli canon there are many statements clearly denying the existence of God. There are two terms usually used to refer to God in the Pāli canon: one is '*brahma*' or '*mahābrahma*' and the other is *issara*, a derivative from the Sanskrit *īśvara*. In the popular Brahmanic belief of the trinity, Brahma is the creator, whereas Vishnu and Maheśvara are credited respectively with continuation and destruction of what has been created. The belief that the world has been created by an all-powerful God is called *issara nimmāna vāda* (God-creation-view) in the Pāli canon. A discourse in the *Aṅguttara Nikāya* refers to three religious views that are rejected by the Buddha as unsatisfactory. The creationist view which holds that everything is due to God's creation has been included as one of them. The Buddha criticizes this view as causing inactivity and lack of moral responsibility and initiative. The Buddha says:

> Thus for those who fall back on the creation of a Supreme Deity as the essential reason there is neither desire to do, nor effort to do, nor necessity to do this deed or abstain from that deed.[6]

The following statement attributed to the *arahant* called Raṭṭhapāla—'*attāno loko anbhissaro*'[7] ('the world is without protection; there is no over-lord there')—is another clear example of rejecting the creationist view. In this statement God has been referred to as '*abhi-issara*', '*abhi*' being a prefix meaning higher or superior.

Buddhist non-theism emerges sharply in the discussions criticizing the Brahmanic belief in the superiority by birth. The most outstanding example in this regard in the canon is the *Ambaṭṭha Sutta* of the *Dīgha Nikāya*. Here the Buddha criticizes the Brahmanic belief that they are born from the mouth of Brahma. The Buddha is presented here as laughing this idea out of existence by saying that there cannot be any manner of birth peculiar only to Brahmins other than that which is common to all human beings. The Buddha indicates that there is no need to believe in any creator other than one's biological creators, namely, one's parents. Buddhism calls one's parents '*brahma*'[8] in the sense that they are the real creators of their children.

In addition to the rejection of the idea of creation, belief in the creator Brahma having a responsibility for the final liberation of beings is also rejected by the Buddha. The Brahmanic belief was that they become united with Brahman after death: *brahma-śavyatā*. In the *Tevijja Sutta* of the *Dīgha Nikāya*, the Buddha compares those who claim that they will be united with Brahma after their death to a succession of blind people guided by one who is equally blind. The idea is that none of those who claimed that they will be united with Brahma have seen him and therefore they are talking of something about which they do not have any personal acquaintance. In making these assertions the Buddha shows that he is rejecting, purely on empirical grounds, the idea of Brahma as the source of salvation.

The main reason, however, why Buddhism cannot accept the idea of a transcendental God is a philosophical one.

This has largely to do with the Buddhist understanding of reality as dependently co-originated. The early Buddhist term which articulates this understanding is '*paṭicca-samuppāda*' (dependent co-origination). The reality originated in this manner is described as '*paṭicca-samuppanna*' or dependently co-originated. The teaching of *paṭicca-samuppāda* is basically used to explain how suffering arises and ceases conditioned by a series of psycho-physical factors. The contemporaries of the Buddha described this phenomenon as either wrought by oneself, or by another, or by both oneself and another or by accident. The Buddha rejected all these positions and explained the origin and the cessation of suffering as causally conditioned.[9] God and soul were not among these causes. Why god and soul were not among these causes is because they do not form a part of dependently co-originated phenomena. God and soul, by definition, are independent, and do not depend on anything for their existence. According to the *paṭicca-samuppāda* understanding of reality there cannot be anything independent and the only reality that is available is dependently co-originated.

It is in the context of this state of affairs that the Buddha's teaching of the four noble truths becomes meaningful. According to this teaching human beings or all beings who have not realized *nibbāna* are subject to suffering caused by one's own defilements. The cessation of this suffering is *nibbāna* and it has to be realized by following the ethical way of life described in the noble eight-fold path. According to this analysis suffering is one's own doing and no one else is responsible for that. The task of getting rid of it too is one's own responsibility. Neither the Buddha nor anyone else is capable of bringing the final release on behalf of someone else. If God exists one does not need to take the responsibility for this arduous task. The Buddha says very clearly the following: 'you must strive yourself; the Tathāgatas are only the pointers of the path.'[10] Furthermore, the Buddha says that one is one's own protector (God); how can there be a protector from outside?[11] It is quite clear from the very teaching of the four noble truths that there is no God who can save one from suffering. Therefore the most convincing argument for the Buddhist non-theism comes from the basic philosophical understanding of reality as dependently co-originated.

III. A Decentralized Concept of God in Buddhism?

Although Buddhism denies the concept of God as the creator and the giver of salvation through his grace this does not mean that the ordinary people who started following the Buddha were so advanced that they were able to do without any gods at all. As is clear from the textual and architectural traditions of Buddhism, gods have been made to associate closely with the life of the Buddha. The discourses such as *Mahāsamaya* and *Āṭānāṭiya* clearly demonstrate how the Buddhist tradition has incorporated a large number of Brahmanic gods into its own belief system.[12] Usually the gods in Buddhism are ordinary beings who enjoy the fruits of their good past *karma*s. They do not have any specific role to play with regard to human life. Nevertheless, there are certain gods attributed with such functions as the protection of people and providing them with help in their day-to-day life. In addition to these gods who are attributed with ordinary functions there are a few gods, mentioned in the Buddhist tradition, to whom certain specific tasks have been assigned and these gods become very important owing to the functions attributed to them.

Three gods that are particularly outstanding in this respect are Yama who is described as the king of hell, Sakka or the king of gods who is the helper and the protector of the good, and Brahma who is the embodiment of good and who plays the role of the highest being in the world except the liberated ones including the Buddha and the *arahant*s. In the remainder of this paper we will examine how each of these gods has been portrayed as performing a special task which has been attributed to God in traditional theistic religions.

A. Brahma

In the Brahmanic tradition Brahma is the supreme being who is considered to be the creator of the universe. In the complex Hindu mythology the position of gods does not remain constant and therefore it is not easy to say anything about them with certainty. Brahma does not appear as the supreme being in the *Ṛg Veda* period. It is because there wasn't any such being at this stage. On the evolution of the concept of *brahma* Eliot Deutsch says thus:

> The term "Brahman" first appears in the *Ṛg Veda* (ca. 1200 B.C.) in close connection with various sacred utterances that were thought to have a special magical power. Originally, then the term may have meant "spell" or "prayer"; an utterance that was used for the magical attainment of worldly wishes and other worldly desires. Later, in the Brāhmaṇas, Brahman comes to signify that which stands behind the gods as their ground and source, and in the Upaniṣads generally it becomes the unitary principle of all being, the knowledge of which liberates one from finitude.[13]

The original idea of the personal *brahma* given as a masculine noun gets established in the Purāṇa period. Of the 18 main *Purāṇas*, six (namely, the *Brahma*, *Brahmāṇḍa*, *Brahmavaivarta*, *Markandeya*, *Bhaviṣya*, and *Vāmana Purāṇas*) have creator Brahma as their central deity.[14] The very same idea of a supreme being was presented through the neuter gender in philosophical discussions. This distinction was later systematized as *saguṇa brahman* or *brahma* with qualities and *nirguṇa brahman* or *brahma* without qualities, an impersonal principle.

Early Buddhist tradition does not seem to know the concept of Brahma as the supreme being in the philosophical sense (*nirguṇa brahma*). It uses the word to refer to *brahma* as creator God as well as to refer to a group of divine beings, as we mentioned earlier, who are born in the *brahma*-worlds as a result of their achievement of developed states of mind.

Those who attain *rūpa* or *āruppa jhāna*s and those who are in the third state of sainthood, namely, *anāgāmi* or non-returner, are said to be born in the *brahma*-worlds.[15] The life-span of those who are born in these worlds are described as much longer than that of those who are born in the heavens.

It is significant to note that, among the many *brahma*s, some are referred to as '*mahābrahma*' or great *brahma*. For instance, Sahampati, the one who encouraged the Buddha to teach his doctrine when he was hesitating to teach, was closely associated with the life of the Buddha, and is always described as 'great'. In addition to such *brahma*s, the discourses refer to a *brahma* who is simply called '*mahābrahma*'—the great *brahma*—who is described as the highest in the thousand world system. What this account says is that there is one *brahma* who is the greatest and the highest among all the inhabitants of the ten thousand world system. The reader of this account is apt to think that what is referred to here is the *mahābrahma* traditionally believed to be the creator God. It is not, however, the case. The message of the discussion is that *mahābrahma* too is subject to change and hence one must not aspire to it. The Buddha says:

> Monks, in the ten thousand systems of world the Brahma is reckoned highest. Nevertheless, monks, even with regard to Great Brahma there is otherness and there is change. Seeing this, the noble disciple would become dispassionate even in it. One who gets dispassionate in that is the one who gets dispassionate in the highest. There is no question (of him getting dispassionate) in what is lower.[16]

What is conveyed in the statement is that to be a *brahma* of this calibre is the highest form of life to which one can aspire within saṃsāric existence. But that too is not more desirable than the attainment of arahanthood which is to escape from *saṃsāra*.

A discourse occurring in the *Aṅguttara Nikāya* discusses the impermanent character of the *brahma*-world. It says that the cessation of the self-view is more desirable than to be born in the *brahma*-world which ultimately is impermanent and promotes one's self-view.[17] Another discourse in the *Aṅguttara Nikāya* shows how the self-(mis)understanding of a *brahma* as being Great Brahma is generated. The *Brahmajāla Sutta* of the *Dīgha Nikāya* has the same account given in the context of explaining the origin of the partly eternalist and partly non-eternalist views. According to the former, a religious teacher called Sunetta is born in an empty *brahma*-world when the universe was contracting and subsequently, when he was feeling lonely and longing for others to come there arose some others. What occurs at that point to him and also to the new-comers is described in the following words:

> And, then, monks, that being who first arose there thinks: "I am Brahma, the Great Brahma, the Conqueror, the Unconquered, the All-Seeing, the All-Powerful, the Lord, the Maker and Creator, Ruler, Appointer and Orderer, father of All That have Been and Shall Be. These beings were created by me. How so? Because I first had this thought: 'Oh, if only some other beings would come here!' That was my wish, and then these beings came into this existence!" But those beings who arose subsequently think: "this, friends, is Brahma, Great Brahma, … and Shall Be. How so? We have seen that he was here, and that we arose after him."[18]

According to these accounts the very idea of a Creator God is a mistake on the part of that particular *brahma* who had that idea and the others who believed it. The discussion is concluded with the assertion that even Sunetta possessing much power and longevity is subject to suffering characterized by birth, old-age, death etc. and that he too is not liberated from suffering (*aparimutto dukkhasmāti vadāmi*).[19] It is customary that Brahma is described as endowed with infallible vision (*aññadatthu-dasa*). In the like manner, in traditional theistic accounts, God is attributed with omniscience. The Buddhist literature contains stories not only denying this attribution but also positively attributing ignorance to this so-called Great Brahma. According to the *Kevaḍḍha Sutta* of the *Dīgha Nikāya*, a disciple of the Buddha goes to see the Great Brahma in order to find an answer to a question he had. On being asked the question by the monk, the Great Brahma did not answer it but merely announced how powerful he was. After a time, Brahma took the monk aside by the hand and said the following:

> Monk, these *devas* [gods] believe there is nothing Brahma does not see, there is nothing he does not know, there is nothing he is unaware of. That is why I did not speak in front of them. But, monk, I don't know....[20]

According to this admission by Brahma himself not only does he not know he is also boastful, arrogant and full of vanity. '*Braham-sahavyatā*' or the union with Brahma, the Brahmanic religious goal, was known to Buddhism. As in the case of many Vedic religious concepts, this concept too gets a new interpretation in the hands of the Buddha. In the *Tevijja Sutta*, mentioned earlier, the Buddha, having shown that union with Brahma advocated by the brahmins is not based on personal experience, explains to his interlocutors the Buddhist view of the way to union with Brahma. The path according to Buddhism is the path of mental concentration characterized by the attainment of the fine-material and the immaterial *jhānas*. The following statement occurring in the discourse to a brahmin called Māgandiya shows how the Buddha adapted his teaching to suit his listeners: *Ime kho brāhmana brahmalokādhimuttā ... yannunaham dhananjānissa brāhmanassa brahmānam sahavyatāya maggam deseyyanti* (These brahmins are devoted to the *brahma*-world. Suppose I show the Brahmin Dhananjāni the path to the union with the *brahmas*).[21] It is important to note that what is usually given in the singular as '*brahma-sahavyatta*' – "union with Brahma' is given in plural as '*brahmānam sahavyatā*' – 'union with *brahmas*,' an idea closer to the Buddhist reading of the concept.

As evident from the above discussion, although Buddhism does not reject the idea of the Great Brahma it effects considerable changes to it. The creator and saviour aspects of Brahma are clearly rejected. Nevertheless the idea is retained as a moral ideal. It is believed that the Great Brahma maintains four sublime attitudes toward all beings. They are loving kindness (*mettā*), compassion (*karuṇā*), altruistic joy (*muditā*) and equanimity (*upekkhā*). In commenting on the statement that one's parents are Brahma (*brahmāti mātāpitaro*)[22] the commentary says that the parents share these sublime virtues with Brahma. The difference is whereas the former have these virtues toward their children the latter has them toward all beings all the time.[23] Although the Great Brahma has these virtues toward all beings, like parents who are creators of their children, Brahma is not attributed with creation in the Buddhist tradition. The equation of parents with the Great Brahma, however, seems to be the Buddhist response to the Creator God concept of the theists. This suggests that the Buddhist tradition did not deny the concept of Great Brahma as a universal moral being. As in theistic traditions, in Buddhism, Brahma is the embodiment of virtue. The Great Brahma Sahampati begging the newly enlightened Buddha to teach the doctrine to 'those who have little dust in their eyes' has to be understood in this context.[24]

B. Yama

Yama is understood as the king of death. He is one of the leading and most powerful gods in the *Ṛg Veda*. According to Radhakrishnan his origin is not Indian, he is Yima, the son of Vivanhvant of the Avesta. In the *Ṛg Veda* there are several hymns dedicated to him. In Vedic belief Yama is the one who reigns in the world of departed fathers (*pitṛ loka*). It is said that he has two messengers, dogs, who assist him in his work. There he judges the departed souls. And it is believed that he is the king of justice.[25] Radhakrishnan summarizes the position of Yama in early Hindu tradition:

> He is the chief of the dead, and not so much a god as a ruler of the dead. He was the first of mortals to die and find his

> way to the other world, the first to tread the path of the fathers. Later he acts as the host receiving newcomers. He is the king of that kingdom, for he has the longest experience of it. He is sometimes invoked as the god of the setting sun. In the Brahmaṇas Yama becomes the judge and chastiser of men. But in the *Ṛg Veda* he is yet only their king.[26]

In the Yama-Naciketas conversation appearing in the *Kaṭha Upaniṣad,* Yama is portrayed as the knower of the secret of winning over re-death (*punar-mṛtyu*).[27] In the story, Yama reveals this to Naciketas though with some reluctance and hesitation. This characterization of Yama as one with a high ethical sense goes well with the development of the concept in the Buddhist tradition.

It is possible that the Buddhists adapted this concept from the Brahmanic tradition. The locus classicus of Yama in the Pāli discourses is the *Devadūta Sutta* of the *Majjhima Nikāya.* According to the account given in the discourse, when a person who did not behave in a righteous manner is dead he is conducted by the attendants of Yama to him. At that point he would ask a few questions from this person. The questions concern whether or not this person saw the messengers of gods (*deva-dūtā*), namely, an infant lying on its back, an old person, a sick person, a robber being punished by the king and a dead person.[28] The person would answer that he has seen these things but it never occurred to him that he must learn a lesson from these events and behave well. At that point Yama becomes silent and his wardens would drag him and fling him into hell and subject him to various forms of grave suffering. The discourse gives a detailed account of the suffering one is to undergo.

The commentary to *Majjhima Nikāya* has the following comment on Yama:

> The king Yama is a hungry-ghost king living in a mansion (*vemānika-peta-rājā*); at times he enjoys in that divine mansion such divine pleasures as a divine wish-fulfillment tree, divine gardens and divine dancers; at other times

> he experiences the results of his (bad) *karma*. He is a righteous king. He is not one; there are four of them at the four entrances.[29]

As is clear from this account, though Yama is the ruler of *apāya* he is not a part of it. If he is in the hell itself as one who pays for his misdeeds he cannot be the judge and the ruler of it. On the other hand, if he is a total outsider it cannot be in conformity with the teaching of the Buddha which considers *karma* and its result as a natural process not requiring an agent to activate it. The commentarial description of Yama as a righteous king is significant. What it really says is that Yama is a just king for justice in the Indian context as denoted by '*dhamma*'. If Yama does not play an active role in the process there is no need to lay emphasis on this aspect of his character. In the Judeo-Christian tradition God is always described as a just God. It is the same in the Hindu tradition.

An examination of this whole account shows how the Buddhists were trying to incorporate an idea that cannot be an intrinsic part of their belief system. According to the Buddhist *karma* theory it is impossible that there is a person or group of persons who, while staying above the law of *karma*, are responsible for distributing due rewards and punishments for the *karmas* committed by people. *Karma* has been described as a natural process similar to the process in the cultivation of a crop. One receives according to what one has sown; the doer of good receives good and the doer of bad receives bad.[30] There is no need for a person to dispense good and bad results. What is required is the combination of all the necessary conditions.

For a non-theist religion like Buddhism belief in the existence of hell poses a serious problem. The belief does not tally with its denial of a creator God. In a theistic tradition God is beyond his laws and he can also have a group of helpers who are equally beyond such laws. The king of hell and his men seem to belong in this category. Buddhism cannot accept the idea that certain beings are over and above karmic effects.

That may be the reason why both Yama and his men are said to belong to the realm of hungry ghosts and considered as undergoing suffering and paying off their own bad *karmas*. The significance of the admission by the commentator that Yama is not one single unique being but a class of people, although that class does not seem to contain a very large number too, has to be understood in this context. All these can be viewed as how Buddhists were trying to incorporate an eschatology which is not their own with the least harm to their basic philosophy.[31]

The presence of Yama and his men was not received unanimously in the Buddhist tradition. The commentary to the *Devadūta Sutta* (mentioned above) reports a controversy among the Buddhist teachers on this matter. The commentator says:

> Some are of the view that there are no wardens in hell, but, as in the case of a machine, the actions take place by themselves. But this view has been rejected in the *Abhidhamma* by answering affirmatively to the questions: "Are there wardens in hell?" and "Are there those who implement?" Like there are executioners in the human world there are wardens in hell.[32]

This account refers to the *Kathāvatthuppakaraṇa* of the *Abhidhamma Piṭaka* as the authority. The *Kathāvatthu* discusses this problem and concludes that the view that there are no wardens in hell is wrong.[33] According to the commentary to the *Kathāvatthu* the view is held by the Andhakas.[34] In support of their view, they produce the following statement:

> Not Vessabhu nor yet the Peta's king—Soma, Yama, or king Vessavana.
>
> The deeds that were his own do punish him—who ending here attains to other worlds?[35]

The Theravādin interprets this statement as underscoring the affinity of *karma* with its result (*kamma-sarikkhatā*). Looking back at this debate one gets the impression that

Andhakas who raised this doubt were motivated by deeper philosophical reasons. Although the philosophical question is not discussed directly their view that the activities in hell are happening mechanically indicates that they had recognized the difficulty in believing that there are agents who are vested with the power of implementing *karma*. The Theravādin analogy with the human world where there are both actions and those who do them does not seem to catch the point.

Finally, the manner in which the *Devadūta Sutta* ends is instructive in this regard. Seeing how the wardens of hell treat those who come under their power the following occurs to Yama:

> Those in the world who do evil unwholesome actions indeed have all these many kinds of tortures inflicted on them. Oh, that I might attain the human state, that a Tathāgata, accomplished and fully enlightened, might appear in the world, that I might wait on that Blessed One, that the Blessed One might teach me the *dhamma*, and that I might come to understand that Blessed One's *dhamma*.[36]

This thought of Yama implies that he himself considers that to be born as a human would be better than his powerful position. Being born as a human being is superior solely because it provides one with the opportunity of advancing on the path to liberation from suffering. According to the Buddhist belief human beings are situated more favourably than any other beings in this context. Therefore it is understandable that even Yama aspires to become a human being and to achieve higher realizations. The concept of Yama belongs to a culture which is dominated by the belief in many gods, each responsible for a specific aspect of human life. In the Indian context, polytheism gradually developed into a form of monotheism with a supreme God having all the essential characteristics in himself. Buddhism which denied the existence of such a God nevertheless accommodated a form of polytheism in which certain gods are more powerful than others. The story of Yama in the Buddhist tradition is a good example of this innovation.

As the above discussion shows the Buddhist Yama is an effort to incorporate certain popular theistic characteristics without undermining Buddhism's fundamental tenets.

C. Sakka

Sakka in the Buddhist discourses is described as 'the king of gods' (*devānam inda*). It is believed that king or '*inda*' of gods is none other than the Indra in the Vedic tradition. The Vedic god Indra is usually depicted as a warring god. In the Buddhist tradition, however, Sakka is not a warring god but an admirer and follower of the Buddha. When the newly enlightened Buddha entered the city of Rājagaha it is said that Sakka announced the arrival of the Buddha by chanting appreciatory stanzas.[37] In this particular instance, he acknowledges to the inquisitive onlookers that he is an attendant of the Buddha. On other occasions he is seen visiting the Buddha and asking questions regarding the doctrine. In the *Saṃyutta Nikāya* there is a whole section containing twenty-five discourses connected to Sakka.[38] Of these twenty-five discourses eleven have some reference to Sakka's dealings with *asuras*. Many of them have references to the battles between the two groups. In the well-known *Dhajagga Sutta*, Sakka says to his fellow gods to look at the flags of the four chiefs including himself if they find themselves in trouble in the battle field.[39] According to the *sutta*, the Buddha, however, adds that although Sakka instructs his people in that manner there is no guarantee that it is going to work because Sakka himself is 'not without lust, hatred and delusion' and hence is bound to get scared and run away (leaving his own followers behind).[40]

Sakka as the divine helper gets highlighted particularly in the *Jātaka*s. The commentaries too have a few references to him. The commentary to the *Dhammapada* reports how Sakka helped Cakkhupala, the blind *arahant*, who was forsaken by his attendant.[41] In the Buddhist *Jātaka* stories Sakka appears very often as the divine helper who watches the world and comes forward to assist good people who get into trouble. In the *Jātaka* stories, very often the benefactor is the future Buddha who finds himself in a helpless situation as a result of his goodness. For instance, in the *Guttila Jātaka*, Sakka comes to rescue Guttila, the future Buddha who was faced with an imminent defeat and humiliation at the hands of his pupil.[42] In his excellent treatment of 'Sakka' Malalasekera has summarized this characteristic of Sakka and refers to relevant instances from the *Jātaka*:

> Sakka appears as the guardian of moral law in the world. When wickedness is rampant among men, or kings become unrighteous, he appears among them to frighten them so that they may do good instead of evil. He is on the side of the good against the wicked, and often helps them to realize their goal. Instances of this are seen in the *Ambacora, Ayakūṭa, Udaya, Kaccāni, Kāma, Kāmanīta, Kumbha, Keḷisīla, Kharaputa, Culladhanuggaha, Dhajavihetha, Biḷārikosiya, Maṇicora, Mahākaṇha, Vaka, Sarabhaṇga, Sarabhamiga* and *Sudhābhojana Jātakas*.[43]

It is interesting to note that all these stories mention that the stone seat where Sakka usually sits would get heated when something drastically wrong happens in the human world. It is through this heat that Sakka comes to know that his intervention is needed somewhere. This particular aspect suggests that Sakka's intervention is not something personal to Sakka but has a broader universal character. Sakka's seat or the position seems to indicate the seat of righteousness or goodness. In other words, it is to say that Sakka is closely connected to the moral nature believed to exist in the universe. This makes Sakka not an ordinary kind of god who is willing to help but a universal phenomenon which is a part of the reality in which righteousness ultimately triumphs over what is unrighteous.[44] The protection of the good is an important task attributed to God in theistic religious traditions. It is clear that in Buddhism's non-theistic tradition Sakka has been assigned this task. Key virtues of Buddhism's social philosophy seem to be implied in Sakka reaching out to help others. In this respect he can be regarded as representing the active aspect of compassion and loving-kindness (*mettā* and *karuṇā*).

IV. Conclusion

Early Buddhist literature, arts and architecture bear ample evidence to the belief that gods had close association with the life of the Buddha and his disciples.[45] Their interconnection with the Buddha is seen when they come to him or his disciples to ask questions or to pay homage. Gods are usually given a position below the Buddha and his disciples. This is understandable in the context of the Buddhist standpoint that one's greatness ultimately depends on one's inner purity and not on the material wealth one possesses or pleasures one enjoys. The close association these gods have with the Buddha and his Order may be a later development. Nevertheless, this association has been executed in such a way that it does not come into conflict with the philosophy of the system.

A problem, however, seems to arise in the existence of certain gods attributed with characteristics usually associated with God in theistic religious traditions. The presence of such gods suggests that, in spite of the fact that one is one's own Lord and one does not need any external intervention in the path to *nibbāna*, some followers needed the help of these divine beings for their daily existence. It is admirable that the early Buddhists did not dismiss this need as unnecessary, irrelevant or inappropriate. Their challenge was to incorporate these divine beings in a way that they do no contradict the fundamental teachings of the Master. In the above discussion we found that they have done their best to be faithful to the Buddha's teaching despite having had to accommodate gods in his system of philosophy.

Sociologists of religion are fond of talking about great and small traditions within traditions. Obviously the gods belong to the small tradition of Buddhism, and even the slightest exposure to the traditional Buddhist cultures would show that this small tradition is thriving today as it has been down through the ages. A curious fact, however, is that even in these cultures, with the possible exception of Thailand where Brahma is popularly worshipped,[46] one does not find those particular three gods discussed above being worshipped as popular gods. How can this be explained? We know that the three gods discussed have their origin in the Vedic tradition. But even in this tradition within which these gods originated they are not worshipped as popular gods. Yama is still invoked at funerals but none of those gods are worshipped daily. The historical reasons for their absence may equally explain why their counterparts are not worshipped in Buddhist societies. In the history of Vedic religion we know that there were several stages in the evolution of the gods. We know that there was a large number of gods at the earliest stage. But most of them were relegated to a subordinate position with the evolution of Vedic thought. This is the fate that befell the three gods discussed in this account. For instance, in the Vedic tradition, as in the Buddhist tradition, Brahma was the highest of all divine beings. With the evolution of the religion and the philosophy of the Veda, Brahma who was a person at the beginning, gradually became an impersonal concept. It is only subsequently that the concept of *brahma* was reintroduced as the creator God in the Brahmanic trinity of gods. According to Garrett:

> In this mythological character of creator of the universe, he is mentioned in the *Bhagavad Gītā* and *Vishnu Puraṇa*. When, …the idea of one Supreme Being was again brought forward, Brahma was considered the chief of the existing trinity, and was at first identified with that idea of an unknown god; and though afterwards Shiva and Vishnu were each in turn identified with the Supreme Being by their respective followers, the Shaivas and Vaishnavas, the name Brahma, *in the neuter*, was still retained in the language of philosophy to designate the universal Supreme One.[47]

As Garrett's account shows the popular Hindu religion gradually bifurcated into *Śaivism* and *Vaiṣṇavism* and the belief in *brahma* as creator God seems to have become a subordinate belief in the system. Furthermore, with the philosophical developments in Advaita Vedanta the term '*brahman*' came to be used exclusively to refer to *brahman* as the essence of reality or the absolute soul (*parama ātma*). This may have caused the idea of *brahma* as the creator and highest being in the masculine sense to recede gradually into oblivion.

In a Theravāda Buddhist country like Sri Lanka the above mentioned three gods are not worshipped; nor are there shrines dedicated to them. Nevertheless, they exist very much in the Buddhist consciousness. As for the gods the Sri Lankan Buddhists worship, a larger majority of them have their origins in Sri Lanka itself or in the Southern part of India. The small tradition has not ceased to exist; only it has evolved. Now there are different gods to perform these very same functions. The admirable aspect in the tradition is that even the most uneducated Buddhist would not attribute any of the characteristics of God to the Buddha for they know that he is no more. Nor would they go to the Buddha in search of mundane assistance. They seek the help of gods either by offering merit or by making some kind of 'payment' to them. The two traditions and the practices associated with them seem to go smoothly, unhindered by the other, each maintaining its distinctiveness.

Ultimately, what all this about gods has to do with a person like Godwin who devoted his life to seek and strengthen the inner tranquility of oneself and others according to the teaching of the Buddha may not be clear at once. Godwin belonged in a Buddhist universe in which gods are a very important class of occupants. His message, nevertheless, was that we, all the sentient beings including gods, must ultimately rely on our own selves which can be refined by meditation. This is an essential aspect of the original message of the Buddha who is 'the incomparable teacher of gods and human beings (*satthā deva-manussānam*).

Notes

1. This essay is in honour of the late Godwin Samararatne who was a fine example of a man with a developed mind (*bhāvita citta*). Among the most striking personal characteristics of Godwin were his simplicity, unassuming demeanor and unpretentiousness. He was such a serious meditator he never looked like one! He was extra-ordinary in being very ordinary. With his life he illuminated the lives of men and women who came to associate with him.
2. D II 89. All references to Pāli texts are to Pāli Text Society (PTS) editions.
3. Ram Nath Sharma, *Indian Philosophy* (Delhi: Orient Longman, 1972): 2-3. The following distinction made by T.R.V. Murti corresponds to these two characterizations: "There are two main currents of Indian philosophy—one having its source in the *atma*-doctrine of the Upaniṣads and the other in the *anatma*-doctrine of Buddha," (*The Central Philosophy of Buddhism*. (London: Unwin Ltd, 1955): 10).
4. M I 140.
5. In more recent times, scholars have focused their attention on the issue of Buddhist non-theism again. Anthony Fernando and Leonard Swilder, *Buddhism Made Plain: An Introduction for Christians and Jews* (New York: Obris Books, 1985): 104, Raimundo Panikkar, *The Silence of God: The Answer of the Buddha* (New York: Obris Books, 1989): 62, and John Hick, *An Interpretation of Religion* (Connecticut: Yale University Press, 1989): 246 are some representative examples.
6. F.L. Woodward, trans., *The Book of the Gradual Sayings* (London: Pāli Text Society, 1979): 158.
7. M II 68.
8. *brahmāti mātā pitaro* "parents are called the Brahma" (*Aṅguttara Nikāya* I 132).
9. An example is the Buddha's discussion with Acela Kassapa (S II 19-20).
10. *tumhehi kiccam ātappam – akkhātāro tathāgatā* (Dh 276).
11. *attā hi attano nātho – ko hi nātho paro siya* (Dh 160).
12. *Dīgha Nikāya,* discourses number 20 and 32 respectively.
13. *Advaita Vedanta* (Honolulu: East-West Center Press, 1968): 9, n. 1.
14. Gavin Flood, *An Introduction to Hinduism,* First South Asian paperback edition (Cambridge: Cambridge University Press, 1998): 110.
15. *Jhānas* mentioned in the Buddhist path of purification are states achieved by developing concentration of the mind to different degrees. The four preliminary states are described as *rūpa* or belonging to the fine material realm and the subsequent four are described

as belonging to immaterial (*āruppa*) realm. It is said that one is born as a Brahma as a result of attaining these states.

16. *yavatā bhikkhave sahassalokadhatu mahābrahmā tattha aggam akkhāyati. Mahābrahmunopi kho bhikkhave atth'eva aññathattam, atthi viparināmam. Evam passam bhikkhave sutavā ariyasāvako tasmim pi nibbindati, tasmim nibbindanto agge virajjati, pageva hīnasmim* (A V 59-60).

17. *brahmaloko pi kho avuso anicco addhuvo sakkayapariyapanno* (A V 410).

18. Maurice Walshe, trans. *Thus Have I Heard*, (London: Wisdom Publications, 1987): 76.

19. A IV 105.

20. Maurice Walshe, trans. *Thus Have I Heard*, (London: Wisdom Publications, 1987): 178.

21. Ps I 194.

22. A I 132.

23. *yathā maha brahmuno catasso bhāvanā avijahitā honti, mettā karuṇā muditā upekkhāti, evam eva mātāpitunnaṃ puttesu catasso bhāvanā avijahitā honti* (*Manorathapūrani* II 204).

24. See the *Ariyapariyesana Sutta* of the *Majjhima Nikāya* for details.

25. *Manu* 7: 7.

26. *Indian Philosophy,* vol. I (Delhi: Oxford University Press, 1994): 85.

27. R. E. Hume, *The Thirteen Principal Upanishads,* 2nd ed. (Delhi: Oxford University Press, 1993): 341-361.

28. The idea of Messengers of Yama is *Ṛg Vedic*. In Buddhism it has been an ethical concept.

29. Ps V 231 (see also Mp II 278).

30. *yādisam vapate bījam—tādisam harate phalam kalyānakārī kalyānam—pāpakāri ca pāpakam* (S I 227).

31. Discussing the role of Yama in the Pāli Canon and in particular, in the *Devadūta Sutta*, M.M.J. Marasinghe holds that Yama does not play any role in the process of *karma* and that he definitely does not play the role of the judge (M.M.J. Marasinghe, *Gods in Early Buddhism* (Colombo: University of Sri Lanka, 1974): 268-270). I think Marasinghe's view of Yama as 'merely a sympathetic onlooker' is a result of reading the discourse only at its literal level. What is implied both in the *sutta* and its commentary is that he does play a role in the process. The reluctance to admit this openly, on the part of the *sutta*, has to be viewed as resulting from the recognition of the basic philosophical difficulty of the position.

32. Ps V 231 (see also in Mp II 228).

33. *Kathāvatthu* 596-98.

34. *Kathāvatthuppakaraṇa Aṭṭhakathā* 187.

35. Shwe Zan Aung and Rhys Davids, *Points of Controversy* (London: Pāli Text Society, 1979): 346.

36. Bhikkhu Bodhi, *The Middle Length Discourses of the Buddha* (Kandy, Sri Lanka: Buddhist Publication Society, 1995): 1035.

37. Vin I 36.

38. *Sakka Saṃyutta* (S I 216-240).

39. S I 218-220.

40. *sakko hi bhikkhave devānam indo avītarāgo avītadoso avītamoho bhīru chambhī utrāsi palāyī ti* (S I 219).

41. DhA I 14.

42. J II 248-57.

43. G.P. Malalasekera, *Dictionary of Pāli Proper Names* II (London: Pāli Text Society, 1960): 963.

44. No instances of such help are recorded in the later history. A somewhat relevant case is reported in the *Mahāvaṃsa*, the chronicle of Sri Lanka. When there was a famine during the reign of Vattagamani Abhaya it is said that Sakka provided a large raft for those monks who wished to go to India in order to escape the famine. (The incident reported in the *Sammohavinodanī*, the commentary to the *Vibhaṅga*, pp. 445-6 has been discussed by E.W. Adikaram in his *Early History of Buddhism in Ceylon* (Colombo, 1947): 73-4.) It is interesting to note that the story also suggests that the Buddhists were aware of the limitations of Sakka. The initial request of the monks was not a raft but destruction of the enemy that has arisen. Sakka is reported to have responded by saying that even he cannot do away with an enemy that has arisen but he can be of help in some other manner. It is at this juncture that he provided a raft.
It is further said that the pre-Buddhaghosa commentary known as *Maha Paccari* was so named because it was compiled in this vessel (*paccari*) (Adikaram, *op.cit.* p.12).

45. There are so many discourses in the Pāli canon showing how a number of non-human beings, a larger majority of whom are divine beings, had close association with the Buddha and his disciples. These encounters have been described in more detail in the subsequent Buddhist literature and portrayed in the Buddhist art. Some prominent examples from sculpture are available at Mathura and Sanci in India.

46. Maurice Walshe, op cit., p. 43, refers to Brahma shrine outside Eravan Hotel, Bangkok.

47. John Garrett, *A Classical Dictionary of India* (Delhi: Low Price Publications, 1990).

Part Three

Rebirth and Mental Culture

The Ultimate Goal of Early Buddhism and the Distinctive Characteristics of Buddhist Meditation

P.D. Premasisi

Meditation, which is believed to be part of the common heritage of Indian thought, is largely shared by the Buddhist tradition as well. Buddhism has recently been greatly appealing to many intellectuals of the Western world searching for a new spirituality, primarily because they believe that Buddhist meditation can bring about an effective transformation of personality.[1] However, it is to be noted that a clear theoretical understanding of the philosophical foundations of Buddhist meditation and its goals and objectives is important to any one who ventures into the practice of Buddhist meditation. In this essay an attempt will be made to clarify some of the distinctive characteristics of the underlying philosophy of the theory of meditation in early Buddhism based on the material embodied in the *Sutta Piṭaka* of the Pāli canon. In this attempt some comparative references will be made to the classical *yoga* tradition of Indian philosophy primarily to show in what respects the Buddhist theory of meditation differed from that tradition.

The starting point of early Buddhism[2] is an experiential fact concerning living beings. In this respect early Buddhism radically differs from most other metaphysical religions that have as their starting point a metaphysical absolute. The Buddha's noble search (*ariyapariyesana*) was motivated by a solution to the experiential fact of unsatisfactoriness (*dukkha*) in life. Living beings are subject to birth, aging, disease, death and rebirth. This process is characterized by intense craving of three kinds, described as the craving for sense gratification, the craving for becoming and the craving for annihilation. It involves very little satisfaction but a great deal of anxiety, pain, frustration and disappointment. The ultimate goal of the Buddha was to find a final end to this process. Early Buddhism explained this predicament of living beings without postulating any metaphysical entities, external or internal that could be responsible for it. The Buddhist explanation was in terms of a psychological theory of dependent arising. The concepts of *Brahman*, *Ātman*, *Puruṣa*, and God do not play any role in the early Buddhist teaching about the liberation of man from the cyclic process of unsatisfactoriness (*dukkha*). The liberation taught in the original teaching of the Buddha is to be attained by a total transformation of the emotive and cognitive structure of personality. This transformation involves a modification in respect of a person's bodily, verbal and mental behavior. The Buddhist tradition uses the term *bhāvanā* as a general term to signify the personality culture that conduces to such a transformation. The Buddha experimented with many existing methods of mental culture practiced by his contemporaries in order to overcome *dukkha.* However, he found them to be unsatisfactory. The Buddha conceded that they led to extremely subtle and blissful levels of experience, but according to him, even after attaining such high levels of mental rapture some residual clinging that prevented a person from crossing over to the incorruptible peace of *nibbāna* persisted. After many years of intense and austere search, he claimed to have discovered a unique method of such crossing over (*pārāyana*) eradicating all the residual clinging. It was this method of crossing over that came to be emphasized in the Buddhist method of meditation known as the method of insight (*vipassanā*).

The *Sutta Piṭaka* of the Pāli canon, which may be considered as the most acceptable literary source for the reconstruction of early Buddhism shows that practices of mental culture (technically described as *yoga*) were known in India during the time of the Buddha. The *Brahmajāla Sutta*, which enumerates as many as sixty-two philosophical theories that existed during the Buddha's time mentions some theories classified by the Buddha among eternalist theories (*sassatavādā*), extentionalist theories (*antānantikā*), casuistic originationists (*adhiccasamuppannavādā*) as theories derived from some form of meditative experience. The method adopted by the theorists as described in the *sutta* is one of meditative application of the mind and the attainment of a certain concentrated and rapturous state of mind consequent upon a deliberate direction of the mind with resolute effort (*ātappamanvāya padhānamanvāya anuyogamanvāya sammā manasikāramanvāya tathārūpaṃ cetosamādhiṃ phusati*). It is pointed out that just as much as different philosophical theorists derived divergent theories of reality from their sense experiences so did they derive divergent theories from the meditative experiences also. The Buddha points out that his insight transcends all these divergent metaphysical constructs (*diṭṭhi*) about the nature of reality, and seeks only to attain the calm, peace and tranquility of mind characteristic of the experience of *nibbāna*. It is not within the range of speculative reason (*atakkāvacaro*). The *Ariyapariyesana Sutta* of the *Majjhima Nikāya* mentions the Buddha's encounter during his striving for the 'Noble Search,' with the then known teachers of *yoga* Ālārakālāma and Uddakarāmaputta. These teachers were capable of guiding the Buddha on the path of attaining the rapturous states of meditative mind known as the experience of the sphere of nothingness (*ākiñcāyatana*) and the sphere of neither perception nor non-perception (*nevasaññānāsaññāyatana*). Later, in the Buddha's own formulation of the meditative progression of the mind leading to the fruits of recluseship (*sāmaññaphala*) he introduced certain meditative stages of attainment known as the *jhānas,* four of them in ascending order. These states of *jhāna* are elsewhere considered as meditative attainments that are within the sphere of consciousness of form (*rūpa*) and are supposed to precede the subtler meditative attainments that belong to the spheres of formless consciousness (*āruppa*). The Buddha also claimed to have discovered a new level of rapturous meditative experience that involved a complete cessation of all sensation and perception (*saññāvedayitanirodha*), conceived in the Buddhist tradition as the culmination of the path of tranquility meditation. The Buddha used the method of tranquility meditation (*samatha*) not as an end in itself. *Samatha* is considered in early Buddhism as an indispensable support for the development of insight (*vipassanā*) that leads to liberating knowledge (*paññā* or *vimuttiñāṇadassana*). Early Buddhism also warns against the possibility of stagnation in some stage of tranquility meditation, misconceiving it as the eternally blissful state of Being that that the so-called soul attains, transcending the unsatisfactory existence bound up with the transient processes of mind and matter. It is with respect to this point that one can discern a distinctive approach in Buddhism to the employment of methods of *yoga* as a means to liberation. The significance of the Buddha's repeated emphasis of the Middle Way teaching involving the avoidance of the metaphysical extremes of eternalism (*sassatavāda*) and annihilationism (*ucchedavāda*) is closely related to this point.

Eternalism, according to the Buddha involved unobservable metaphysical entities underlying the experientially observable phenomena. The solution of the riddle of life in eternalist terms involved the notion of some eternal Absolute with which the individual merges and continues to eternity, or the notion of an immortal Self or Soul which survives in an eternal realm after death. Eternalist teachings were the usual alternative presented to counter the materialist philosophy that denied any survival after death, and affirmed the annihilation of the individual. The Buddha described them as the metaphysical extremes. The first affirmed that what exists, exists eternally, maintaining the dogmatic position 'Everything exists' (*sabbaṃ atthi*). The second denied all continuity and affirmed the dogmatic position 'Nothing exists' (*sabbaṃ natthi*). In responding to a question raised about the right view by a person named Kaccāyana, the Buddha explains that the above are two extreme views to which people in the world mostly tend to cling dogmatically. According to the Buddha, one who sees with proper insight the way things arise, will not fall into the extreme of annihilationism, and one who sees with proper insight the way things pass away, will not fall into the extreme of eternalism. Both erroneous beliefs are, according to him, a consequence of being tied to attachment, clinging and dogmatism (*upāyupādānābhinevesavinibandho*). The right view of the nature of reality can be expressed only in terms of the principle of dependent arising (*paṭicca-samuppāda*). The Buddha maintained that erroneous views not only involved a difference in the metaphysical description of the ultimate goal of the religious life, but also the practical consequence of being bound to the cyclic process of re-becoming due to the residual craving for existence (*bhavataṇhā*). While the materialist was not concerned with the religious life because of the belief in utter annihilation at death, the eternalist was searching for eternal survival of the Self and interpreted the principles of the religious life based on the metaphysics of the Self. The Buddha considered both as hindering the goal of a final end to the empirically observed process of *dukkha*. This is a fundamental difference between early Buddhism and all other systems of religion and philosophy that Buddhism described as imprisoned within the clutches of metaphysical dogma (*diṭṭhi*). This fundamental difference involves a difference in the Buddhist methods of meditative practice and the Buddhist theory of meditation, expressed in terms of the distinction between tranquility meditation (*samatha*) and insight meditation (*vipassanā*). However, those who interpret Buddhism overlooking this fundamental distinction attempt to impose upon the Buddhist goal and the Buddhist theory and practice of meditation some of the metaphysical trappings characteristic of non-Buddhist systems of meditation.

The emphasis in the Buddhist method of mental culture is not on the attainment of some extra-empirical Being, but on having insight into the existential reality involving impermanence (*anicca*), unsatisfactoriness (*dukkha*) and soullessness (*anattā*), resulting in the extinction of all unwholesome psychological traits. The empirical world (*loka*) is considered in Buddhism as consisting of the five aggregates of personality (*pañcakkhandhā*) or the twelve spheres of sense and sense objects such as the eye and material form, ear and sounds, etc., (*dvādasa āyatanāni*) or the eighteen elements which include the sense faculties, sense objects and the corresponding sense consciousness (*aṭṭhārasa dhātuyo*). In some instances the Buddha points out that there is nothing other than these elements of existence that can meaningfully be talked about. "Everything" (*sabba*) falls into these empirical phenomena. The insight to be gained by the culture of the mind is not concerned with the existence of some enduring and eternal entity other than these phenomena. According to early Buddhism, the liberating insight is the penetrative vision into the impermanence, unsatisfactoriness and soullessness of these phenomena. Such insight leads to disenchantment with them (*nibbidā*). Disenchantment leads to dispassion (*virāga*) and dispassion to liberation (*vimutti*). Early Buddhism repeatedly emphasizes the fact that the elements of the empirical world cannot be an Ātman or anything that belongs to an Ātman (*attā vā attaniyaṃ vā*). Suffering is due to the attempt to cling to them with a sense of ownership. When this sense of ownership is abandoned suffering itself comes to an end. There will be no more conditioning of the aggregates of clinging. The aim of meditative culture of the mind is this insight, this penetrative vision.

We notice here a significant difference in approach between

the Buddha's teaching and the eternalist doctrines that the Buddha rejected. Eternalists could agree with the Buddha that all mental and material elements of existence are impermanent, characterized by suffering and lacking in Self-nature. The disagreement between the Buddha and the eternalists arise regarding the claim of the former that liberation is possible only by the pursuit of some extra-empirical eternal Being, not subject to change. The Buddha considered any attempt to identify any component of empirical reality such as any one of the five aggregates with a permanent self as mistaken. He also considered any attempt to seek a substantial self outside the empirical personality as equally mistaken. The Upaniṣadic and the Vedantic theory of the Self that explained final liberation in terms of monistic metaphysics as merging of the individual Self (*Ātman*) with the cosmic Self (*Brahman*) with the realization of their identity does not seem to be acceptable to Buddhism. In the *Alagaddūpama Sutta* the Buddha refers to a certain view that affirms the survival after death of the individual Self that is identical with the cosmic Self and remains eternally without any change (*so loko so attā so pecca bhavissāmi nicco dhuvo sassato avipariṇāmadhammo sassatisamaṃ tatheva thassāmi*).

The Buddha points out in the *Alagaddūpama Sutta* that the sense of fear, insecurity and agitation (*paritassanā*) often felt by people may be due to the prospect of loosing something that they desire to retain in the outside world, or it may be due to something they desire to retain in the inner self. The following account of the *Alagaddūpama Sutta* that occurs after it refers to the way in which a well taught noble disciple puts aside all notions of the self deserves special attention:

> When this was said, a certain *bhikkhu* asked the Blessed One: "Venerable sir, can there be agitation about what is non-existent externally?"
>
> "There can be, *bhikkhu*," the Blessed One said. "Here, *bhikkhu*, someone thinks thus: 'Alas, I had it! Alas, I have it no longer! Alas, may I have it! Alas, I do not get it!' Then he

sorrows, grieves, and laments, he weeps beating his breast and becomes distraught. That is how there is agitation about what is non-existent externally."

"Venerable Sir, can there be agitation about what is non-existent internally?"

"There can be, *bhikkhu*," the Blessed One said. "Here, *bhikkhu*, someone has the view: 'This is self, this the world; after death I shall be permanent everlasting, eternal, not subject to change; I shall endure as long as eternity.' He hears the Tathāgata or a disciple of the Tathāgata teaching the *dhamma* for the elimination of all standpoints, decisions, obsessions, adherences, and underlying tendencies, for the stilling of all formations, for the relinquishing of all attachments; for the destruction of craving, for dispassion, for cessation, for *nibbāna*. He thinks thus: 'So I shall be annihilated! So I shall perish! So I shall be no more!' Then he sorrows, grieves, and laments, he weeps beating his breast and becomes distraught. That is how there is agitation about what is non-existent internally."[3]

A comparison of the early Buddhist standpoint on what is to be achieved by meditation with the standpoint of other meditative traditions such as the *yoga* tradition of India systematized by Patañjali makes evident the marked distinction between them.[4] According to almost all scholars who interpret the *Yogasūtras* of Patañjali, suffering is due to the enslavement of the spirit to matter. The *yoga* philosophy that derived its metaphysical basis from the Sāṃkhya doctrines, considered even the mental processes as an evolution of matter. A distinction was made not only between gross matter and the spirit but also between the mental processes and the embodied spirit. Suffering is explained as a consequence of the spirit being shackled to matter. The series of incarnations to which the spirit is subjected is conceived as an expression of this enslavement.[5] Ignorance that leads to suffering, according to the *yoga* philosophy, is not as in the early Buddhist teaching confined to the ignorance regarding the transient, suffering and unsubstantial nature of mental and material phenomena. Ignorance is the confusion of spirit with our psycho-mental experience. This makes us attribute "qualities" and predicates to the eternal and autonomous principle that is Sprit. Eliade describes it as a metaphysical ignorance. Eliade also observes that according to *yoga* philosophy "...it is natural that it should be a metaphysical knowledge that supervenes to end this ignorance. This metaphysical knowledge leads the disciple to the threshold of illumination—that is, to the true "Self."[6]

According to the Sāṃkhya doctrine, there exists a matter (*prakṛti*) from which everything is derived, including the mind with its processes. The spirit (*puruṣa*) exists in contradistinction to matter, which is totally different and separate from it. The aim of *yoga* is considered to be the attainment of *kaivalya* interpreted as isolation of *puruṣa.* The Buddha is seen in his teachings to consistently deny the theory that there exists a spirit completely separate from the body (*aññaṃ jīvaṃ aññaṃ sarīraṃ*). This theory, according to the Buddha, belongs to the class of eternalist doctrines, and is equally objectionable as the opposite materialist or nihilist extreme that affirms that the spirit and the body are identical (*taṃ jīvaṃ taṃ sarīraṃ*).

All descriptions of the aims of *yoga* seem to imply the idea of the supreme Self or Spirit. *Yoga* is considered as the reunion of the living self with the Supreme Self (*saṃyogo yoga ukta jīvātmano paramātmanah*).[7] This, we have already found to have been refuted by the Buddha in the *Alagaddūpama Sutta*. The *yoga* tradition describes *yoga* as the silencing of the mind's activities which leads to the complete realization of the intrinsic nature of the Supreme Person (*puruṣasyātyantikasvarūpāvasthiterhetuscittavṛttinirodho yoga iti*).

The consequence of the metaphysical standpoint of those who followed non-Buddhist systems of meditation appears to be that their sole aim was to attain a certain state of deep *samādhi*, which they described as an integration of the individual soul with Supreme Being or the cosmic Spirit.

According to the Buddha, such an aim involves a metaphysical presupposition which is difficult for many people to discard, namely, the presupposition of some eternal entity, an Absolute, that is the primordial source of everything that exists. When a certain blissful and rapturous state of mental calm is experienced through the practice of methods of tranquility meditation, there is a tendency to describe erroneously those states of mind which, from the Buddha's point of view are yet within the sphere of the conditioned and dependently arisen, as experiences of merging with Supreme Being. The underlying cause for this is the fear of annihilation. Craving for survival (*bhavataṇhā*) that still persists in a subtle form creates an agitation of mind at the thought of the annihilation of the self. This is due to the presupposed metaphysical self of the dogmatist who all along conceived of liberation in terms of the immortality of the self. In Buddhism, this presupposition is never made. Therefore the question of the annihilation of an existent metaphysical entity does not arise. The Buddha was often accused by his contemporaries as teaching a doctrine of annihilation due to this misunderstanding. The Buddha brushed aside this accusation in a number of instances, pointing out that throughout his career as a teacher he has taught only the arising of misery and its cessation. In the *Alagaddūpama Sutta*, for instance, after rejecting numerous attempts by soul theorists to cling to some notion of a metaphysical self the Buddha points out the common misunderstanding of his teaching on the part of the eternalist metaphysicians thus:

> "So saying *bhikkhus*, so proclaiming, I have been baselessly, vainly, falsely, and wrongly misrepresented by some recluses and *brahmin*s thus: 'The recluse Gotama is one who leads astray; he teaches the annihilation, the destruction, the extermination of an existing being.' As I am not, as I do not proclaim, so have I been baselessly, vainly, falsely, and wrongly misrepresented by some recluses and *brahmin*s thus:..
>
> "*Bhikkhus*, both formerly and now what I teach is suffering and the cessation of suffering..."[8]

The Buddha's position regarding the questions raised about the after death state of the liberated person also can be explained in terms of his consistent avoidance of the presupposition of a metaphysical self.

The Buddha insisted that this difference is not restricted to a mere difference of interpretation of meditative or the so-called religious experience. According to the Buddha, such a metaphysical view (*diṭṭhi*) is a hindrance or a stumbling block to final liberation of the mind, and therefore, the attainment of the ultimate goal of Buddhism, the cessation of misery through the overcoming of all clinging. The mind cannot attain the liberation described in Buddhism as *anupādāya āsavehi cittaṃ vimuccati* (the mind is released from the cankers due to non-clinging) as long as it is obsessed with the dogma of a metaphysical self.

The special significance of the Buddhist method of insight meditation (*vipassanā*) should be seen in the light of the above discussion. It needs to be reiterated that the aim of Buddhism is not the attainment of some rapturous experience, which could be described as the mystical experience of integration with the Supreme Spirit. The stillness of mind (*samādhi*) attained by tranquility meditation is a prerequisite for the skill with which the three characteristics of all empirical reality needs to be grasped by the meditative mind. The consequence of harnessing the stilled mind to see the rising and falling nature of things results in the final break through that liberates the mind from all cankers. When the mind is stilled it is possible to see things as they really come to be (*samāhito yathābhūtaṃ passati*). The aim of Buddhist meditation, stated briefly, is the attainment of the knowledge and insight that leads to the eradication of the cankers (*āsavakkhayañāṇa*).

The early Buddhist evaluation of the rapturous states of meditative mind attained by means of the development of *jhāna* and *samāpatti* could also be understood in the light of the above discussion. These various levels of experience attainable by means of meditative cultivation of the mind were no doubt considered by the Buddha as delightful and pleasant. They were conceived as belonging to a hierarchical order of mental experience far more delightful than what is obtainable in the gratification of the senses. However, any tendency to cling to these experiences or to identify any such experience with a metaphysical self was considered by the Buddha as a hindrance to liberation. The Buddha and many of his senior disciples who were described as liberated in both ways (*ubhatobhāgavimutta*) had the skill to attain those states of experience, and emerge from them in forward order, in reverse order, and in both forward and reverse order wherever they wanted, whenever they wanted, in whatever way they wanted, and as long as they wanted. Early Buddhism does not appear to have considered such skill as indispensable for the attainment of liberation. A class of liberated beings is identified in the *sutta*s as those liberated by insight (*paññāvimutta*) who by merely contemplating the three characteristics of being and the rising and falling nature of phenomena in terms of dependent arising had attained full liberation. This shows that the minimum degree of tranquility of mind required, according to the Buddha's teaching, for the attainment of final liberation is the stillness of mind that enables a person to direct one's attention to the three characteristics of being without being disturbed by the five hindrances. Liberation through insight, according to early Buddhism, is not elevating one's spirit to a special metaphysical plane of existence. It is merely a transformation of attitudes, a total emotive and cognitive transformation of the person.

Nibbāna, the ultimate goal of Buddhism is neither something out there, nor something deep within, but the quenching of the thirst and agitation (*taṇhakkhayo*), the eradication of greed, hatred and delusion, the destruction (*samugghāto*) of the conceit associated with the ego (*asmimāna*), and the destruction of the "I-making" and "mine-making" latent tendencies of the mind (*ahaṃkāramamaṃkāramānānusaya*).

The transformation of thought and attitudes leading to this liberation of mind is brought about by the contemplation on impermanence, unsatisfactoriness and insubstantiality leading to a process of disenchantment and dispassion. The realization of the three characteristics of being through the contemplation of this reality concerning all empirical things needs to be established both at the cognitive and the affective levels of personality. According to Buddhism, the various stages of enlightenment, beginning from stream entry to the attainment of sainthood (*arahatta*), is a consequence of the strengthening of this vision. Insight meditation cultivated with a view to strengthening this vision, results in the weakening of one's suffering relative to the degree to which this vision has been strengthened both cognitively and affectively. Therefore, it is reasonable to conclude that the philosophical foundation of the Buddhist theory of meditation differs very significantly from that of other Indian traditions such as the Vedānta, and the *Sāṃkhya-yoga*. This difference is also evidently reflected in the way early Buddhism characterized the ultimate goal of all techniques of meditation and mental culture.

Notes

1. The subject of this essay is very appropriate for inclusion in this volume which is published in memory of Mr. Godwin Samararatne, one of the greatest Buddhist meditation teachers who devoted nearly three decades of his life solely to the practice and the propagation of what he conceived as genuine Buddhist meditation. I wish to mention here with immense gratitude my indebtedness to the practical benefits as well as the theoretical clarity I was personally fortunate to acquire through my association with Mr. Godwin Samararatne.
2. In this essay the expression "early Buddhism" is used to refer to the Buddhist teachings contained in the *Sutta Piṭaka* of the Pāli canon. The author subscribes to the view that the literature preserved in the *Sutta Piṭaka* of the Pāli canon and the parallel literature that is preserved in the Chinese *Āgamas* belonged to a time prior to the appearance of sectarian divisions within the Buddhist tradition. At least the major part of this literature can reasonably be believed to

have contained the original teachings of the Buddha although some parts of it could have been later additions. There are some sections like the *aṭṭhaka* and the *pārāyana vagga*s of the *Sutta Nipāta* belonging to the *Sutta Piṭaka* of the Pāli canon which undoubtedly belonged to a very early period.

3. Bhikkhu Ñāṇamoli and Bhikkhu Bodhi, trans. *The Middle Length Discourses of the Buddha , A New Translation of the Majjhima Nikāya* (Kandy, Sri Lanka: Buddhist Publication Society, 1995): 230-231.

4. Patañjali is the reputed author of the key scripture of classical *Yoga*, the *Yogasūtra*, also known as the *Patañjala Sūtra* or *Sāṃkhyapravacana*. The most likely date of Patañjali is the 3rd century C.E. However the traditions from which the author draws are undoubtedly much older. See Mircea Eliade ed., *The Encyclopedia of Religion,* vol II (USA: Macmillan 1995): 206.

5. Fernando Tola Carmen Dragonetti, *The Yogasūtras of Patañjali*, trans. K.D. Prithipaul (Delhi: Motilal Banarsidass, 1987): xv.

6. Eliade, *Yoga: Immortality and Freedom* (Princeton: Princeton University Press, 1958): 14.

7. Christopher Johnson, *Yoga: The Method of Reintegration* (London: Alcuin Press, 1949): 7.

8. Bhikkhu Ñāṇamoli and Bhikkhu Bodhi, op cit., p. 234.

Reconstructing the Path:

Two Case Studies from the Lay Meditation Movement in Sri Lanka

George D. Bond

Introduction

In 1952 a delegation of Buddhist lay followers led by H. Sri Nissanka traveled from Sri Lanka to Burma (Myanmar) to visit the fountainhead of the new and vibrant lay meditation movement there, the Mahāsī Thathana Yeiktha. After practicing meditation at this center with Mahāsī Sayādaw, the Burmese monastic who led the revolution in lay meditation,[1] the Sri Lankans returned home and began working to kindle this movement in their own country. Excited by the religious ferment in Burma and anticipating the great event of the Buddha Jayanti that was due to occur in 1956,[2] Nissanka and other Buddhists founded a society, the *Lanka Vipassanā Bhāvanā Samitiya,* and invited Burmese meditation teachers to Sri Lanka to hold classes for the laity. Within a few years they established a meditation center called Kanduboda, to teach this "new Burmese method" of *vipassanā*. In the following years, thousands of Buddhists went to Kanduboda to practice the "new Burmese method" of meditation. These meditators generated a resurgence of lay meditation in Sri Lanka which in some ways resembled the developments in Burma, but in other ways followed its own course and developed differently from the Burmese movement. For example, although the *vipassanā* movement in Burma was supported by the government of U Nu and the forces of nationalism, in Sri Lanka the lay meditation movement was never linked closely to Sinhala Buddhist nationalism. In contrast to the central place the *vipassanā* movement was given in Burma, in Sri Lanka the meditation movement was not included or recognized in the government's official and elaborate Buddha Jayanti celebrations. Although some nationalist leaders, such as J.R. Jayawardene, then a young minister, were among those who welcomed the original delegation of Burmese monks to the country, the meditation movement never became a significant or official part of the Buddhist nationalists' quest for identity.[3] In Sri Lanka the lay meditation movement followed a different trajectory, a trajectory that in some ways was more bound by classical Theravāda but in other ways was more open to other factors that emerged in Sri Lanka and led the movement to break with both classical and contemporary Theravāda.

This article seeks to explore the legacy of the lay meditation movement in Sri Lanka by considering two case studies of contemporary meditators who "graduated" from Kanduboda and were influential in charting the course of the meditation movement in the island. Having learned the "new Burmese method" at Kanduboda, both of these meditators went on to become influential teachers with large followings. The first teacher we consider is Godwin Samararatne, to whom this volume is dedicated, and the other is D.C.P. Ratnakara who was a close friend and associate of Godwin Samararatne.

The careers and teachings of these two teachers illustrate some of the distinctive features of the lay meditation movement in Sri Lanka and indicate some of the directions in which it has developed. The movement's ties to the early Buddhist revival can be seen in features such as the laicization of meditation and the practice of meditation for instrumental purposes.[4] The influence of the "new Burmese method" can be seen in the emphasis on the accessibility of both the path and the goal. However, the contemporary meditation movement has not been constrained by the "new Burmese method" or at least there is not much accent on or debate about method in the current context. For example, a key feature of the "new Burmese method" was its emphasis on the ability of meditators to proceed directly to *vipassanā* without first developing *samatha*.[5] But the contemporary lay meditation teachers freely employ *samatha* when it is useful for their students. In this respect, the movement has become very eclectic and even global in its choice of methods. The two teachers examined in this article exhibited this eclectic approach to the path of meditation. Through their construction of new ways of practice they also expressed the meditation movement's critique of what Scott has termed "contemporary Buddhist orthodoxy."[6] For both Samararatne and Ratnakara, the meditation movement derived its authority not from contemporary orthodoxy but from the "privileging of experience."[7] Through privileging experience both of these men became teachers/gurus to their followers and taught them to rely on their own attainments in meditation to liberate themselves from suffering.

A. Godwin Samararatene

Our first case study focuses on the teacher to whom this volume is dedicated, Godwin Samararatne. He was a pupil at Kanduboda and considered the abbot of Kanduboda, Venerable Kahapiṭiya Sumathipāla as one of his main teachers. Another person whom he acknowledged as his teacher was the Venerable Nyanaponika, the German-born monastic who directed the Buddhist Publication Society from his forest retreat near Kandy. A further influence came from D.C.P. Ratnakara, the meditation teacher whom I will discuss below. This lineage establishes that Samararatne had ties to both the "new Burmese method" of meditation and the Orientalist and textual influences of the early Buddhist revival.

Godwin Samararatne's primary position as a teacher of meditation was as the head of the Nilambe Meditation Center near Kandy. The Nilambe Meditation Center was founded by the Society of the Friends of the Dhamma (*Sadaham Mithuru Samuluwa*) in the late 1970s as a place where the Society could hold meetings and retreats. However, its remote location high in the foothills of the mountains made it somewhat impractical as a meeting site for the group and so it gradually became primarily a meditation retreat center catering to both Sri Lankan and foreign meditators. Samararatne, who was then the head librarian at the Kandy Library, was selected to be the resident director and meditation teacher at the idyllic center. After he took up the post at Nilambe, Samararatne became a very popular and influential meditation teacher. In addition to residing at Nilambe and teaching meditation there, he also led several meditation groups in the Kandy area and frequently traveled abroad to teach meditation. He was in great demand as a meditation teacher because of his wise and compassionate approach.

While he was himself one of the principal figures in the contemporary meditation movement, Samararatne was also a keen observer of the movement. His frequent trips abroad probably enabled him both to draw comparisons with foreign movements and to have a more objective perspective on the developments in Sri Lanka. In discussions that I had with Samararatne, he commented, for example, on the increase in the number of lay teachers, noting that there are now significantly more lay teachers than monastic teachers of meditation.[8] Teaching according to the authority of their own experience, these lay teachers have emerged as lay gurus with their own societies of followers. Samararatne observed that this emergence of lay gurus was a new phenomenon in Sri Lanka because in the past in Sri Lanka a meditation teacher would have been regarded as a *Kalyāṇa Mitta*, rather than a guru. Samararatne raised the question of whether there have been any contemporary monks who have been regarded in this same way. With the possible exception of Ānanda Maitreya, he did not think that there have been, and this makes the emergence of the lay gurus even more interesting.

When I discussed with him the question of how he thought this change came about, he attributed it to the influence of the Burmese. He did not disagree, however, with my suggestion that Indian influences were also at work given the impact that numerous contemporary Indian meditation teachers such as Sri Goenka and Vimala Thakar have made on Sri Lanka. The emergence of lay gurus represents a significant development in the meditation movement because the lay gurus have become increasingly independent from what we might call contemporary Buddhist orthodoxy as well as from the lineage of Kanduboda. Kanduboda was founded for the purpose of disseminating the "new Burmese method" to the laity; however, these new gurus now teach a variety of meditation methods to their own societies of followers. The experience and charisma of these lay teachers authorizes their teachings and gives them true guru status.

Godwin Samararatne can be counted among these new "lay gurus" of the last half of the twentieth century, although he would have never described himself thus. He preferred to be regarded as a *kalyāṇa mitta* and in his low-key style of teaching he related to his followers as a good friend. Samararatne wore the mantle of a guru very lightly and did not take himself too seriously, unlike some of the other contemporary gurus. He taught his followers with great compassion and a good sense of humor. For their part however, his followers clearly regarded Samararatne as their teacher and deferred to him as their authoritative leader on the path of meditation.

Since gurus cannot exist without followers, it is clear that the emergence of this new kind of lay teacher is closely related to shifts in the lay Buddhist clientele for meditation. The key shift here is probably the expansion of the middle class as well as the increasing Westernization or globalization of this class. Samararatne was well aware of these developments and adjusted his teachings to meet the needs of these new middle class meditators. Describing the changes that were taking place, Samararatne said that in the past the practice of village Buddhists centered on merit making. Village Buddhists did *sīla* and *dāna* and had a strong sense of community. However, they did not pursue meditation in a systematic way, nor did they aspire to any higher attainments on the spiritual path. In the present, however, the expanded middle class is turning to meditation to find ways to cope with the demands of their new situation. Samararatne commented on how different this use of meditation is from the classical model of a monastic going to the forest to do meditation in order to seek enlightenment.

Although Samararatne tailored his teaching of meditation to this new audience, he did not yield completely to the instrumentalist aspirations of the contemporary lay meditators. While understanding that it is normal for people to need help with problems in their lives, he also tried to elevate the aims of his students by showing them that they could begin by viewing meditation as a means of solving practical problems and then could progress to develop greater wisdom on the spiritual path. In describing his general goal in teaching meditation, Samararatne said that he viewed meditation as a means of overcoming suffering. He understood this to be a traditional Buddhist goal, but he also had in mind the various dimensions of suffering present in contemporary society. He wanted to use meditation to enable people to overcome suffering on a variety of levels, from the most mundane to the supramundane. He was somewhat skeptical, however, about the extravagant claims that some contemporary lay gurus make about the possibility of attaining advanced stages on the path. Samararatne commented that these kinds of claims of arahantship and other advanced states were unheard of even a decade ago and represented another new feature of the meditation movement.

Samararatne's Methods of Meditation:

For Samararatne the primary purpose of meditation was to alleviate suffering or *dukkha*. He assumed that meditation represents a way of life, something that can be done in all aspects of life, rather than a retreat from life. True meditation should result in a shift in the way one views life and the most important shift would be away from suffering and toward joy. Samararatne noted that some people may practice a certain technique of meditation very successfully, but that alone may not bring any transformation of their life. Meditation, as he taught it, required not only a technique but also a kind of self reflection and self-knowledge. This approach was evident in the structure of the meditation sessions that he led. His sessions often consisted of a period of silent meditation followed by discussion of questions and problems brought up by the meditators. In responding to the meditators' problems, he attempted to enable his followers to observe their thoughts, feelings and emotions to see how they develop and create suffering. This practice elucidates the meaning of the second Noble Truth, which is that we cause our own suffering because we have desires and expectations for the way things should be, and when events do not conform to our plans, we suffer. If we could just accept the present and not impose our desires, however, we could avoid most of this suffering. According to Samararatne, this method is not a matter of merely accepting suffering, but it represents a way of eliminating suffering because it enables us to see that suffering is a construct that we superimpose on the events that happen.

One of the meditation topics that he emphasized was *mettā* or loving-kindness meditation. He felt that this practice was crucial for overcoming our suffering and generating joy in life. He often stressed that meditation offers the promise of helping people to live by joy rather than suffering. In discussing *mettā*, he noted that we often do not show *mettā* toward ourselves because we are too critical of ourselves. Godwin called it "giving ourselves a minus." To deal with this he would lead a guided meditation in which he asked the group to think about an event in the past when they did this and to try to feel *mettā* toward themselves and the past situation. Without criticizing or blaming, they should try "just to be okay with it." He also led a meditation where he instructed the meditators not to be critical or judgmental about anything that was happening in their minds or bodies. He spoke about other ways that we do not show *mettā* toward ourselves, such as by comparing ourselves with others and by seeking to achieve what others have achieved. He said that some people are never satisfied with anything they do and that people should try to break out of this pattern. One way of doing this, he noted, was to keep a "merit book" in which you write down the positive and virtuous things that you do. He also encouraged people to react with *mettā* toward any unpleasant things that happened to them in their daily lives. Clearly Samararatne saw that this form of meditation could help overcome suffering and move people toward finding joy in living. He recognized that as *mettā* meditation enabled people to overcome psychological or emotional scars from the past, it could also enable them to show loving-kindness not only to themselves but also to others.

Another aspect of his meditation technique that was directed toward the goal of joy was *ānāpānasati*, meditation on the breath. He summarized his approach by saying that the meditator should do *ānāpānasati* to develop *samatha*, when the mind becomes calm through this practice, the hindrances are cut off and the *jhāna* factors arise. One of the textual *jhāna* factors is joy, which links this practice to *mettā* meditation and to Samararatne's overall understanding of the function of meditation. In focusing on the hindrances or *nīvaraṇa*s, Samararatne sought to enable people to overcome negative emotions and experience positive emotions. But he taught that one should not be attached to either kind of emotions. Rather we should view them as empty and not-mine, as states that arise without a sense of ownership. To illustrate the kind of non-attachment that he wanted to teach, Samararatne told a story about the Thai monastic Ajahn Chah. Once a pupil who had been studying with Ajahn Chah for some time asked the teacher why he always preferred to have his tea in one particular cup. The visitor wanted to know if that was his favorite cup and whether it was proper for a meditator to be so attached to a particular cup. What would he feel if it broke? Ajahn Chah said, "You see this cup; to me it is already broken. While it is still intact on my table, I use it. It has beautiful colors and makes a nice sound if I tap it with a spoon. But for me, it is already broken."[9] The point that both Ajahn Chah and Samararatne were making is that the meditator should have no attachments to anything in order to live in freedom and joy. Samararatne applied the point here to our attitude toward our bodies, noting that we enjoy our bodies, we take care of them, we use them, but we must realize that they are ultimately not ours and not us, because we finally cannot control what happens to them. The same applies to our relations to others. We should enjoy our friendships with other people, without a sense of attachment, or possessiveness.

I discussed this analogy of the cup with Samararatne and suggested that some people might regard this as a pessimistic or at least a stoic approach to life. His response, however, was that he felt that it was not a pessimistic view but rather a realistic view of life. He saw approaching life without a sense of ownership of our bodies or our relationships or possessions as a very positive approach that frees us to enjoy life and not be attached. He regarded this as a very joyful and liberating way to live—and I think it was the way that Godwin himself lived.

A related form of mindfulness (*sati*) meditation that Samaratne employed to eliminate suffering involved teaching his pupils to be mindful of thoughts and emotions and their arising. He asked the meditators to recall something that someone did that made them angry. When one remembers an incident in this way, the anger might arise again. The goal of the meditation was to try to observe this incident in the present without reacting to it, to observe the anger with an awareness of *anicca*, impermanence. Samararatne asked the meditators, "Is it possible to observe the anger without anger, is it possible to observe the anger without reacting to it, is it possible to see that it will pass away?"[10] The meditator should observe it as not "my" anger, but should see it objectively, as a case of anger that arose from a certain cause and will pass away. If people can deal with remembered anger, then they can also deal with anger in the present, the key being to observe the cause of the anger. When you see that the cause of your anger is an expectation that you have had, then you see that the cause of suffering is within your own mind and not with the other person. The point, according to Samararatne, is not whether we react emotionally, but how quickly we recover. We are bound to have emotions, but we should not allow them to control us. This focus on the meditator's reactions recalls the teachings of Goenka, although Samararatne did not adopt either Goenka's complete theory about the centrality of reactions (*saṅkhāras*) or his technique for getting rid of past reactions. Samararatne did, however, give a more or less popular explanation of how reactions affect our *karma* if we are not mindful of them. To document his point about reactions, Samararatne used the same *sutta* illustration that Goenka employs in the book, *The Art of Living*. This *sutta* contains a teaching from the Buddha which says that anger—or other emotional reactions—in the mind can be of three kinds: like letters written on the surface of water, like letters written on sand or like letters written in stone. The goal advocated by both Goenka and Samararatne, of course, is that our reactions to events should be like "letters written on water."[11]

To illustrate the kind of non-attachment to emotions that people should strive for, Samararatne told a story about one of his teachers, Venerable Nyanaponika. One day Venerable

Nyanaponika was translating a Pāli text in his small house in the forest above Kandy when some robbers broke in looking for valuables. The teacher explained that he had no valuables, but the robbers ransacked the house and struck the teacher several times in an attempt to get him to hand over his valuables. Finally the robbers gave up and left. When they had gone, Venerable Nyanaponika just went back to translating the text. A little later, the police heard about the robbery and came to investigate. Samararatne said that Nyanaponika told him that the robbery was not so bad because he just got up and went back to work, but when the police came things became more difficult.

Although for the most part, Samararatne's methods of meditation could be considered fairly orthodox—and he regarded them in that way himself—he did have a couple of very innovative elements in his work. First, he incorporated *yoga* in his teaching of meditation, something not done by many Sri Lankan meditation teachers. He was probably influenced in this by D.C.P. Ratnakara who has also included *yoga* in his teaching about meditation for many years. Meditation retreats at Nilambe often interspersed periods of *yoga* with the meditation. Second, he employed meditation as a means of healing illness and relieving pain, which he saw as more explicit forms of suffering. Since meditation is not commonly employed for healing in Sri Lankan Buddhism, this emphasis might reflect a further influence from Goenka's teachings, for Goenka has said that purification of the mind may affect the course of illness. Samararatne worked with doctors and medical students to help them understand the intention of meditation. He has also went directly to the cancer wards of the hospitals to teach the patients meditation. He instructed the patients to visualize their bodies and to radiate thoughts of *mettā*, loving kindness, onto their bodies at the place of illness. Another aspect of this work involved helping the patients cope with feelings about themselves because he discovered that they usually did not like themselves and had a sense of self pity. In such cases, Samararatne said, the meditation on loving-kindness could be very useful in helping them to deal with both psychological wounds and physical illnesses.

A related method of healing involved using *mettā* to try to relieve pain. Samararatne taught patients to simply be with the pain and see how they could view it. They should see if they could observe the pain without desiring the pain to go away because the pain becomes suffering when there is resistance and dislike concerning it. But if a meditator could "be with the pain" for a few minutes then it might be possible to reduce or eliminate the feeling of suffering. Samararatne recalled a woman patient who used this technique and reported that "the pain is there but I am not there." He explained that, "She had a kind of *anattā*, or not-self, experience by focusing on the pain." But he admitted that it was not easy for patients to do this.

Some of the meditation steps that he set out for the patients to follow in doing *mettā* meditation on pain are outlined here:

1. Take the pain as a point of meditation. Reflect on it with awareness, observation, understanding.
2. Pain is not mine. It is of the body and does not belong to me.
3. Accept it in a friendly way, without reproach. Do not escape from it or run away from it.
4. If the mind is tranquil, the body will be also, and vice versa.
5. Pain should not induce *dukkha*, suffering.
6. Pain in the body may be due to repressed emotion.
7. Dealing with emotions with equanimity is essential. To get rid of repressed emotions, one should observe and understand the causes for them.

In sum, Samararatne's approach to meditation represented an interesting combination of orthodox and post-modern themes. He did not stress the attainments, *ariya puggala*, or promise instant enlightenment, rather his approach was pragmatic in helping people to cope with suffering. He did, however, believe that meditation has practical benefits that people can access. This theme seems to reflect the "new Burmese method" which had been part of his training as a pupil at Kanduboda. He maintained that this is what liberation or enlightenment really means in Buddhism: the overcoming of *dukkha*, suffering, in practical ways. He described his method of meditation as a "practical, direct model that is in accordance with the texts—*nīvaraṇa*s, *jhāna*s, *vipassanā*." In this way, he saw his approach as very textual and based on his comprehensive understanding of the Buddhist scriptures. He also was very well versed in the literature of contemporary Buddhism from various parts of the world, however, and his teachings reflected global influences from sources such as Ajahn Chah, Goenka and other Burmese meditation teachers as well as Zen teachers. Somewhat surprisingly, he had little interest in socially engaged Buddhism which he regarded as largely a Western import. Although he devoted himself to social service through projects such as his work with the hospitals, helping needy children and his meditation groups, Samararatne questioned whether one could find a textual basis for socially engaged Buddhism, at least in the form it had taken in Sri Lanka. He pointed out that none of the (Sri Lankan) forest dwelling monks had ever taught that meditation could coexist with social activism. He had great respect for the forest dwelling monks and seemed to place them on a par with the Pāli texts as the great authorities for Theravāda Buddhism. Samararatne walked the Theravāda path represented by these authorities but with an awareness of the global context in which we live. He both dressed and lived as one who was on the path; and his followers respected him both for his learning and for the aura of experience that surrounded him. Samararatne was, until his recent, untimely death, a teacher who was greatly revered by his followers and friends.

B. D.C.P. Ratnakara

Mr. D.C.P. Ratnakara was the founder of one of the earliest lay meditation societies in Sri Lanka and until his death in 2000 he was one of the senior lay meditation teachers in the country. In the teachings of this guru and the life of his society, we glimpse other developments of the lay meditation movement and note how far some aspects of this movement have moved toward sectarianism.

The Guru:

D.C.P. Ratnakara was the "lay Patron and Founder" of the Society of the Friends of the Dhamma (*Sadaham Mithuru Samuluwa,* or S.M.S.). Before his retirement in the early 1980s, Mr. Ratnakara was a lecturer in educational psychology at the Peradeniya Teachers Training College near Kandy. Along with Godwin Samararatne, Ratnakara was in the first generation of lay meditators during the 1950s revival of meditation. He studied the "new Burmese method" of meditation at Kanduboda and also studied with several teachers including some Sri Lankan forest monks. As a youth he was very interested in Theosophy and also read many books by Indian teachers such as Vivekananda and Krishnamurti. For almost four decades, the members of his society accorded him great respect as a guru who had reached an advanced stage of the spiritual path. But Mr. Ratnakara was not the sole authority for this society; his wife, Siri Ratnakara also has had a key role.

The Society:

The Ratnakaras founded their society in 1962 and since that time it has grown to have almost one thousand members and many local branches. The story of the founding of the society reveals some key facts about the nature of this movement. Mr. Ratnakara explained that it was not his idea to found a society, but it became necessary to do so because of the "revelations" that he and his wife were receiving and the demands of their "teachers." To abbreviate the history of these revelations, which I have given in full elsewhere, Mr. and Mrs. Ratnakara began receiving transcendental messages through a relative who served as a medium. Mrs. Ratnakara was also very receptive to these messages and eventually served as the chief contact with the spiritual beings whom they believed to be the authors of the messages. The messages consisted of comprehensive *dhamma* teachings about such topics as cosmology, ethics, meditation and healing. The Ratnakaras came to believe that these *dhamma* teachings emanated from a pantheon of higher beings, including "masters," yogis, gods and goddesses. Especially important in this pantheon were the goddess Sarasvati and a "Buddha from another planet." Eventually, these higher beings told the Ratnakaras to form a society to study and follow these teachings, which is how S.M.S. came about. The charter of the S.M.S. states that "Masters or Spiritual Teachers mentioned in the Buddhist Theosophical Literature...do even now exist, and one could communicate with them by developing certain meditative states of consciousness...or through a trained medium." Today the society continues to follow these teachers and to be interested in some more recent cross-traditional influences such as the teachings of the Indian gurus Vimala Thakar and Sai Baba.

The members of the society study and live by the *dhamma* given by the spiritual teachers rather than the *dhamma* of the *tipiṭaka*. The charter of the society explains that "the oral teachings of the Great Sage were committed to writing long years after the *parinibbāna* of the Founder. By that time interested parties changed the original teachings and one can hardly ascertain how much." So the written canon is not to be trusted, but this *dhamma* mediated by the deities is pure. Accordingly, the members do not study the traditional texts but instead study the teachings given by the deities to the Ratnakaras.[12]

The content of this celestial *dhamma* is too voluminous to explain fully here, but I will mention some of the chief categories. There are elaborate teachings on the nature of the pantheon of deities, which is extremely complex. For example, one of their main deity teachers is described as the "42nd assistant to the goddess Sarasvati" although this deity teacher also goes by the name Sarasvati. One aspect of this *dhamma* prescribes new forms of *sīla* or ethical conduct, therefore the society lives by a number of special regulations, such as rules concerning simplicity in dress and lifestyle. Members are advised to arise at 4 a.m., to observe a vegetarian diet and to avoid people who engage in "wrong activities."

A major topic in the celestially revealed *dhamma* is the path of meditation. Mr. Ratnakara explained that having these spiritual beings as teachers is a great help since *saṃsāra* can be compared to a prison and the *deva*s resemble beings who, having liberated themselves from the prison, can now show others the way out. It is these liberated *deva*s who have revealed the path of liberation to the Ratnakaras. The form of meditation that Ratnakara's society teaches, however, seems—despite the esoteric source of the teachings—relatively conventional, stressing concentration (*samādhi*) and mindfulness (*sati*). The teachings received from the spirit beings, however, provide some new explanations of the nature of the meditation process. One such idea that they teach is that "nature" or *jīvitendriya* can be described as a force that seeks to elicit karmic reactions in order to keep human beings trapped in *saṃsāra*. The goal of meditators, therefore, must be to recognize nature's scheme in order to avoid getting caught in it any further. Through these teachings Ratnakara attempted to show his followers how to overcome suffering in this life. S.M.S. holds meditation retreats and camps for the members and encourages them to meditate daily. They seek to attain *nibbāna* in this life, or as one S.M.S. member explained, "We cannot visualize or even hope for *nibbāna*…but if we can be peaceful, not in conflict and not reacting, then that must be *nibbāna*, or at least a glimpse of it." Ratnakara claimed that people in S.M.S. have attained higher states, but he did not put as much emphasis on these attainments as some contemporary meditation teachers do. Rather Ratnakara stressed that the idea of reaching *nibbāna* in this life really means that one can come to understand reality as it is or the dhammic nature of all things.

With this celestial *dhamma* as its guide, S.M.S. breaks sharply with the *saṅgha* and contemporary Buddhist orthodoxy. The members who began the society were not content with the *dhamma* given by monks "which stressed going to heaven or the Brahma realms." D.C.P. Ratnakara explained that "the common Buddhism practiced today, with its innumerable rituals, ceremonies and alms feasts has drowned the real practical aspects of the sublime *dhamma*." Needless to say, the S.M.S. members do not go to the temples or seek the services of the monks. They do, however, perform some rituals of their own, such as a form of *pirit/paritta* chanting done by lay persons as well as *pūjā*s to the deities who are the guardians of their society.

Other significant features of this society are its emphasis on healing and its interest in social engagement. Mrs. Siri Ratnakara explains that she has had the power to heal for about 10 years. She attributes this power to her contact via the medium with the *deva*s, *rishi*s and other spiritual beings, including Hippocrates, whom they believe is now living as a deity. She also received, by supernatural means, *ayurvedic* advice from other spiritual sources such as one teacher whom she calls a "*Rishi* Doctor" in India who had been a physician for Mahatma Gandhi. He would tell her how to make *ayurvedic* potions to heal people and she would prepare the mixtures and plants that he prescribed. This "*Rishi* Doctor" had various means for healing that went beyond those of ordinary medicine, for example he could see a person's "*saṃsāra*" and take that into account in healing them. She worked with the medium and this "Guru Doctor" for about 10 years although she no longer does so. During this time, she says that she healed many people. She even tried to heal some cancer patients, but says that they were too ill to respond to the treatments. She related a story about working with a Muslim couple who had been unable to have children. Since the husband's mother was threatening to force the couple to divorce unless the woman could conceive, Mrs. Ratnakara called on the medium to communicate with the *deva*s to get an answer for this problem. After the medium and Mrs. Ratnakara met with the woman and conveyed the *deva*s' instructions, the woman conceived and the couple had 3 children in 5 years and were very happy.

In addition to this emphasis on healing, the society also has had a socially engaged focus. It carries out social relief work on a small scale and has some environmental projects. These are not major aspects of the society but neither are they insignificant. The younger members of the society are especially interested in the ecology projects and other kinds of outreach that they have undertaken.

Conclusion

The lay meditation movement, as exemplified by Samararatne and Ratnakara, could be said to represent an expression of what Obeyesekere has termed the soteriological sense of the *sāsana* because it seeks to reconstruct the spiritual path and apply it to the contemporary context.[13] But in doing so, the meditation movement reinterprets the soteriological sense fairly extensively. Clearly breaking with orthodox Buddhism as well as with Sinhala Buddhist fundamentalism, some aspects of the lay meditation movement suggest new forms of sectarianism within Theravāda.[14]

The two case studies I have discussed here give us some idea of the spectrum of reconstructions of the soteriological path and the extent to which these teachers tend toward sectarianism. Clearly, Godwin Samararatne's reconstruction remained largely within the bounds of Theravāda, for he appealed to the Pāli texts and to a lineage of Theravāda teachers. In his meditation method and teachings, however, he was open to global influences and followed a somewhat eclectic approach. Ratnakara and the S.M.S. represent a clearer move toward independence and sectarianism. This society demonstrates "the privileging of experience" and the way that this is related to earlier reforms with Western roots such as Theosophy.[15] In the case of S.M.S., the earlier Western influences are now mingled with more global influences to support the authority of experience and enable the group to challenge contemporary Buddhist orthodoxy. The formal structure of the society with its charter and by-laws indicates that they recognize and accept a sectarian status. The current leaders of the society explicitly say that S.M.S. is not Theravāda Buddhism and that because of the celestial source of its *dhamma* the society has ties to Mahāyāna and Vajrayāna. The charter of the society reads, "The S.M.S. does not differentiate between Mahāyāna and Theravāda teachings. Senior members study both with an open mind and accept what is true irrespective of the label."[16]

In the end, however, these two lay meditation teachers seem to have been less concerned with establishing sectarian positions and more concerned with reinvigorating the spiritual path for people today. They sought to fill a spiritual void left by the dominant Buddhist fundamentalism and nationalism. Undoubtedly, the tumultuous situation in Sri Lanka during at least the last two decades has increased the need for this kind of spiritual sustenance. Recognizing this need and drawing on the new global context, these two lay teachers reconstructed the path while remaining true to the soteriological goals of Buddhism. As Godwin Samararatne said, they desired to help people to overcome suffering and they employed a variety of means to do this. In Samararatne's teachings, this is what liberation or enlightenment really means for Buddhists: the overcoming of *dukkha* and the attainment of joy.

Notes

1. Mahāsī Sayādaw was, of course, not alone in leading the Burmese *vipassanā* movement. His teacher, U Narada, is given credit for originating the "new Burmese method" which Mahāsī Sayādaw popularized.
2. The Buddha Jayanti was the 2500th anniversary of the Buddha's entry into final *nibbāna*. It became a significant event because the Buddhists in Sri Lanka, Burma and other places promoted the belief that the Buddha had prophesied that his *dhamma* would endure for five thousand years and at the mid-point it would undergo a great regeneration. Thus, an almost millennialist fervor surrounded the Buddha Jayanti.
3. One possible reason for the nationalist politicians' reluctance to endorse the *vipassanā* movement was that some elements of the Sri Lankan *bhikkhu saṅgha* voiced strong opposition to what they viewed as an intrusion by the Burmese monks. These same elements of the Sri Lankan *saṅgha* also critiqued the "new Burmese method" as inauthentic and non-textual. For a summary of this debate, see George D. Bond, *The Buddhist Revival in Sri Lanka: Religious Tradition, Reinterpretation and Response* (Columbia, S.C.: University of South Carolina Press, 1988): ch.4.
4. On the reformulation of meditation during the earlier period, see Richard Gombrich and Gananath Obeyesekere, *Buddhism Transformed: Religious Change in Sri Lanka* (Princeton, N.J.: Princeton University Press, 1988): 237ff.
5. On the earlier debates between the Sri Lankan *saṅgha* and the Burmese teachers, see Bond, op cit., Ch. 4.
6. David Scott explains "contemporary Buddhist orthodoxy" as "that complex of religious power organized through the *saṅgha*." David Scott, *Formations of Ritual: Colonial and Anthropological Discourses on Sinhala Yaktovil* (Minneapolis: University of Minnesota Press, 1994).
7. The idea of the privileging of experience has been discussed by Robert Sharf, in "Buddhist Modernism and the Rhetoric of Meditative Experience," *Numen* 42 (1995): 228-283.
8. The discussions that I refer to in this article took place during the period from April 1997 to November 1998.
9. Cited by Ayya Khema, "The Glass is Already Broken," *Walking on Lotus Flowers*, ed., Martine Batchelor (London: Harper Collins, 1996).
10. Comment made in a discussion about meditation on 7/2/97 in Kandy.
11. Goenka cites as the source of this quote, the *Lekha Sutta*, A III 130 (S.N. Goenka, *The Discourse Summaries* (Bombay: Vipashyana

Vishodhan Vinyas, 1987): 28 and William Hart, *The Art of Living: Vipassana Meditation as taught by S.N. Goenka* (San Francisco: Harper San Francisco, 1987): 38).

12. This idea represents another common theme among many of the contemporary meditation teachers. It probably reflects Orientalist influences from an earlier period.

13. Gananath Obeyesekere, "Buddhism, Nationhood and Cultural Identity: A Question of Fundamentals," *Fundamentalisms Comprehended*, ed. Martin E. Marty and R. Scott Appleby (Chicago: University of Chicago Press, 1995): 231-256.

14. Gombrich and Obeyesekere note that "laicization that is the hallmark of modern Buddhism contains within itself the seeds of sectarianism." *Buddhism Transformed* (1988): 324.

15. Robert H. Sharf, op cit., 228ff.

16. Charter of Incorporation for Sadaham Mithuru Samuluwa, 1991, Sri Lanka.

A Conversation with Godwin Samararatne:

Buddhism, Emotion and Therapy

Susan A. Reed

In the summer of 1997, I had the privilege of spending many hours in conversation with Godwin Samararatne discussing issues related to Buddhism, emotion and therapy. I was in Sri Lanka to begin a new research project on culturally appropriate psychotherapy, and one of my first goals was to explore the range of therapies available there. Since the early 1980s, Godwin had been using meditation to aid in the treatment of psychiatric patients referred from the Peradeniya Hospital. As most of the psychiatric treatment available in Sri Lanka is based on Western medical models, I was especially intrigued by Godwin's work in Buddhist therapy as a culturally sensitive mode of treatment.[1]

However, the conversations recorded here go well beyond Godwin's work with the Peradeniya patients, expanding to more general discussions of culture, emotion and concepts of the person. Indeed, I began the interview by focusing on cultural difference, inquiring about the meditation experiences of Westerners and Sri Lankans. Attention to these differences shape much of our conversation throughout, as we speculate about explanatory factors from kinship to Christianity. However, while Godwin recognized culture as an agent of "strong conditioning," it is clear that he felt that Buddhist teachings were applicable and beneficial for all. In this sense, then, Godwin did not conceive his therapeutic approach as especially "culturally sensitive"—if by that we mean relevant only to Sri Lankan Buddhists, or even only to Sri Lankans—but rather as universalistic.

The interviews which follow are transcriptions of two tape recorded conversations I had with Godwin at the Lewella Meditation Centre, Kandy, in August 1997. While Godwin and I had discussed many of these issues off and on over the course of many years, these interviews were the first opportunity I had taken to systematically record Godwin's views. I have only edited out those portions of the interviews that I have deemed not especially pertinent to the topics at hand—mostly personal asides and digressions on my part. Almost all of Godwin's words have been retained.[2]

Interview. Lewella Meditation Centre August 19, 1997.

Meditation Experiences: Westerners and Sri Lankans

S: One thing that you and I have discussed before are the types of emotional problems that people come to you with at the meditation center. And you have indicated to me that there are some differences between the types of problems that Westerners have, and the types of problems that Sri Lankans have.[3] Could you tell me more about how you see the differences, and the source of the differences?

G: Yeah, right. One thing is about childhood. As you know, Westerners invariably relate problems to what happened in childhood. But the Sri Lankans won't attribute their present problems to what happened in childhood. So I just have a theory about this (we both laugh).

S: I like theories.

G: So one possible reason is that in Asian countries still there are extended families. So maybe a child growing up here will get a lot of attention and affection from the family members around them. So they have a choice. But whereas in the West, you are brought up only with the parents. And whatever happens in childhood can create a very deep impression. This is one possible reason. The other is, the Buddhist culture here where you are brought up with the idea that you have to be *grateful* to your parents. So, the idea of blaming them would never arise. And perhaps maybe Freud, who also influenced Western thinking. But there again you can't blame the poor man (laughing).What he discovered in talking to patients in Vienna at that time was that mostly they were having problems in childhood. He did not invent the theory, but he just presented what he discovered. But somehow or another that idea might have gained currency. So these are my theories to account for these differences. In the beginning, these things really interested me. So that is one.

Another is Westerner's problems of suffering from problems of guilt. And, arising from guilt, they would be very hard on themselves. So the practice of loving-kindness, the idea of being friendly to themselves, they find it very difficult. They find it easy to be friendly to others... But maybe, anyway it has something to do with this problem of guilt.

A third difference is trying too hard. Again, there may be a cultural reason…Westerners are very hard on themselves. And Sri Lankans are generally more laid back. (Laughter.)

And another difference which I am exploring is tensions in the body. The relation to physical pain and physical discomfort among the Sri Lankans. And the Sri Lankans, generally speaking, their pain has obvious physical reasons. But in relation to Westerners, in some cases you don't see any physical reasons, but more, that it seems to be repression which manifests itself as a tension or pressure.[4]

Another difference is the tradition, hmm…? In Western countries there is no tradition of meditation, and in Sri Lanka there is a tradition. It can work in both ways. One thing, the

Westerners are much more open, they are not conditioned by the tradition. Whereas, Sri Lankans can be conditioned by the tradition. But it's also... [5]

S: By "the tradition" you mean...?

G: The Buddhist tradition. Then because of an absence of a tradition in the West, there is a something like a spiritual supermarket, they try various things, they don't know why they are doing it. But here in Sri Lanka, the people who come to meditation, generally speaking their goals are very clear, because of the tradition. So these are the cultural differences.

S: Actually, I am interested in this "body" thing. It's interesting because in some of the anthropological literature they say that Asians tend to "somatize" their psychological problems.[6] But you are saying almost the opposite…

G: Yes, I know what they say. What they say is the usual *vāte*. *Vāte* thing, you know? *Vāte*, you loosely use that Sri Lankan term to try to understand the somatic situation. But I am talking in the context of meditation.[7]

S: Oh, I see, so not in general.

G: No, certainly this *vāte* shows up in a psychosomatic situation. This is why I am still exploring this. This doesn't mean that there is no repression in Sri Lanka. But there seems to be some indications that it doesn't seem to affect their body. But I don't know.

S: I notice it among the way people carry themselves, more relaxed generally.

G: Right, right.

S: Very unusual to see someone really tensed up.

Meditation with Psychiatric Patients

S: What are the types of problems that Sri Lankans come to you with?

G: One thing is, they don't come with a problem, they want to become enlightened in this life. Another is, some may come carrying wounds, grief, someone had died in the family, someone close, and they would come to get some help through meditation. And, well, sometimes students come to find out how meditation can help in their studies. And of course people I meet at the clinic, those who have psychiatric, so-called psychiatric problems, some of them are there.

S: Could you tell me more about how you started in that work in meditation?

G: Actually, I started when I was in the [Kandy] library. I got to know Professor Rodrigo. And he was very interested in exploring the possibilities of meditation. And he asked me whether I would mind seeing some of his patients in the library. So he would send them to the library, and I would meet them, and then we realized the library is not a suitable place, the patients were reluctant (laughing). But after he left, that was the introduction [to this kind of work].

S: This must have been quite some time ago?

G: Yes, the 1980s. And then I started working with Dr. Abeysinghe and Dr. Rodrigo at the Peradeniya Hospital, and they were also sending me patients with neurotic problems.[8]

S: Like anxiety…?

G: Like anxiety, sadness, and personality disorders in the sense that they feel inadequate with themselves, so these were some of the problems they were having. Sometimes I would offer them some meditation techniques in addition to medication, which they tried to do in their homes. And others, I would take them to Nilambe.

S: Did you talk to them also?

G: (Strong assenting gesture.) Oh, yes. I would have a long chat with them. The first point is to get to know the person, and the other is to get to speak openly about it. That can be therapeutic. And then to offer specific techniques, in relation to their symptoms. So I would use techniques like loving-kindness, focusing, being aware of the breath, and general awareness. So it is really, as I would say, to learn to be their own psychotherapist, learn to handle whatever arises.

S: Generally, when people had come to that point, had they come to a point where they couldn't talk to other people, or it hadn't helped...talking about it, the usual thing they would have done with friends or with family people.

G: Well, they would have spoken to them, but apparently they haven't gotten any relief, that is why they are seeking the help of the psychiatrist.

S: Do they have any of their own theories of why they were suffering? Or would they just be coming with symptoms.

G: Yeah, especially the younger people I was meeting, it was mostly younger people, and they would come just with some symptoms.

S: And they didn't have a theory?

G: No, they didn't have a theory about it.

S: Did you provide a theory?

G: Well, no, but one of the things I would emphasize to them was—"don't think that you are sick." I would say that everyone is having this, it is normal. I would say sometimes I have these things also. It's normal. To impress on them not to think of the sickness. So, this is interesting. I think that this idea that they are sick, that this is my neurotic problem, is something recent in Sri Lanka.[9]

S: And you think that is a Western...?

G: Maybe, maybe.

S: Were most of the patients Sinhala-speaking, urban...?

G: Sinhala-speaking urban, and some from the village also. Sometimes rural, mostly urban.

S: Would it surprise you to find someone from a remote area coming to the clinic with a problem?

G: No, no...

S: So you would have a long conversation with them...Then would you follow up in any way?

G: Yes, yeah. Of course, if I take them to Nilambe that would arise.

S: You would have an interview with them there.

G: Yeah, I would relate to them individually, see what is happening, and meet with them subsequently. And those who come to the clinic without visiting the meditation center, I would see them, and see whether they are making any progress, are they having any difficulties, whether their symptoms are continuing.

S: And normally at the clinic were you seeing them as individuals?

G: *Oh, yes, yes.*

S: The families aren't involved?

G: If there is a need, some of them. Otherwise... But sometimes there was a problem between a couple, he was paranoid about his girlfriend, and so I would summon both of them. For jealousy. A common problem. That is the point I made—some years ago that wouldn't be considered a mental illness. Just "*irisiyāva*," I would have jealousy.

S: But it is still a problem, even if it's not a mental illness.

G: Yeah, but they would try to work with that symptom without meeting a psychiatrist. This is the point that I am making.

S: So do you think that the psychiatrist has become...That is, in the West, I feel that because people need someone to talk to about these things, and the friends and family become problematic for various reasons, they decide to go to the psychiatrist. Do you think the psychiatrist is coming to have that kind of role here?

G: I don't know. Because here it is very simple. They think that they are suffering from some sickness, mental sickness, so they go to a doctor.

S: "Mental doctor..." Now, I talked to Dr. Abeysinghe mostly when I was here before,[10] and the impression I got was that they didn't have time to do long-term counseling, so in a sense you were the person doing that more long-term...

G: Yes, so I was doing therapy with them. And maybe that's what they needed. And by they I mean Abey and Rodda, because they don't have time, they thought, to do this. Whereas a person like me would have more time.

S: And normally, would the people be on medication of some sort?

G: Yes. Sometimes in addition to meditation, they would be trying medication. And sometimes without medication. Sometimes they would have stopped medication.

Techniques for Emotional Problems

S: Could you talk about the meditation techniques, and what worked and what didn't seem to work. Once you told me that for Westerners, sometimes meditation seemed to aggravate certain types of problems. Do you find that among the Sri Lankans?

G: Let me tell you how I try to help them. For the first point, is to make a connection with them, where the patient feels supported.[11] The other is to try to explain that it is not a sickness, so therefore they can try to help themselves.[12] So using a technique like focusing on breathing, they may learn, for the first time, how to handle thoughts and emotions. Just try letting go of them. Another is, because of this "illness," they actually don't like themselves. They think of themselves as a failure. So loving-kindness can be extremely helpful. And another point I try to impress on them that is sometimes very helpful is to see the connection between the thoughts and their symptoms, how they are related. So it is mostly their thoughts that are creating and constructing some of these symptoms. So, if they can see the mechanism of this, through awareness, through that they are able to understand and make a shift. And the other thing that is helpful, is just tell them, when they don't have the symptoms, is just to *know* that I don't have symptoms. So I feel that the key is the self-confidence that comes. If the symptoms come, I know how to handle them. That can be a kind of breakthrough. And when the symptoms are not there, they are not there. If in both situations you can have, as it says in the *dhamma* "equanimity"—not liking one, not disliking the other—that would be extremely helpful to them.

S: Were most of the patients that you saw Buddhist?

G: No, sometimes I would see non-Buddhists. So I wouldn't mention the word "*bhāvanā*"—meditation—I would speak about relaxation techniques.

S: I was wondering if you noticed a difference between Christian and Buddhist in terms of their "guilt" for example. Or the way they conceptualized the problem.

G: No, I don't think I saw a difference in relation to understanding their symptoms. They would say I am having this tension. I would not try to make an effort to understand how *they* conceptualized it. Just that it was a real problem for them.

S: And how were you presented to them, as the healer?

G: Yeah, what exactly was Dr. Abeysinghe telling them (laughter). Sometimes I think he would also be selective and say there is a meditation teacher, maybe you want to go and talk to him. And maybe other times he would say [there is a mental health worker], maybe you should talk to him.

S: And they didn't know who you were.

G: No, no. Sometimes they didn't know. Sometimes they would address me as "Doctor."

S: Yeah, that's what I'm wondering.

G: And after some time I would say I am not a doctor.

S: Did any of them develop a relationship that became problematic? A dependency relationship with you, wanting to see you too much. Or wanting you to…?

G: Yes, I think it happened.

S: What do you do then?

G: Help them,…

S: Do they see... Is there a concept of an inherent flaw in the person, that some people are born with more vulnerability to emotional problems than other people. Or did they see, as you seem to be suggesting, that something happened to them at a certain point in their life?

G: Yeah, yeah.

S: So, they don't feel that they themselves attracted the problem. But is it that first the problems come and then they start having some conceptualization of themselves as becoming a "sick" person?

G: I think I did not go into that area, because that area did not interest me very much. Because I was giving them meditation, some techniques to practice…

S: Do you think that would have been problematic, so you avoided it?

G: I didn't deliberately avoid it, but I thought… But maybe I did not have any thoughts about it. I was more interested in presenting them with techniques and seeing how they work. It was a more practical approach. And now that you raise this question, I wonder in what way it is relevant?

S: I'm very curious about this issue with Western therapy. The idea of suggestibility, of the therapist introducing elements like the childhood, when the therapist starts asking about your relationship with your mother and your father and maybe it creates problems there… [Studies have shown] that people are highly suggestible. And I think sometimes that thinking too much can just exacerbate the problem. A lot of therapy, I think, is not just neutral, it's harmful…[13]

G: Is there anything written on this, because I am very interested in this.

S: There are some people who are very critical of certain kinds of therapy. Some people think that a lot of what happens is some kind of "flashback" from the past. Basically, if you have that view, you can't get over it.

G: Right, right.

S: Because everything you do is going to be a reflection of what happened in the past, and the past can't be changed. So, some people have the idea that you can't get over this. No matter what, your parents were always wounding you. Actually there has been a backlash against therapy. But, the general idea floating around in the culture is that the present is dependent on what happened in the past, so "scapegoating" of the parents and family, that is present in the culture right now.

G: Right.

S: Blaming, "projection" in American culture is very pervasive...

G: Not taking responsibility. This is where meditation can be helpful, it really enables you to take responsibility, where you are your own therapist. Maybe it is due to something that happened in the past, but what are you doing now? This is the question I raise with them.

S: Yeah.

G: There may be something, but do something about it now.

S: In most of the cases you worked with did they find the meditation helpful?

G: I think it is effective when they have the motivation…

S: Normally, how long would they stay at Nilambe?

G: It varies. Maybe a few days, maybe a couple of weeks.

S: Let's take a specific case. You worked with a number of phobia patients. Agoraphobia, people afraid to go out. How did it work with them?

G: A person with some kind of phobia. One, is to get them to relax with meditation, then to bring up that phobia. It can be very effective.

S: Within the meditation?

G: Yeah, yeah… They come to a state when the thoughts in relation to the phobia come unexpectedly. So I tell them to make friends with the phobia. So this is one thing. Another thing is to get them to gradually confront that phobia. Before that I might get them to draw that phobia. So make friends with it. And then as I said earlier, I get them to see how thoughts are created.

S: How did you come to some of these ideas about how to deal, making friends with phobias? Were you reading a lot of Western therapy?

G: No. Buddhist ideas. And also, learning from helping them. So I knew it was helping them, and it was helpful to me to really understand, it was very interesting for me. [Long pause.] So these are really issues in meditation, the connection between thoughts and emotions.

S: Have you thought of teaching to other meditation teachers? Are there others doing this? Are you still working with the patients at the University?

G: No, I stopped, but I meet with them privately. Sometimes they come to Nilambe. I find I am very busy now.

S: How did Dr. Abeysinghe and Dr. Rodrigo interact? How did they get involved?[14]

G: They would see them, and then just ask them if it's helping them, and if it's helping them, then maybe they would try to reduce their medications. And maybe there were some cases when meditation wasn't helpful at all, maybe because of lack of motivation. And then they would continue to treat them with medication.

S: What were the ages of the people?

G: Young people, most of them, some middle-aged.

S: Men and women?

G: Men and women, both.

S: Did you see any differences between men and women in terms of how they discussed the problems?

G: I didn't really pay attention to that.

S: When I've been to Nilambe a few times, mostly there have been Sinhala men there. Is that just a coincidence or are there more men involved at Nilambe?

G: I think it varies. Sometimes we have more men, sometimes we have more women. At the moment, there are more women.

S: Do you think that meditation can solve most of the normal emotional problems?

G: (Pause.) I would say that they can at least have a handle on...I have thought of about seven or eight, I call them tools to work with emotions. The first tool is to be open to these emotions. Because usually they don't like these things. They hate them, and I think that can give them more power and more energy. And that is a really strong conditioning, and of course very difficult to really be open, just to let those emotions come. That is the first tool. Second tool—having a friendship with them, being open to them, exploring and investigating them, because we take them for granted. And here something very interesting is that I ask them to see whether the thought comes first, or if the emotion comes first. To observe, to learn by themselves. And the third tool is, when they are not there, just to know they are not there.

S: Can you say a little bit more about that?

G: Yes. So if they are suffering from anxiety, just to know that that anxiety is not there. So they say "wow, I don't have anxiety. For one day, I didn't have that anxiety." They have a choice. They realize they have a choice. So when they are there, they know when to use these tools.

So another tool is to experience these emotions without the word. Take away the word "anxiety." Take away the word "fear." And see what *exactly* is happening.

S: Hmm. That's interesting.

G: *Yeah*. Then they realize it is just a sensation (laughing). Anxiety or fear, why it's just some negative thoughts they are having.

Another thing is, while seeing that emotion is there, to see what else is there. Because they have given that emotion such power, they think that is the only thing that is happening. I tell them to see what other thoughts and sensations are there. This creates a sense of separation [from the problem].

The sixth is that you don't "own" your anxieties, emotions.

There is a nice line in the *dhamma* where it says to see them as "visitors"—the idea of impermanence. You are the "host."

The next is, to have self confidence, whether the emotions are there or not there, you know how to handle it. A major problem is no self-confidence, low self-esteem.[15] I see it as three stages. First, you are nobody; then you get confidence and you are somebody; and then finally you are being "nobody." I talk about giving yourself pluses. Most people give themselves minuses, but people need to give themselves pluses. The third stage is beyond pluses and minuses.

S: What about relationships?

G: Relationships are very important. And also the need to relate to yourself.

S: What about relating to people who are not helpful to you, people who you are very angry with?

G: Do not avoid a negative person—but use the experience as a teacher. The problem is not the other person. And guilt: this is having unrealistic expectations of ourselves and of others. The idea that I "must" behave this way. Put ourselves on a pedestal, put others on a pedestal.

Repression and Control of Emotions

S: I want to ask about repression and control. How did you distinguish between control of emotion, what you would see as a positive expression of emotion, and repression?

G: In the *dhamma*, it is said to avoid repression, and also to avoid expression. In the *dhamma*.

S: But, in practice how do you…?

G: Yeah, a practical example. Anger, if it comes, so you don't give it a "minus." It's only when you give it a minus, that you push it away. That you deny it. By pretending it's not there, that's giving it a minus. But allowing doesn't mean breaking plates with anger (laughter).

S: If it's with someone else, in a relationship...?

G: If you want the relationship to continue (laughter), again you can stay until the anger is over, and once you recover from that. So this is the ideal. I would say the next stage is, if you express it....

S: So, the first one is the ideal, to just let it go, and don't make an issue of it.

G: Let it be. Yeah, and sometimes in the *dhamma*, they also use the word "restraint, " the Buddhist ideal of restraint. If you fail in restraining, you can reflect on it later; that's the next phase: "maybe I should say sorry about it."

S: That's for anger, what about sadness?

G: So pushing away sadness is a reaction to it.

S: I don't know if this is correct, but someone told me that a Western Buddhist monk living here said that he feels the Sri Lankans repress anger too much, and that is why some of these problems have developed.[16] Do you have any theory about the cultural…?

G: Yes, there seems to be an element of repression here, that is true. But... I don't know. Certainly, there is repression, maybe it is one way of explaining this violence. You also see it clearly when people get drunk. So, it shows. But in other ways, now at a funeral for example, they don't repress there.

S: I haven't been to a funeral actually, there are people who cry?[17]

G: Aah, they cry.

S: Men and women, both?

G: Yes. I'm very, very interested in this area. And then the Buddhist texts draw a distinction between suppression and repression. Suppression is consciously putting something away. Repression is doing it unconsciously. It's complicated.

This is an interesting distinction.

S: Who makes the distinction?

G: You come across this in some things.

S: Is it in the Buddhist texts?

G: One of the texts, I think one could say it is suppression, and not repression, when thoughts come, gently knowing when thoughts are coming, without giving it a minus. Without judging. You are then deliberately, consciously being aware of it. In certain situations, there is suppression. In sexual situations, there is repression. I don't know. I don't know, I would like to know (laughter).

S: It's interesting that you brought up sexuality, which is actually something that I hadn't thought to talk about, but it's related to all these things...

G: Why? (Laughing...)

S: I don't know, I just hadn't thought about it, but now *you* brought it up (laughing).

G: Yes, I would like to…

S: One of the papers at this conference.[18] You know there is a sociologist here in Sri Lanka doing this big project on sexuality. He contends that this is a massively repressed culture. Do you think that's true? Or what is the meaning of it, actually?

G: Yes, that's the point. We can see repression, but what is the meaning of it?

S: And what is the standard? Is it just the West because…?

G: Yes, it is possible that people may be shy, reluctant to hug each other in public, now is that repression? Then when they are alone, they would not be like that. I would say that repression comes when you give it a "minus," in my terms: "I should not be having these feelings."

S: Having feelings?

G: Having feelings, and also feeling bad about it, either cognitively or emotionally, and pushing it away. That may be very close to repression and suppression, because still the emotion is there, because when you push it away, where does it go? So there has to be an outlet for that. But if someone is a meditator, that is a difference, using awareness. Then they are aware, so maybe it would come close to suppression and not repression.

S: Yeah, right. Because they are consciously aware, but they don't have to act on it.

G: Yes. They do not have to act on it. So was there a time in Sri Lanka, even if they were not openly meditating, that meditative way of life was a part of Sri Lankan life? I don't know. Now is there a shift, and because of that is there repression? Because Sri Lanka is definitely violent. Look at the recent killings, look at what happened recently. What happened...?

S: To cause that?

G: One needs to explore, but how does one do it?

S: All the suicide people are trying to do that. I don't know what the current theory is about it. Jeanne Marecek is doing research on suicide. And one of the things she found is that people commit suicide to hurt others, not that people don't do that in the West, but the percentage of people who do that is higher here.[19]

G: Maybe due to shame. Not a guilt culture, but a shame culture.[20]

S: Right, humiliation and shame culture.

G: And another thing is losing the reverence for life. Your own, killing yourself or killing others.

S: Have you ever had anyone come where you decided they weren't quite ready?

G: Some who were diagnosed as manic depressive. When they are manic, meditation makes them more.... Psychotics, especially schizophrenics, they only withdraw into themselves. Some stability is necessary.

S: Once you told me that for some Westerners, meditation seemed to create more problems for themselves.

G: *Yes*. Now I am realizing it more and more. Especially, staying at Nilambe, isolated, into themselves. Now I'm encouraging them to relate to people. Unless they are very mature, unless they are able to handle what comes up...

S: That's a big cultural difference. In terms of having to encourage them in having to relate to others.

G: Yes, yes. Because they [see themselves] as individuals.[21]

S: What about the role of faith?

G: I encourage more the faith in themselves, but if someone is inclined that way, faith in the *dhamma*, trust in the *dhamma*...But what I tend to emphasize generally is faith in themselves.

S: How about faith in the gods?

G: If someone comes with that, I would encourage them to develop along those lines, yeah. When I read the texts, that is what the Buddha did. To create a prop—I call them props, to hold onto the props until they can...

S: Until they are ready...

G: Un-hunh.

Interview. Lewella Meditation Centre
August 26, 1997.

Responsibility and the Roots of Psychological Problems

S: Last time, also, we talked a lot about blaming others for problems. And actually I was saying that in the U.S. now, in American culture, the way it's constructed now, it's a pervasive theme in the culture. There's been a lot of discussion of it, the victim in U.S. culture. I don't know if you were saying, given your experience in many cultures, whether it is a common thing for people to blame others for their problems?

G: Common? You mean, is it universal? I think I would say it is universal—and then I wonder, and this is related to it—I encounter people, especially in the context of meditation—they are highly critical about themselves. So in a way they blame themselves. And my guess is, because of this, they start blaming others (laughing). Because you know the phrase I often use is "giving minuses." And you start giving minuses to yourself, and then of course you start giving minuses to others. In the context of meditation, how one can work with it is to see what you are doing to yourself with the minuses. And especially from this very critical aspect, too, as they say in the *dhamma*, which I emphasize very much, "learning to be your best friend." And then with that, then you can extend that to others. If this can be achieved, then the question of either blaming yourself or blaming others does not arise.

But the danger is in blaming others you don't take responsibility. This is quite common for Westerners who blame their parents for what happened in childhood, and they continue to blame them. So one of the points I make to them, whatever they did—what are you doing *now*? What are *you* doing about it? Again taking responsibility and trying to make a shift. And I say the same thing to people who say something about their *karma*. Well maybe, I say, all of these things are connected with the past.

S: But what are you doing now?

G: And in a way, this ties up with, if you like, Buddhist therapy. The need to go back, the need to go back and start digging. So what you dig is not very pleasant. *Is that necessary? That's the question mark...* What is your... Do you have any thoughts about it?

S: Because I think I was raised in such a culture, it's very hard not to do that, not to want to do that type of analysis.

G: Hmm, strong conditioning, huh? Psychoanalysis.

S: But, it depends. I think the idea of going back is almost inevitable, trying to figure out *what* has happened. Whether you blame people is a separate issue, I think. But that you look at the past, that somehow you have to. That is, if you keep reacting in a patterned way...

G: Right, right, right.

S: To the same kinds of situations, it seems sort of automatic. If you can't figure out *why* that is happening.

G: Yeah, I would still say it has a use, but it has a limited use. And *overemphasizing* the past, and *disregarding* the present is what I am really exploring. But then wasn't there a shift from psychoanalysis, to behavior therapy, and Gestalt therapy and other therapies where the emphasis is more in the present than in the past. I thought…

S: Yes, there are a lot of approaches, maybe it depends on the people I've been talking to. Most of the therapy I'm familiar with, still the emphasis is on the past, childhood, the parents, the relationship with the parents, what was the relation. Even if they are not Freudian psychoanalysts strictly… In this field, therapists employ a variety of methods, but still many of them think that the critical period is very early, for the basic formation of the personality. So that you have to understand what was happening. So, did this person develop a strong basis, or a weak basis for confidence during that period? And I think that even if a person isn't…?

G: But I think in Europe, I'm not sure, there has been a kind of reaction to this. There are some books written questioning these assumptions. This is interesting. So in a way, wouldn't you say that it is controversial, or is it…?

S: It's controversial, but I tell you it is so pervasive in the culture, that it's hard to get away from it.[22]

G: Right, right.

S: Even if you don't go to therapy. If you never go to therapy, this idea is there, that things were formed very, very early on.

G: And I think with this thing of sexual abuse, this has become much more prominent.

G: So, back to Sri Lanka (both laughing).

S: So, we were talking about blaming, things like that. And you were saying that people tend to blame themselves.

G: Blame can be, I would say, sometimes more self-destructive. People can start hating themselves, can start punishing themselves. This is a really important area to work with.

S: So how do you help people distinguish between blame and responsibility?

G: Hmm, good question. Blame. So that's what I was saying earlier. So I would say *now stop blaming and take responsibility*. Because blaming someone else will not help you at this stage. Supposing you are blaming your parents, how is it going to help you *now*? So try and work out what happened between you and the parents. Can you, if you have hatred to them, can you bring up the hatred, and once that is over, is it possible to forgive them? I find that in the people who have problems in childhood, they have what I call a selective memory. One way of working with this selective memory is, I suggest to them, try to reflect in a meditative situation, what are the difficulties that *you* created to your parents?

S: Hunh, see no one asks that question (lot of laughter from both). That's actually true. In a therapeutic situation, generally they wouldn't ask that.

G: Oh, what were the *good* things the parents did for you. And then what were the difficulties you created to the parents. And then when they start reflecting, they come and say "now I feel guilty." And then I realize it is helping (laughter).

S: It's a good sign.

G: Yeah, it's a good sign because it clarifies more and more how this selective memory is working. And in a way they are the victims of this selective memory. Maybe what is happening by some therapists is that they are reinforcing this selective memory. So even the therapy is a bit superficial. So here it is really working through that conditioning.

S: I think a tricky thing about therapy in the West is that very often the therapist wants to keep the client in therapy, not get them out of the therapy.

G: This must not be in the hospitals.

S: Most therapy is private. In hospitals, they want to pull you out, they may not do enough there. Actually, there is a really good book I should send you about psychotherapy and moral responsibility.[23] This is a therapist who says that sometimes it is necessary to strongly disagree with the patient. The general mode is that you don't challenge the patient's interpretation, right? That you go along with the patient's interpretation, you support the patient. This guy is arguing that… If he sees that someone is making a moral judgment in the situation that is affecting other people negatively, he feels the therapist should intervene and say that. Or say: I think you're thinking of this problem in a wrong way. But, 90% of therapists won't do that.

G: I think I know the reason. Because they may assume that the patient is not in a position to handle this. Because in a way I see this in some meditators. If I say something very, very firmly to them where sometimes they have to take responsibility, sometimes they don't like it. So I think it has to be done in a very gradual way.

S: Right, he is arguing that too. That you shouldn't do it too soon. Timing is the most important thing, and he has a lot of cautions about doing this.

G: That's very important, I feel.

S: But, some therapists will never do it.

G: Talking of books, I came across a title, *Humor and Psychoanalysis*.[24] I would like to know in what way humor can be used. And so that shows it is possible to have a kind of "lightness"—that can make a difference. Otherwise, it becomes so serious and heavy (laughter).

S: That is true, yeah.

Positive Emotions: Affection, Compassion and Joy

S: I wanted to ask you some questions I had about the *Dhammapada*, and the more positive emotions, like joy and compassion.

G: Yes, yes, yes.

S: There is the chapter on affection. It seems to say not to develop too much affection for someone, because then the separation from that person is very painful. Is this aimed at monks or at laypeople?

G: I think ideally at monks. Supposing there is a very serious layperson. At Nilambe, it's a lay meditation center. So how does a serious layman relate to his family? And what are the boundaries? This is how I try to tackle this. The idea, ultimately, in the *dhamma* is to realize that we don't *own* anything. No sense of ownership. But having no ownership doesn't mean having no affection. So, I often take the example of a cup. One can use the cup, one can have a connection with the cup, one can protect the cup, wash it, even have affection for the cup, if you want to. But you can relate to the cup with the realization that it doesn't belong to you.[25] So in the same way you can relate to the body. Care, affection, all that. Care, affection and beautiful sensitivity, but realizing that the other person doesn't belong to you. That can really result in a kind of *unconditional love*, which is different from a very possessive love which can be very destructive. So I think it is really important to develop this kind of quality of understanding affection and use it. Not become a victim of it. Does it make sense?

S: Um-hmm. Very difficult.

G: Very difficult. Of course! Very difficult, very difficult. But I feel that this would be more effective than, how shall I say it, taking up the position that you should not have affection. So here it's a kind of, I wouldn't call it a compromise, but I think it's a really interesting *model* to work with. And then to realize when there is hurt, disappointment, to see how it is directly related to affection. And then when there are moments when you still have concern, you are still concerned, and still not to be suffering. This is very, very important.

S: And also it seems that for it to work the best, both people would have to have the same idea.

G: Yes, that is why in Buddhism they encourage that you should be spiritual friends. Spiritual friends grow together. So one can say it can be an ideal in the context of laypeople. And it's an interesting challenge, an interesting challenge. One can work with your possessions, one can work with your body.

S: Do you think marriage in that sense, let's say if people aren't interested in having children, would you suggest marriage for them?

G: Yeah—I would say two spiritual friends coming together and they want to grow in the *dhamma*. And I think in a way if they take up the position that having a child would be like having Rahula. It might be a hindrance. So I think it depends on one's views.

S: What I've seen in the US is that somehow it's easier for people if they are not married, not to develop that possession…In the West marriage really implies possession, otherwise what is necessary about it, why do you need to do it, then, really?

G: Yes, that's why, because the idea of spiritual friendship is not there. So I think, if spiritual friendship was there, then it would be emphasized.

S: So—back to the *Dhammapada*—do you disagree with it?

G: No, no, no. What I'm saying is that there is a place for affection, but what is important is not to get *stuck* with affection. The relationship should be used in such a creative way where, one, there is a place for affection, and then you can have a different kind of affection, which can be described as unconditional. And I think that is something very beautiful. And as it is said in the *Karaṇīya Mettā Sutta*[26] what is encouraged is to relate to others like the mother related to her only son, her only child. That is a *lot* of affection. That's the *ideal*. So it is not having no feelings. I have often mentioned this. People are confused: the idea is to overcome desire, not to overcome feelings. In the name of overcoming affections, they overcome feelings. That is *worse*! [Very emphatic.] Then you become like a block of wood. No feelings, no affection. The phrase "block of wood" comes from the Zen tradition.

S: What about joy?

G: Oh, that's my favorite (said with much feeling). That's my favorite. There is a statement in the *Dhammapada* which I often quote: "you can overcome suffering with joy." And what is happening is they try to overcome suffering with suffering. So I say that there are two models. One model is to overcome suffering through joy; the other model is to overcome suffering with suffering, which some people, for some reasons prefer (laughing).

S: Can you say more?

G: Yeah. Trying too hard. And sometimes blaming themselves. In a way, self-mortification.

S: Do you find that more among Westerners?

G: Oh much more, *much more*.

S: It's a very Christian theme, of course. The fact that you can't achieve without suffering.[27]

G: Yes, yes, I see that happening.

S: You can't achieve without suffering. And the more you suffer, the better. The better, the more you suffer.

G: Yes, yes.

S: And again I think, it doesn't matter whether you are brought up as a Christian or not, it's one of those themes that's very much in the culture. Which is why the work ethic works very well in the U.S. If you work seventy hours a week it's better than working forty hours a week. But you feel guilty when you are not working. Very negative, actually.

G: Yes. Oh, right. It's a vicious circle. Then you feel guilty, and you are sort of blaming yourself, a *lot of suffering*. Then, there is no room for joy. And then I think some of the Buddhists I meet, for some reason I often tease them, saying you are stuck with the first Noble Truth.

S: The suffering.

G: Yeah, only the suffering, *dukkha*. What about the other truths? For some reason, it's there.

S: People get stuck there.

G: Yeah. So there is this idea of joy and lightness. So I make it a point to really emphasize this. Even in meditation, I have a very simple model. Actually, it's based on Buddhism. First to work with the negative emotions, what are called the hindrances in Buddhism. And then through working with them, to experience the positive emotions. And then once you have the positive emotions, try to see them as impermanent, you know, not to cling to them. A very simple model. And for joy to arise one factor is loving-kindness. Make a connection with themselves.

S: It's a paradox in the U.S., known to be very fun-loving as a culture, but often that guilt is there when you are enjoying something. Maybe it depends on the ethnic group of the family, also. But among some ethnic groups, like those of German descent, there is a lot of discipline, control, very closed.

G: Yeah, that's another aspect of this. Giving a lot of power to suffering. Here we encounter it, too.

S: With Sri Lankans?

G: I think I encounter it more among Westerners. It's very difficult, for example, when they are focusing on breathing. They start controlling breathing.

S: That's what you were talking about a few weeks ago at the meditation session in Kandy. Just to breath naturally, instead of thinking there is one right way.

G: Another thing that is helpful in developing joy is a sense of humor. Especially learning to laugh at oneself, and also laugh at life.

S: To me, that seems one of the really positive things about Sri Lankan culture. A lot of people comment on this—the self-deprecating sense of humor that people have. Generally, most of the people I know are very good at making jokes.

G: Yeah, yeah, so light (laughing.)

S: Yeah, all the time, joking around... (laughing).

G: Yes (laughing), so light-hearted. One can even cultivate this, and practice it.

S: Yes, really (laughing).

G: (laughing) That's why I'd like to see this book, *Humor and Psychoanalysis*.

G: By the way, do you know that there is no Sri Lankan word

for guilt, no Sri Lankan word for depression?

S: Yeah. What about remorse?

G: Yes, [the Sinhala word is] *pasutävilla*.

S: Actually, how do you distinguish between guilt and remorse? Last time you talked about people feeling really bad, like if they think they did something that might have hurt you, they feel bad. But that's not guilt, right? Later they are really thinking about it, did I hurt that person? That kind of thing.

G: Yeah, I think that element is there. But, I think in guilt, there is um…When I meet meditators, I see it in these terms, that they find it very difficult to *forgive* themselves. So, then they carry that wound [muffled]. So I draw a distinction between regret and guilt.

S: Regret, ok. So regret doesn't carry that connotation?

G: Well, I regret it. I did this, and I aspire now to be different.[28] But that's ok, I am human. That's another aspect I touch on, that aspect of being human.

S: What is the word for joy?

G: The Sinhala word is *prīthi*. Actually, it comes from a Pāli word "*pīti sukha*."

S: What is "*muditā*"?

G: "*Muditā*": that's an interesting word. It is sympathetic joy in relation to the joy of others.

S: The joy of others.

G: The opposite of jealousy and envy. And that is the traditional interpretation. But I emphasize that *muditā* should begin with your own—giving pluses and being happy. So it's completely the opposite of blame, remorse. This is mentioned in the texts: *Saṃyutta Nikāya* some parts of the *Sutta Nipāta*, *Majjhima Nikāya*. Actually, if you can read these three, it's really inspiring, some of the references.

Acknowledgments

I am grateful to the American Institute for Sri Lankan Studies for funding my field research in Sri Lanka in the summer of 1997. During that summer, I had the good fortune to live in the home of two of Godwin's closest friends, Harilal and Visaka Wickramaratne. I would like to acknowledge here the Wickramaratne's kindness and generosity, and thank them for providing me the opportunity to enjoy many splendid dinners, with much laughter, with Godwin and the Wickramaratne family.

Notes

1. By "psychiatric treatment" I mean the kinds of treatment available in institutionalized medical settings such as government hospitals and doctors' offices.
2. Ellipses in the text usually indicate pauses, though occasionally I employ them to indicate deleted sections of the interview. Italics indicate words or phrases that were emphasized by the speaker. The interview is transcribed verbatim, with the exception of repetitive words or phrases. I have retained all Sri Lankan-English constructions.
3. For the purposes of my discussion here, "Western" refers to the predominantly Protestant cultures of northern Europe and North America.
4. In this passage, I understand Godwin to be saying that he has noticed Western meditators in bodily pain due to repressed emotion much more frequently than Sri Lankan meditators. He is thus not making a statement about repression in the culture generally, but only in the context of meditation.
5. A number of meditation teachers and Buddhist scholars have noted differences between "Westerners" and "Asians" in their experiences of meditation. Godwin's view here seems in accord with the views of well-known Buddhist teachers such as the Dalai Lama and Mahāsī Sayādaw who have noted that Westerners appear to suffer considerably more than Asian meditators from feelings of low self-esteem, self-blame and guilt (see e.g., Mark Epstein, *Thoughts without a Thinker: Psychotherapy from a Buddhist Perspective* (New York:

Basic Books, 1995): 30; and Jack Kornfield, *A Path with Heart: A Guide through the Promises and Perils of Spiritual Life* (New York: Bantam Books, 1993): 245-246). These observations call out for much deeper ethnographic inquiry, as well as for more nuanced analysis of the categories of "Western" and "Asian."

6. Medical anthropologists Arthur and Joan Kleinman define somatization as "the expression of personal and social distress in an idiom of bodily complaints and medical health seeking" ("Somatization: The Interconnections in Chinese Society among Culture, Depressive Experiences, and the Meanings of Pain" *Culture and Depression: Studies in the Anthropology and Cross-Cultural Psychiatry of Affect and Disorder*, ed. Arthur Kleinman and Byron Good (Berkeley: University of California Press, 1985): 430).

7. *Vāte* is the spoken Sinhala term for the humor of wind/air, one of the three humors in *Ayurvedic* medicine (see Gananath Obeyesekere, "The Impact of Ayurvedic Ideas on the Culture and the Individual in Sri Lanka," *Asian Medical Systems: A Comparative Study*, ed. Charles Leslie (1976): 201-226). In Sri Lanka, it is believed that an imbalance of *vāte* causes general bodily aches and pain.

8. Dr. E.K. Rodrigo and Dr. Ranil Abeysinghe are both in the Dept. of Psychiatry at the Unversity of Peradeniya.

9. Though I did not pursue the point, it strikes me that Godwin was suggesting that these notions derive from Western medical discourse, a discourse which is now permeated with discussion of "disorders" and "syndromes"—labeling what had previously been regarded as normal feelings and bodily processes as illnesses. If so, his ideas are thus in accord with the observations of of Gananath Obeyesekere (and possibly were influenced by him) who has argued that the affects pertaining to sorrow, which in the West are labeled as an illness—"depression"—were traditionally regarded in Sinhala Buddhist culture as the normal conditions of everyday life. Obeyesekere argues that it is only in recent years that some Sri Lankan Buddhists label such affects as "illness"—an indication of the growing power and prestige of Western medicine ("Depression, Buddhism and the Work of Culture in Sri Lanka," *Culture and Depression: Studies in the Anthropology and Cross-Cultural Psychiatry of Affect and Disorder*, ed. Arthur Kleinman and Byron Good (Berkeley: University of California Press, 1985): 134-152).

10. In the late 1980s, I sat in on occasional interviews with the patients of Dr. Abeysinghe at the Peradeniya Hospital. These open interviews were conducted as part of student training in psychiatric medicine, with the full consent of the patients and their families.

11. Godwin is here discussing the patients who were referred by the psychiatrists at Peradeniya Hospital.

12. Godwin's reiteration of the point that meditators should not view

their problems as "sickness" again indicates the extent to which Western ideas of "mental illness" have come into circulation in Sri Lanka. In his Buddhist therapy, Godwin sought to make the person self-reliant: able to be aware of their emotions and deal with them in a productive way, without needing to rely on psychiatrists and the medical establishment.

13. Though I did not elaborate on this with Godwin, I was thinking here primarily about the epidemic of psychiatric diagnoses in the U.S. of multiple personality disorder. Studies have indicated that certain therapists, noted for their work with multiple personality disorder, actually introduced the notion of multiple personality to their clients, who then began manifesting the classic symptoms of the disorder.

14. Here I was asking to what extent the psychiatrists remained involved with the patients once they were referred to Godwin.

15. Godwin's statement here appears to complicate his earlier statements about the relatively stronger sense of self that he posited for Sri Lankans. It may be that in this case Godwin is referring to his psychiatric patients, and not to his "typical" Sri Lankan meditation students.

16. I was referring to the problem of violence in Sri Lankan society.

17. This may strike the reader as an odd question. But there are, in fact, some cultures where crying at funerals is not considered appropriate.

18. American Institute for Sri Lankan Studies Conference, held in Kandy in August 1997.

19. See Jeanne Marecek, "Trends in Psychiatry" (talk delivered for NEST, Colombo, Sri Lanka, 2001), "Culture-specific Meanings of Women's Suicide and Self-harm" (paper presented at the American Psychological Association convention, San Francisco, CA, August 2001), and Jeanne Marecek and Lakshmi Ratnayake "Suicide in Rural Sri Lanka: Assessing a Prevention Program," *Suicide Risk and Protective Factors in the New Millenium*, ed. O. T. Grad. Ljubljana, (Slovenia: Cankarjev dom., 2001).

20. Godwin is referring to the distinction between "guilt" (Northern Euro-American Protestant) and "shame" (Asian, Mediterranean) cultures which has its roots in the early psychological anthropology of Margaret Mead and Ruth Benedict. For more on the guilt-shame dichotomy and its relevance for Sri Lanka, see Gananath Obeyesekere, *The Cult of the Goddess Pattini* (Chicago: University of Chicago Press, 1984): 499-508.

21. On a number of occasions, Godwin had discussed the notion of Westerners as isolated individuals in contrast to the Sri Lankan "we-self," to borrow Roland's term (Alan Roland, *In Search of Self in India and Japan: Toward a Cross-cultural Psychology* (Princeton: Princeton University, 1988). The extensive anthropological literature

on South Asian concepts of the person discusses these distinctions; see Sarah Lamb, *White Saris and Sweet Mangos: Aging, Gender and Body in North India* (Berkeley: University of California Press, 2000) for a detailed and insightful critical review. It is important to note that several anthropologists have critiqued the notion of the Western self as a bounded individual. See e.g. D.W. Murray, "What is the Western Concept of Self?" *Ethos* 21,1 (1993): 3-23.

22. I was thinking here about the extent to which American culture is permeated by Freudian views concerning the role of childhood in psychological development. Indeed, the power of these ideas is such that Epstein has argued that Buddhism must be presented in the language of psychoanalysis in order to be effective in American culture (Epstein, op cit., 7).

23. William Doherty, *Soul Searching: Why Psychotherapy must Promote Moral Responsibility* (New York: Basic Books, 1996).

24. I have not been able to find a book with this exact title.

25. Godwin's use of the analogy of the relationship with a cup is discussed in Bond (this volume).

26. The third part of the *Mahā Piritta*.

27. Here I made a very broad statement in an attempt to compare a "Buddhist" perspective with a "Christian" one. Obviously, this is a broad generalization, applicable primarily to certain aspects of Protestantism.

28. This notion of "remorse" as an emotion is in accord with the Buddhist conception that emotions are "visitors"—transitory states—and not permanent aspects of one's person.

Children Who Speak of Memories of a Previous Life as a Buddhist Monk:

Three New Cases[1]

by Erlendur Haraldsson and Godwin Samararatne

INTRODUCTION

In several countries of Asia, as well as in other parts of the world, children can be found who at the age of two to four years start to speak of past events which they or persons around them believe to arise from memories of a previous life. Usually these alleged memories fade away after a few years and seem in most cases to disappear in the early years of primary school.[2] In the majority of these cases the child speaks of a life that ended with a violent death, usually through some accident. Most of these children speak of a previous life that they claim to have lived a few years before their present birth. They almost never report having lived in earlier centuries and rarely in foreign countries.

A fairly large number of such cases have been found and some of them have been meticulously investigated, particularly by Stevenson, Mills, Pasricha, Keil, and the authors of the present paper.[3] The first author (E.H.) has investigated 60 cases in Sri Lanka in the last nine years with the assistance of the second author (G. S.) and other Sri Lankan associates.

G. S. has investigated a large number of cases since the early sixties, in association with Ian Stevenson and Francis Story,[4] and on his own. Two authors have raised strong criticism of the investigations of cases involving alleged memories of previous lives.[5] Regretfully, neither of them has had direct exposure to such cases.

The focus of these investigations has been to ascertain what statements the child has been making by interviewing the child and relatives who live with and daily observe the child, as well as other independent witnesses. Secondly, every effort has been made to search for and find a deceased person whose life seems to correspond—to a greater or lesser degree—to the statements made by the child. When such a person is found (or under consideration as a match) we examine the correctness of each of the child's statements for that person.[6]

In about two-thirds of the cases in Sri Lanka it has not been possible to trace a person who fits the description made by the child. We call such cases 'unsolved.' There may be several reasons for this; among them, the statements were too general or too few, or they were found to be incorrect.[7] However, in about one-third of the cases some resemblance is found to a person who actually lived. Among these, a fair number show a rather striking correspondence between a child's statements about a previous life and the facts in the life of a particular person who has died.

Sri Lanka is a multi-religious society. Buddhism is the predominant religion, accepted by two-thirds of the population. There are also Hindus (16%), Muslims (8%), and Christians (7%). Cases of the reincarnation type have been found in all these religious communities.[8]

Among the cases of children in Sri Lanka who at an early age speak persistently of another life, we have found three young boys who claim to have been Buddhist monks in the previous life. What makes these three cases particularly interesting is not only the alleged memories but also the behavioural features that the children display. Each child shows behaviour that is considered appropriate and even ideal for monks. At the age of two to three years they began to show an active keen interest in Buddhism. They aspired to live like Buddhist monks, their behaviour seemed to correspond to these aspirations and they often expressed a desire eventually to join a Buddhist order. Such behaviour sometimes caused considerable concern and distress to their parents. In two of the three cases the child was born of Buddhist parents, in one of Roman Catholic Christians.

Reincarnation and Previous-Life Memories in Buddhism

The concept of reincarnation is an important doctrine in Buddhism, both in Theravada and Mahayana Buddhism. Monasticism plays an important role in both traditions. In Theravada as well as in Tibetan (Vajrayana) Buddhism children may enter monastic orders at a relatively early age; in Sri Lanka, for example, at the age of 8-10 years, and in the Tibetan orders even earlier.

In the ancient Pali scriptures of Theravada Buddhism which were first recorded in writing in the first century B.C., there are references to a special faculty or knowledge involving the memory of previous lives, through which it is possible directly to verify in one's personal experience the truth of reincarnation and *karma.*[9] It is stated that this faculty can be obtained through special training or cultivation of the mind. However, the Pali canon also mentions instances of "skepticism about the Buddhist claim to have super-normal faculties of knowing in general and also the claim that these faculties can be used to verify the truth of rebirth and *karma.*"[10] This skeptical view has generally been rejected throughout the history of Theravada Buddhism.

In the famous, voluminous 5th century *Visuddhimagga* a special chapter deals with how this faculty of previous-life memories can be developed. In this text no mention is made of spontaneous recall of previous lives, nor of the possibility that children may have such recollections.

Monastic Orders and Cases of the Reincarnation Type in Theravada and Mahayana Buddhism

In Vajrayana Buddhism many children are admitted into monastic orders. Some of them are considered monks reborn (called *tulku*s) whereas the majority are not. The *tulku*s usually rise in time to leading positions within the monastic orders, and in some cases they are 'discovered' as specific reborn personalities, such as in the case of the Dalai Lama and the Panchen Lama. There is rather scanty information about the methods used by the monks to determine whether a boy has been a monk in a previous life or not, but there are some interesting descriptions by Tibetan *lama*s and scholars of Tibetan culture that throw some light on this process.[11]

Sometimes a dying *lama* may give intimations about the manner of his rebirth; oracles may be consulted (e.g. in trance the oracle may give a clue as to the direction in which to search); leading monks may experience omens or have visions; and monks (sometimes in disguise) are sent on searching expeditions with objects that belonged to the deceased *lama*. The monks then observe whether a potential *tulku* selects the objects of the deceased *lama* from a pool of other similar objects. Similarities of physical features may also be taken into account.

Gould thus describes the search for the present Dalai Lama:

> At Jeykundo the party under Kyitsang Tulku received news of three remarkable boys in the direction of Amdo. The Tibetan Government had provided each of the search parties with a number of articles which had belonged to the thirteenth Dalai Lama, and with exact copies. It was anticipated, as had happened at the discovery of former

> Dalai Lamas, that the genuine reincarnation would pick out the things which had belonged to his predecessor and would show other signs of superhuman intelligence, and that no other child would succeed in these tests. And so it proved. Of the three boys, one was found to have died and the second failed to display any interest in the things that had belonged to the late Dalai Lama and ran away crying. But Kyitsang Tulku, on approaching the home of the third, felt a great uplifting of heart. He found himself in surroundings already familiar from the description that the Regent had given of his vision of the lake. When Kyitsang entered, the child at once went up to him, said 'Lama, Lama', and seized his necklace, which had belonged to the Dalai Lama.[12]

It is added that this child made further correct choices. Norbu and Turnbull write: "Some may go to investigate claims or rumours of wonder children, others may concentrate on an area which various oracles and omens have indicated as being likely."[13]

Some cases in Tibetan Buddhism have features that have some resemblance to the Sri Lankan cases to be reported in this paper but these seem to be few. Norbu and Turnbull write: "Sometimes a boy is born with such unmistakable signs of greatness that word reaches the authorities who immediately send delegates to investigate the claim."[14] Of still greater interest is the following: "It has been known for boys to come forward on their own and demand to be returned to their monastery and recognized."[15] It should be added that among exiled Tibetans there have been disputes about the genuineness of the claims about *tulku*s and skepticism expressed about their alleged previous identities.

In the Theravada Buddhism of Sri Lanka, Burma (Myanmar) and Thailand there is no tradition of selecting child novices through alleged indications that they have been monks in a previous life. Occasionally, however—very rarely in fact—children may appear among Theravada Buddhists who at the age of two to four speak of memories of having been a monk in a previous life, or are interpreted to possess such memories. They express a desire to become a monk again. Their alleged memories and monk-specific behaviour and inclinations may lead them into monastic orders. We present a report on three cases of children that we have found and who claim to have been monks in a previous life.

THE CASE OF DUMINDA BANDARA RATNAYAKE

When Duminda Bandara Ratnayake was about three years old he started to speak about a life as a chief-monk at the Asgiriya monastery in Kandy and often expressed his wish to visit that temple. The Asgiriya monastery is one of the largest monasteries in Sri Lanka, and its monks share with the Malvatta monastery the privilege of guarding the Temple of the Tooth, one of the foremost places of pilgrimage in Theravada Buddhism.[16]

Duminda was born on June 16, 1984, of Sinhalese Buddhist parents. He was the second of three sons. He lived with his mother at the farm of her parents, who are small landowners in Thundeniya, a mountainous rural area some 16 miles by road from Kandy.

In September 1988 we learnt about the case and interviewed the principal witnesses to the boy's statements: his mother, grandfather and grandmother. They all had heard him say that he had lived in the Asgiriya monastery, had owned a red car, had taught other monks, had suffered a sudden pain in his chest, fallen on the floor and been brought by some monks to a hospital and died. Duminda mentioned no personal name. His statements are listed below.

Duminda showed some behavioural features unusual for a boy of his age. He wanted to carry his clothes in the fashion of a monk, wanted to be called '*podi sadhu*' (little monk), went every morning and evening to a temple (*vihara*) close to his house, visited the temple regularly, plucked flowers to bring

Duminda's Statements and Behavioural Traits

Table 1

Statements Made by Duminda About his Previous Life

1	He had been a senior monk (*nayake-hamduruvo, loku-hamduruvo, lokusadhu*) at Asgiriya temple.
2	Had pain in chest and fell, was brought to a hospital and died (used the word *apawathwuna,* which is only used for the death of a monk).
3	Had owned a red car.
4	Had been teaching the apprentice monks.
5	Had an elephant.
6	Had friends in the Malvatta Temple and used to visit it.
7	Longed for his money-bag which he had in Asgiriya.
8	Longed for his radio in Asgiriya.

there and placed them down in the typical Buddhist fashion. Cleanliness was very important to him, he did not want to play with other children, and wanted to become a monk and to wear a monk's robe, which his mother only seldom allowed him to do. He liked to recite stanzas (religious statements, usually short) in the way that monks do. He recited these in Pali, which is the ancient language of Sinhalese Buddhism, used and learnt by monks only.

Duminda's mother sought advice from the Ven. Iriyagama Jinorasa, a monk residing in a nearby temple. The monk tried to question Duminda, who did not answer. Perhaps he was shy. He asked for a monk's fan and the monk gave him one. He took the fan, held it in the typical fashion in front of his face and recited one of the Buddhist stanzas. On a later visit to the monk, the boy told him that he had been a monk in the Asgiriya Monastery, that he wanted to see the monastery and his car, and that he had had a room in the monastery with

Table 2

Some of Duminda's Behavioural Traits

1	Often talks about wanting to go to the Asgiriya temple.
2	Expresses early a wish to visit the local temple in Thundeniya.
3	Likes and shows great cleanliness.
4	Wants to visit the Malvatta temple.
5	Wears and treats his clothes like a monk.
6	Goes to *vihara* (place of worship) every morning and evening.
7	Requests a monk's robe and fan.
8	Wants to wear a monk's robe (only seldom allowed).
9	Wants his family to call him '*podi sadhu'* (little monk).
10	Wants to become a monk.
11	Tried to build a *vihara* (place of worship) at home in the fashion that children build toys, e.g. houses.
12	Plucks flowers and brings to *vihara* 2-3 times a day on Poya-days (Buddhist monthly holiday) as monks do.
13	Does not like wrong-doings of anyone and killing of insects.
14	Knows a few stanzas in Pali and recites them holding the fan in front of his face as monks do.
15	Once when his mother wanted to help wash his hands he told her "You should not touch my hands" (as women are not supposed to touch a monk's hands).
16	When brought to Asgiriya Temple, he did not want to sit down until given a white cloth to sit on (as is the tradition for monks).
17	Does not like to play with other children.
18	Displays calmness, serenity and detachment rarely found in children of this age.

some belongings. This is about all that the monk learnt from this boy who behaved so differently from other boys. When Duminda visited the nearby temple he would go straight to the stupa to worship, and seemed to be very religiously oriented. As we questioned Ven. Jinorasa, he remarked that he did not believe that the boy's parents could have taught him this behaviour. In the end the monk advised Duminda's mother to take her son to the Asgiriya monastery.

In October 1987 Duminda was taken to Asgiriya by his mother and grandparents. A journalist from the newspaper *Island* learnt about the case and was present during Duminda's visit. The boy's mother had ambivalent feelings about the visit as she feared that the boy might later leave her to become a monk.

In November 1989 we visited Duminda's family again, when he was five years and four months old. Duminda's mother reported the same statements from two years earlier. The only new statement the boy had made came up when the death of the *mahanayaka* (chief monk) of the Malvatta Monastery had been recently announced over the radio.

Spontaneously the boy said that he had known him. His mother further told us that before the boy had started to talk about a previous life he had wanted to carry a piece of cloth around his shoulder as monks carry their robes. He then asked for a robe and a monk's fan to be used as toys. Once when she had helped him wash his hands, he made the remark that she should not touch his hands (women are not supposed to touch a monk's hands). He had also protested about her calling him "son"; he wanted to be called "*podi sadhu.*" At first when he was brought to pre-school he also protested and did not want to go there because some girls had touched him.

Duminda's maternal grandfather, A. H. Ratnayake, had listened to our interview with his mother. When we had finished that interview and she had left to prepare some refreshments, he told us that two items had not been reported.

Duminda's most frequent statements had been that he had lived in Asgiriya, had been a teacher (preacher), and that he missed his red car, and this was new—that he missed his money bag and radio.

When we asked Duminda's mother about the money bag and the radio, she confirmed that he had mentioned them but was somewhat embarrassed, because these items are not considered appropriate for a monk to have.

When we again visited the family in June 1990 not much had changed. Duminda was adjusting well to school, and his calm detachment and dignity were evident when we compared his behaviour with that of his brothers, who, like normal healthy boys, would never be quiet or still for long.

As far as we could ascertain from Duminda's family there existed no ties of any kind between any member of the family and the Asgiriya monastery. None of them had visited the monastery until they took the boy there, and the name Asgiriya had never come up at his home as far as they could remember. The family had no relative or neighbor who was a monk.

Even before the visit to Asgiriya the family had apparently become convinced that the boy had in fact been a monk at Asgiriya. They found their conviction further strengthened during that visit. This visit is of less importance in our investigation than Duminda's statements because it proved difficult to reliably reconstruct what had taken place. Duminda's statements are more important to us because he repeatedly uttered them over a period of more than two years.

The Search for a Personality Matching Duminda's Statements

Oliver D. Silva, the journalist from *Island* who first reported on the case, quickly concluded that the boy had been referring to Ven. Ratanapala, a senior monk who had died of a heart attack in 1975 in Galatera outside of Asgiriya. We learnt from three monks who had known him that Ven. Ratanapala had not owned a car or an elephant, had no personal income (hence no money bag), did not preach (hence did not use the fan), had no connection with the Malvatta monastery, and had been known for his interest in politics. Thus he was excluded as a candidate whose life might correspond to Duminda's statements.

If Duminda's statements did in fact refer to a certain monk who had lived in Asgiriya, answers to the following questions would seem pertinent in attempting to distinguish him from other candidate monks: Which monks had income from the temple (money bag), had connections with the Malvatta monastery and the Temple of the Tooth, had frequent occasions to visit these places and had friends there? Which monks had preached sermons and exhorted laymen to recite the Buddhist precepts, thus using a monk's fan? Which monks traveled and often used a red car? Which monks had a heart condition, fell down and died in a hospital? Which monks owned a radio? Which monks owned an elephant?

Furthermore, it seemed likely that the monk we sought had lived many years in the Saṅgha (the Buddhist clergy) since he had been a senior monk, had not been a vegetarian (Duminda did not reject non-vegetarian food at home), had not been a 'meditating' monk (Duminda's emphasis was on ceremonies and behaviour), and had been virtuous and strictly obeyed the rules.

Duminda had clearly stated that he had been a senior monk though he never explicitly mentioned the title '*mahanayaka*.' We independently asked his mother, grandmother and grandfather about which Sinhalese word Duminda had used to describe his position. They agreed that he had referred to himself as *'nayaka-hamduruvo'* meaning chief-monk, and less frequently *'loku-sadu'* or *'loku hamduruvo'* meaning 'big' monk. The red car and the money bag also indicated either a senior monk who had died quite recently, or a *mahanayaka* (chief-monk) of Asgiriya who had lived not earlier than right after the first World War. The Asgiriya monastery has only one *mahanayaka*, and he is elected by the monks. Not until the twenties had a *mahanayaka* owned a car, and only in the eighties had other monks than *mahanayaka*s owned cars. The same can be said about possessing money bags; now a few of them may have some personal income but that is quite a recent development.

After detailed and careful inquiries we learnt from various monks in Asgiriya that no monk who had died in the seventies or eighties seemed to match the statements made by Duminda. His description therefore could only fit a previous *mahanayaka*, if anyone at all.

From an 83-year-old senior monk in Asgiriya, Ven. Thoradeniya Piyaratana, we obtained a list of all the *mahanayaka*s in Asgiriya from the beginning of the 1920s (when the first car came to Asgiriya) to 1975, when the present *mahanayaka*, Ven. Gunaratna Chandananda, took office. This list is in Table 3 with the principal statements made by Duminda, and how each of them fits each *mahanayaka*. We gathered this information from various monks in Asgiriya during visits in 1988 and 1989 but mainly from Ven. Thoradeniya Piyaratana, who knew no details about Duminda's statements.

Duminda claimed to have owned a red car. In Table 3, we see that only two *mahanayaka*s had owned cars. Ven. Godmunne, who died in 1975, owned a white Mercedes car. Ven. Gunnepana Saranankara, who had died in 1929, owned a car. In 1988 we interviewed independently two old monks who recognized Ven. Gunnepana in a group-photo to be described below. According to the Ven. Kappitivalana Sumangala, then aged 82 (now deceased), Ven. Gunnepana Sarananakara had owned a car. When we asked if he could remember its colour, the monk said brownish. The same day we independently met for the first time with Ven. Thoradeniya Piyaratana, who also recognized Gunnepana Saranankara in the same group photo. He remembered the colour of his car as red or brownish.

Table 3

List of Abbots of Asgiriya Temple from 1921 to 1975

Name	**Years**	**Car**	**Cause of death**
Gunnepana	1921-29	Red/brownish	Sudden heart attack
Mullegama	1929-47	No car	Paralysis
Yatawatte	1947-66	No car	Paralysis
Udugama	1966-70	Uncertain	Old age
Godmunne	1970-75	White Mercedes	Sudden heart attack
Name	**Radio**	**Preached**	**Elephant**
Gunnepana	Gramophone	Frequently	Had one?
Mullegama	No radio	Famous for it	None
Yatawatte	No radio	No preaching	Had one
Udugama	No radio	No preaching	None
Godmunne	No radio	No preaching	None

In 1990 we learnt through the Ven. Molagoda Dharmaratana, who had become a resident monk in the village of Gunnepana, that an old man, Mr. Sedaraman (born in 1914), had known Mahanayaka Gunnepana Saranankara since he was 12 years of age as he had lived in the village of Gunnepana. He and his father used to drum at festivals for Mahanayaka Gunnepana Saranankara. Mr. Sedaraman told us that all these years when he knew Gunnepana he had owned a red car with a folding roof.[17] In his red car he had often visited his home village Gunnepana where he was born and where he had previously lived in the local monastery. Conclusion: only one *mahanayaka*, Gunnepana Saranankara, had owned a red (or brownish) car.

Two of the *mahanayakas*, Gunnepana and Godmunne,

had died from heart attacks. This item excludes the other *mahanayakas*. Duminda had stated that he had died in a hospital. However, Ven. Thoradeniya Piyaratana and Mr Sedaraman stated that Mahanayaka Gunnepana died in the Asgiriya Monastery after a physician had been summoned to him. Gunnepanna's death certificate could not be traced, but this information seems reliable.

Did any of the *mahanayakas* have a radio? None, according to Ven. T. Piyaratana, but Gunnepana, and he alone, had owned a gramophone, and had records made of Buddhist chanting and recitations which he often played. At Duminda's home there was no gramophone, and Duminda has apparently never seen one, as far as we can ascertain from his family. Gramophones and radios have in common that they play sound. Could it be that Duminda did not recognize the difference since he had never seen a gramophone? If this is the case the evidence again points towards Ven. Gunnepana. Furthermore, according to Mr. Sedaraman, Mahanayaka Gunnepana had been particularly fond of music (drumming and trumpeting) and chanting, and there was more music played in Asgiriya during his time than either before or after his term in office. Sedaraman and his father had become close to Gunnepana as musicians because they had often drummed for the *mahanayaka* in the monasteries in Gunnepana and Asgiriya. This musical interest is likely to have caused Ven. Gunnepana to obtain a gramophone. Mr Sedaraman did not know that Gunnepana had owned a gramophone, but stated that he might have had one without his knowledge.

Every *mahanayaka* taught apprentice monks so this item is of no value in distinguishing between them. Which of the *mahanayakas* preached? According to Ven. T. Piyaratana, Ven. Mullegama was famous for his preaching. Ven. Gunnepana did quite a bit of preaching. Ven. Yatavatte, Ven. Udugama and Ven. Godmunne did no preaching. Again we have two candidates, Ven. Gunnepana and Ven. Mullegama; the latter, however, had no car and died by paralysis, not of a heart attack. The fan used by monks in Sri Lanka is a part of every monk's paraphernalia; however, it is only used by monks who preach and only some monks do that. The holding of the fan and reciting of stanzas, so important to Duminda, is done at the beginning of any formal sermon.

Duminda spoke of having had an elephant. Ven. Piyaratana was not sure whether Ven. Gunnepana had owned an elephant, but he was sure that Ven. Yatavatte had owned one. Again, Mr. Sedaraman's testimony proved informative. According to him, Ven. Gunananda, the chief disciple of Ven. Gunnepana, had caught an elephant and had it brought to Gunnepana village where Ven. Gunnepana Saranankara was a frequent visitor (he had been born there and had lived in the local monastery). Ven. Gunnepana had taken much interest in this elephant, which died shortly before he himself died.

According to this testimony, we may infer that two of the *mahanayaka*s had owned or taken particular interest in elephants, Ven. Gunnepana and Ven. Yatawatte. The latter, however, had no car, died of paralysis and did no preaching. Once more Ven. Gunnepana is the most likely person to match Duminda's statements. Besides, the Asgiriya Monastery owned several elephants which were used on festive occasions.

Mr. Sedaraman did not reveal much to us about Ven. Gunnepana's personality except that he had always been gentle, kind and friendly towards everyone, was very calm and never got excited. He had come from a poor family and the lay-people liked him. Ven. Piyaratana, who also knew Ven. Gunnepana, remembered him as a very virtuous monk who strictly observed all the rules.

Only one *mahanayaka*, Ven. Gunnepana, matches the five principal statements listed in Table 3. Three (Mullegama, Yatavatte and Godmunne) fit one statement, and one (Udugama) none at all. Ven. Gunnepana is clearly the primary candidate to fit Duminda's description.

Possible Effects of Contamination in Duminda's Statements

One of the principal difficulties in investigating cases of children who claim to remember a previous life is to get the child's statements before they may have become contaminated by knowledge of some person that people around the child come to believe to have been his previous personality. One must attempt to distinguish the child's original statements from whatever the child or those around him may have later added or substituted. In this case the possibilities for such contamination were smaller than usual, since the original investigation by the journalist was superficial and the child's statements only to a small extent matched the monk whom the journalist picked as the supposed previous personality. Duminda's family never came to know the family or friends of that monk (or any monk), nor did they seem interested in knowing any details about the personalities whom Duminda might have been. For example, when we asked Duminda's grandfather which monk he thought the boy had been he did not know. For the family, it was enough to know that he had been a monk in Asgiriya.

Hence possible contamination is more likely to be of a general nature, involving the assumed or idealised characteristics of monks in general. Duminda lived in a rural area, and he might have seen a monk on the road and seen how they dress and fold their robes. Also puzzling is his clear and correct recitation of stanzas at three years of age (in Pali, not his native Sinhalese), and the fact that he did it with a fan in a monk-like fashion.

We made many inquiries about how Duminda might have learnt these stanzas. Duminda's grandmother knew most of these stanzas but denied having taught them to Duminda. Another normal explanation was the fact that at five o'clock each morning a monk recites some stanzas on the Sri Lanka radio. The boy was an early riser and may have heard them.

This, however, might not explain it all. E. H.'s first interpreter, Mr. Ranasinghe, commented, when we were pondering about this, that his grandchildren of similar age also were sometimes up early but had never learnt any stanza, nor had he heard of any child, in his family or elsewhere, who had learnt these stanzas, which are in the dead language, Pali. However, we were not able to ascertain that he understood the meaning of individual Pali words.

In the case of Duminda Bandara Ratnayake we find many behavioural features unusual in a three- or four-year-old child and which correspond to the behaviour of monks in general, and, it seems, in particular to the life of Mahanayaka Gunnepana. In addition, the testimony that we were able to gather from witnesses who knew the Ven. Gunnepana Saranankara indicates that Duminda's statements for the most part match what we have found out about the life of the Ven. Gunnepana Saranankara, who was chief monk of the Asgiriya monastery from 1921 to 1929.

THE CASE OF SANDIKA THARANGA

Sandika was born on May 20, 1979 of middle-class Roman Catholic parents in one of the suburbs of Colombo. Our associate, Tissa Jayawardane, interviewed the family on June 20, 1985, when the boy was six years old. At the age of three Sandika[18] had started to talk about a previous life as a monk in a monastery which he did not further identify. According to his parents, he frequently spoke of the chief monk who lived in the monastery. He stated that one day he was going to attend an almsgiving with some other monks, and then heard a big noise, shot, or explosion, and this is the last thing he remembers. An almsgiving is a common religious ceremony where monks are invited for a midday meal by lay-people.

Sandika showed a great fear of crackers and sudden noises.

When he heard sounds of explosions he instinctively placed his hands in fear on the left side of his chest. His parents' explanation was that this fearful behaviour was caused by a shot he had received in his chest and which led to his death in the previous life. There is a small dark birthmark on his chest slightly to the left of the midline, and we were told it was more prominent when he was younger. His parents know of no monk in the area who has died from a gunshot wound. Sandika further stated that four or five monks had lived in his monastery. A list of his statements is given in Table 4. Sandika's statements bring to mind that Sri Lanka has been through periods of violent political turmoil, particularly the Insurgency of 1971, in which a number of monks were killed.

E.H. first met Sandika in 1988 when he was nine years of age. At this time his memories were fading, as is generally the case with subjects as old as he. His main interests were visiting temples and his school work. He was very religious from the time he started to speak of his previous life, and had tried to convert his parents to Buddhism by requesting them to become Buddhists but they did not comply. He was eager to find the monastery where he had lived. At his request Sandika's father took him to 6-7 temples in their wider area when he was 3-4 years old, in the hope that he would find his temple. He did not recognize any of them as his old monastery.

One day his mother took the boy to a temple some two miles away where there lived a pious monk. She told him about the boy. The monk plucked some flowers, gave them to him, and observed what he did. He climbed the steps to the *vihara* (shrine room) and worshipped there, which is an appropriate response for a devout Buddhist. After Sandika was taken to some temples and he became acquainted with the monk, he gradually stopped talking about his previous life unless he was asked to do so.

Table 4

Sandika's Statements about his Previous Life as Reported by his Mother

1	The chief monk lived at the temple.
2	The chief monk had a big bowl.
3	One day he went away for almsgiving with some other monks.
4	Then there was an explosion with much noise.
5	There was a little monk (child monk) in the temple.
6	Four or five monks lived in the temple.
7	There was a jack-fruit tree there.
8	The temple where he lived was close to his present home.
9	He had a brother who was of fair complexion.
10	His younger brother wore no shirt.

What most impressed his Roman Catholic parents, however, was not so much that he spoke of a previous life but his unusual behavioural traits and exemplary behaviour as well as his interests, which differed radically from the religious life and background of his family. The family did not force him to go to church since he only wanted to visit temples.

Like many children who speak of a previous life, Sandika told his mother that she was not his real mother. He asked to be taken to his monastery and to his previous mother's place. Another unusual behavioural trait was that he would at certain times pick flowers and place them on his bed as long as there was no altar or shrine room in the house for him to place them. Placing flowers on an altar is common practice among Buddhists. Furthermore, he chanted religious stanzas (in Pali, his parents thought) and worshipped as Buddhists do. What verses or stanzas he chanted his parents did not know or could not remember as they had not paid much attention to it or understood the words. Sandika had stopped chanting when E.H. first met him. As a child he stammered but he chanted

Table 5

Prominent Behavioural Traits with Sandika, as Reported by his Mother

1	Asks to be taken to his previous temple.
2	Expressed a wish to visit the temple to see the chief monk.
3	Asks to be taken to his previous mother's place.
4	Picks flowers to place on bed or chair before worshipping.
5	Wanted a Buddha image in the house for his worship.
6	Requests family to give alms to monks.
7	On Poya day (full moon, important Buddhist public holiday in Sri Lanka) he requests his father to take him to temple.
8	Requests family to invite monks for alms-giving which they did.
9	His family became more sympathetic to Buddhism because of his behaviour.
10	Does not eat meat.
11	Gets specially high school marks in Buddhism (91 of 100 possible).
12	His main interests are to visit temples and do his schoolwork.
13	Is fearful of crackers and sudden noises, then places his hand on the left side of his chest, as if in defense.
14	Is particularly clean in everything he does.
15	Requests his parents not to cut his hair (as his hair was always cut in the previous life when he was a monk, and he does not want that now).

without stammering, according to his mother.

From the age of three Sandika would worship two to three times a day. At the age of six he was still offering flowers to a picture of Lord Buddha, which at his request was put up for him. Later he was given a small statue of the Buddha. A small shelf was placed on the wall in one room to serve as an altar for Sandika. When we visited the family in April 1996, there was one image of the Buddha displayed in a prominent place in the house, another had been placed elsewhere by Sandika only recently. We noticed no Christian pictures or images in the house. According to his mother, some which they had earlier had been removed at the request of Sandika. The family did not seem particularly religious or seriously committed to Christianity, and Sandika's mother would sometimes visit temples as well as churches, apparently due to Sandika's influence.

As stated in Table 4, Sandika requested his family to give alms to monks and to get monks to have a ceremony in their house (common in Buddhist households) which in the end they did. On the full moon day he requested his father to take him to a temple, in line with a common tradition among Buddhists. From the time he was a small child he abstained from eating meat. He showed unusual concern for cleanliness and was a very pious, gentle and obedient boy. Through his pious behaviour his parents became more sympathetic to Buddhism than they had been previously as they were deeply impressed by their son. He became an outstanding pupil after entering school. His highest grades were in his favourite subject, Buddhism. He also attended from an early age the optional Buddhist Sunday School.

From early childhood Sandika has only gone to the local Buddhist temple. His parents did not take him to church because he refused to go. When he grew old enough, he went alone every Sunday to the temple's Sunday School. He is still in close contact with the monk who is his teacher in the temple school.

Sandika's mother and father believe that their son was a monk in a previous life. In 1988 the mother was still afraid that he might go back to the temple and become a monk. Sandika, however, has never expressed a desire to become a monk. When we met him in 1996 he was still deeply interested in Buddhism, and would often visit temples, but he had no intention of becoming a monk. He had received a scholarship for outstanding school performance and continued to be a very gentle and modest boy. In a class of 40 he had always been among the top three, and had recently been admitted to Ānanda College, the most prestigious Buddhist college in Sri Lanka, where he plans to study mathematics and science.

THE CASE OF GAMAGE RUVAN THARANGA PERERA

Ruvan, as we shall refer to him, was born in August 1987 and was eight years old when we met him and his parents at their home in the Kalutara district. Ruvan looked a normal boy for his age. He was quiet in our presence but attentive. He had a younger sister and was attending school.

According to his father Ruvan started to speak of a previous life when he was 2 years old. He stated that he had been a monk living in the Pitumpe monastery. The name Pitumpe was unknown to his parents. Ruvan said that this monastery was in Padukka, which is some 20 miles to the south of their home. Ruvan also stated that there was a monkey in the temple, and two weeks later he added that the monkey was made of clay. The name Pitumpe led to the identification of a particular monastery. The unexpected verification of his very specific statement, that there was in the Pitumpe temple a monkey made of clay, was seen as evidence that Ruvan had lived in this place.

Ruvan's mother stated that he had been talking about a Pitumpe monastery almost from the time he started to speak, and was keen to become a monk. He did not ask for toys, only for pictures of the Buddha, which he collected lovingly. Furthermore, she described some unusual behaviour that still persists; Ruvan sits in a lotus position when they go to the temple, although no one had taught him to do so; he wants to wear a robe like a monk and knows how to put it on; and he knows how to hold a fan when chanting; he does not want to eat at night and discourages his family from doing so (monks are not supposed to have meals from noon until next morning); and he does not eat fish or meat (a few monks do not); he recites the Buddha's first sermon; can read the book of chants *(Gatha pota)*; and wants the family to perform a *puja* (prayer-like ceremony of worship with recitations and offerings such as of flowers and incense) in the evening and scolds them for not doing so; he does not like to sleep with his mother, tells her that monks do not sleep with women; once when his father brought some liquor into the house with some friends, he protested vehemently.

Furthermore Ruvan would chant stanzas in Pali. His parents recognize Pali from hearing it in the temple and sometimes on radio and television. Ruvan may have learnt the stanzas by listening to radio or television broadcasts but his parents reject that explanation.

A local reporter, Laksman Vithana, learnt about the case, interviewed Ruvan and his parents, and published a report in the newspaper *Lankadeepa* on November 3, 1993, when Ruvan was six years old. In this report some of Ruvan's statements were published (see Table 6). They are particularly important as they were published before attempts were made to learn whether his statements regarding the Pitumpe monastery could be verified.

A monk in the Pitumpe monastery and some laymen associated with the temple read the report in *Lankadeepa*. A few days after its publication they made the 20-mile trip to visit the boy and learn first hand about the case. They questioned Ruvan about his alleged previous-life memories, and tested him to see if he recognized any of them. Some members of the group became convinced that Ruvan was the previous abbot of the monastery, Ven. Ganihigama Pannasekhara (1902-1986), reborn. In particular they were

Table 6

Ruvan's Statements as Reported in *Lankadeepa* Newspaper

1	I lived as a monk in the Pitumpe temple in Padukka.
2	There was a statue of a monkey in the temple.
3	There were six monks living in the temple.
4	I led the flower offering ceremonies in the temple.
5	I organized religious processions in the temple.
6	I motivated many people towards meritorious living.
7	My father and mother were very much devoted to religion.
8	There were frescoes and wall-paintings in the temple.

impressed with his monk-like demeanor and the way he carried his robes. Ruvan's statements published in *Lankadeepa* about his leading and organizing of religious ceremonies and processions could only refer to a senior monk or abbot. However, the incumbent monk and former disciple of the abbot remained skeptical, because Ruvan did not recognize him, and did not know the former abbot's name.

Another disciple of the deceased abbot, Ven. Nawagamuwe Revata, visited Ruvan somewhat later with Ven. Mahagama Tillaka and Ven. Kanugala Medhankara. The late Ven. Ganihigama Pannasekhara had been his uncle and he and Ven. Pannasekhara were disciples of the same high priest. Also accompanying them was Nimal Weerenayaka, Ven. Pannasekhara's sister's daughter's son. All were quite familiar with Ven. Pannasekhara. Ruvan did not recognize any of them and hence they remained skeptical. He told them that he was the reincarnation of a lesser monk who attended on the *loku hamduruvo*, i. e. the chief monk. Ven. Revata began to wonder if Ruvan was referring to the life of a young monk from Pitumpe (Ven. Pannagula Nanavasa), who died around 1986. More about him later.

Ruvan's Statements and his Personality

Our inquiries revealed that Ruvan's parents had shown little interest in what Ruvan was saying and tried to keep the case a family secret. Had it not been for the journalist, Laksman Vithana, who learnt about Ruvan accidentally from a female neighbour, the case might never have become publicly known. When we arrived at the scene in December 1995 Ruvan's parents were co-operative.

A next-door neighbour, Mrs. Karuna Wijeman, knew Ruvan from his birth. According to her, he started at the age of two to speak of a life as a monk but she no longer remembered details of his statements. She was primarily impressed with his monk-like behaviour, his serenity and peacefulness, his wish to be dressed like a monk, and how he frequented the shrine room in her house to sit there quietly alone. Mrs. Wijeman told us that Ruvan's father had a drinking problem and the family had little interest in religion. Through Ruvan's influence his father in due time stopped drinking and the family even became vegetarians. This was later confirmed by Ruvan's mother.

Another neighbour, Mrs. Puspa Ranjani, also knew Ruvan from early childhood. He then talked about having lived in Pitumpe, and about being a monk. Mrs. Ranjani was a teacher in a nearby Montessori school. Ruvan was later admitted to this school and then she came to know him better. He was a very good pupil. There his monkish behaviour became more evident. He did not play with other children. When he was asked to draw he would always draw incidents in the life of the Buddha. He wanted to dress like a monk, and expressed a wish to become a monk. He wanted to eat only vegetarian food.

Sometimes Ruvan would insist that the other children in his class stand as a mark of respect as when a monk is brought in a procession to preach a sermon. He would get them to imitate that they were beating drums, then he would walk into the classroom and sit cross-legged on a chair laid with white cloth. In place of a fan he would take a large leaf and hold it as a fan, then preach for about 15 minutes, ending the session by 'offering merit' as monks do when they preach a sermon. There is a special chant for offering merits and Ruvan would chant it in Pali. Mrs. Ranjani knew this chant. The other children accepted his behaviour, listened attentively and gave him due respect. Among the children he came to be known as 'Ruvan sadhu' (monk).

The Montessori pre-school was on the compound of the Dombagoda temple. There Ruvan had his first contact with monks, and became particularly attracted to Ven. Omatte Hemarama, who soon learnt about Ruvan's memories. Ruvan liked their robes, the pictures of Lord Buddha, and liked to go to their books and handle them. He liked to sketch pictures of the Buddha on the floor, and one day, he spoke of a monkey. When asked what monkey he was talking about, he replied, "the monkey in Pitumpe." Ruvan stated that he had been a monk in Pitumpe, that there were 3-4 monks in his temple and that he wanted to become a monk.

Ven. Hemarama knew there was a temple in Pitumpe and suggested to Ruvan's parents that they make inquiries and take him to Pitumpe. His parents were against this and no inquiries were made. It was not until two years later, after Ruvan had entered primary school, that the journalist published his report and the first contact was made with Pitumpe.

At the beginning of our investigation we expected that Ruvan might have learnt about Pitumpe from the monks in

Dombagoda. However, several witnesses asserted that Ruvan had mentioned Pitumpe before entering preschool where he came to know the monks. The Dombagoda monastery belongs to a different sect than the Pitumpe monastery, the Siyam Nikaya sect. Their monks come from a higher cast and are affluent.[19] There was no connection between the two monasteries, which were over 30 miles apart. We learnt from an old, invalid monk in Dombagoda, Ven. Somaloka, that many years ago he casually met Ven. Pannasekhera at functions but never visited his temple. The old monk looked very frail and complained of lack of memory from which he had suffered for a number of years. Ven. Revata told us at a later date that he remembered that in the late fifties when he lived in Pitumpe, Ven. Somaloka who at this time lived at a temple much closer to Pitumpe, did visit the Pitumpe temple. At this stage we have no way of verifiying either of their statements. Assuming that the old monk did visit the Pitumpe temple, the question arises of whether or not he influenced Ruvan's memories.

According to both monks, Ruvan's connection at the Dombagoda monastery had been almost solely with Ven. Hemarama. If that is true, it is unlikely that Ruvan obtained any information about Pitumpe from Ven. Somaloka. Ven. Hemarama, probably in his forties, stated that he never knew about or met any monk from Pitumpe.

Shortly after the visit of the group from Pitumpe, Ruvan's family went to the Pitumpe monastery with the *Lankadeepa* reporter, Ven. Hemarama, and several other persons. Ruvan's father said that he instructed the party not to tell his son anything or give him any leads in order better to test whether he could recognize something. According to the *Lankadeepa* report, Ruvan helped in locating the Pitumpe monastery after they arrived in the vicinity. The memories of those who made the trip to Pitumpe had become vague about details by the time we interviewed them. It proved impossible to reconstruct reliably what happened there.

According to a second article by the reporter, the group visited the shrine room and there Ruvan pointed to the statue of the monkey made of clay, which is not prominently placed. He said: "That is the monkey I told you about." In the room of the present chief monk at the Pitumpe monastery, the Ven. Mahagama Hematillaka, there were two large framed photographs, each of one monk. Without being asked Ruvan pointed at one of them and said: "This was the chief monk." That photograph was of Ven. Ganihigama Pannasekhara, the former abbot of Pitumpe monastery. This impressed Ven. Hematillaka. The other photograph was of Pannasekhara's teacher who previously had also been a chief monk.

In May 1997 we visited Ruvan's former primary school. It was early morning and a group of children were waiting for the school to open. Some of them had been class mates with Ruvan, who had left school the year before to join a monastery. We asked them about Ruvan, whom they remembered well. He had been a class leader all his three and a half years in primary school, appointed by the teacher. Would they have liked another pupil as a class leader? No, they said, they liked Ruvan as class leader.

On occasions Ruvan got his fellow pupils to recite the Five Precepts, and he preached to his fellow pupils. He sat in an elevated position, but they sat on the floor (according to tradition). In his sermons Ruvan had taught them the importance of behaving well.

Did Ruvan ever get angry? No, three of them replied, he did not get angry, was always calm. What did they think of his becoming a monk? It was a good thing, and they evidently were not surprised by it.

In Sri Lanka a class leader is traditionally the best pupil in the class (usually of 30 to 40 pupils). The principal of Keselheneva Junior School, Milton Dharmasinghe, allowed us to examine the grade books. Ruvan had completed his studies

Table 7

List of Ruvan's Behavioural Features as Reported in *Lankadeepa* Before the Case was "Solved"

1	Does not eat at night (monks do not).
2	Does not want to sleep with his mother (monks do not sleep with women).
3	Recites in Pali part of Buddha's first sermon.
4	Does not ask for toys, only pictures of Buddha, which he collects lovingly.
5	Wants to become a monk.
6	Sits in a lotus position when he goes with his parents to the temple.
7	Likes to wear monk's robes when he is at home.
8	Asks his family not to eat at night and only take refreshments as monks do.
9	Does not eat fish or meat.
10	Likes to read the '*pirithpotha*' (Buddhist texts for protection).
11	Ask his mother to make offering to Buddha in the evenings. He scolds her if she does not.
12	Takes offence when he learns that his father has taken liquor.
13	Knows how to wear a robe as monks do.
14	Plays some tunes on a drum that was given to him at his request (drums were used in Pitumpe temple as in many other temples).

in grade 1 to 3. The first two years he ranked first in his mean school performance, and in the third year another pupil shared with him the first rank. In his fourth year he left the school for the *pirivena* (school for child novices living in monasteries).

According to the principal Ruvan had been a very talented pupil and popular with the other children, a true class leader, although he did not move much with them. He had a keen memory, and even remembered what he heard only once. He was obedient to his teachers, quiet, and peaceful. He did not like to be with girls, not even his sister.

In his early years in primary school Ruvan started to give frequent public *pujas (Bodhi-pujas)* at the request of various persons, and his fame started to spread, also through several articles in the newspapers. We were told that he conducted these ceremonies, which consist mostly of chanting, with the dignity of a senior monk.

On August 9, 1996, Ruvan was ordained into the ancient Pushparamaya Pathawatta temple in Rajgama. The monks there had heard about Ruvan, and happened to know some people where he regularly went for meditation. One day Ruvan's family had visited the temple to discuss the possibility of his entering as a monk novice. Then he told his parents: "I wish to stay here; you can go home." Ruvan told us he is happy in the temple, does not miss home, has time to meditate and that there is much to study. The abbot, Ven. Dhammarama, told us that Ruvan is different from the other child novices, is more calm and composed, and gets on well with them, has a better memory and much greater knowledge of Buddhism. On the last full moon day he had performed the *Bodhi-puja* and did that very well.

Attempts at Verification of the Case

One of the interesting features of this case is that some of Ruvan's statements were published before an attempt was made to find a person who fitted Ruvan's story. Hence it is of crucial importance to find out whether Ruvan might in normal ways have acquired knowledge about the Pitumpe monastery and the clay monkey in the temple. We failed to find such a normal way, both for the name of Pitumpe temple, and for the fact that there was a monkey made of clay in this temple. The monkey was in a scene that depicted Buddha's passing away. Statues of monkeys are almost never found in temples, as far as we have been able to ascertain.

The statement that there were frescoes and wall-paintings in the Pitumpe temple is also correct. However, such wall-paintings and frescoes are not uncommon in temples but those in Pitumpe are of unusual beauty for a temple of such a small size. They were built and painted at the initiative of Ven. Pannasekhara.

The statements about leading the flower offering ceremonies, organizing processions in the temple, and motivating people towards meritorious living, would fit the life of any abbot who is actively engaged in promoting Buddhism among the public, which some (but far from all) abbots do.

We were able to trace a younger sister of Ven. Pannasekhara, now 91. She had been a vegetarian all her life. Furthermore, she told us that her parents had been very religious; they had also been vegetarians for religious reasons, which is rare in Sri Lanka. They had been in close contact with a nearby temple, Sri Pushparamaya (the family still is), and had given her brother to that monastery when he was ten years old. Her brother, at least as long as he lived with his family, had also been a vegetarian.

Of Ruvan's eight statements (see Table 6) one is incorrect.[20] There were 3-4 and not six monks living in the Pitumpe temple, not counting the child novices. If the child monks are included Ruvan may have been right. At present there are four child novices in Pitumpe and one monk.

The Abbot Ganihigama Pannasehhara

The monk that Ruvan is believed to be referring to is Ven. Ganihigama Pannasckhara. He was born in April 1902, became a monk in the Amarapura sect and lived in the latter part of his life in the small and unimportant Pitumpe monastery. In 1972

Table 8

Chronology of the Case of Ruvan Perera

Ven. Ganihigama Pannasekhara	
1902	Born in Ganihigama as I. D. Julis.
1912	Entered a monastery as novice.
1972	Appointed *sanghanayaka* at Pitumpe temple.
January 9, 1986	Died at Pitumpe temple.
Gamage Ruvan Tharanga Perera	
August 2, 1987	Born in Betas.
Late 1989	Starts talk of previous life.
January, 1991	Enters pre-school in Dombagoda.
January, 1993	Enters Keselheneva Junior School.
November 3, 1993	Case published in *Lankadeepa.*
November 7, 1993	Monks from Pitumpe visit Ruvan. Case "solved."
November 10,1993	Second report in *Lankadeepa.*
December 1, 1995	First investigation by EH & GS.
August 9, 1996	Enters the Raigama P. S. Pushparamaya Vihara (monastery).

he was appointed *sanghanayaka* (chief abbot) over the whole Colombo district. This was a great honour and recognition by the authorities of his spiritual and leadership qualities. Thus he came to participate in many important official functions, religious and otherwise, where he was bound to meet other leading clerics of the nation. Ruvan's statements that he led flower *puja*s and processions and motivated people towards a meritorious life seem a fitting description. Ganihigama Pannasekhara died January 9,1986. Ruvan was born 17 months later, August 2,1987.

The Ven. Pannagula Nanavasa

The Ven. Pannasekhara is not the only candidate for Ruvan's previous personality. Some monks involved with the case have considered the possibility that Ruvan is referring to Ven. Nanavasa, who stayed in Pitumpe for two years, disrobed and died two years later in January 1986, then still a young man. However, his personality differed widely from Ven. Pannasekhara. His relatives described him as shy, an average pupil in school, and not particularly good at chanting. In addition he does not seem to have been deeply committed to Buddhism (as Ruvan is) as he abandoned his life as a monk.

Summary of the Case

Ruvan displayed no recognitions of persons, and his statements are few and not specific enough to point clearly to any previous personality. Only by the method of exclusion does Ven. Pannasekhara become a better fit for Ruvan's statements than other monks who have lived in Pitumpe in recent times. Ruvan's personality resembles Ven. Pannasekhara in that his life is strongly oriented towards Buddhism; he has distinct leadership qualities (even in school he organized religious services) and he also enjoys chanting in public and does it with ease.

Sri Lankan Buddhists have a fairly distinct image of the characteristics of the ideal monk: serenity, composure, and harmlessness (in extreme cases this is exemplified by vegetarianism). Some monks are committed to serve the public, conduct religious activities and encourage people to meritorious living. Even as a child Ruvan seems to have these characteristics. Some persons were also impressed by how well he knew how to carry monk's robes. The behavioural features are prominent in this case and they are what primarily lead laymen and some monks to accept Ruvan as a reincarnation of a monk.

Is there another obvious explanation of how Ruvan's behavioural characteristics could have developed at such an early age? Where could he have picked up and identified with the image of the ideal monk? He was not brought up in a religious family, nor were there monks in his extended family or among his neighbours. He apparently received no support (and perhaps even resistance) from his family, but early on found his way to people who shared his religious commitment. We find no easy explanation for his unusual and distinct behavioural characteristics which are so atypical for a child.

DISCUSSION

We have described three cases of children who claim memories of having been monks in a previous life, and our attempts to verify their claims. These are the only cases concerning monks that we have found among over two hundred cases that have been recorded in Sri Lanka.

The majority of children in Sri Lanka and elsewhere who claim previous-life memories speak of an untimely violent death. The cases of Duminda and Ruvan differ for they claim to have lived as senior monks until they died as relatively old men. Sandika's case is more typical, as he speaks of a death in a bomb blast and apparently at a relatively young age. The crucial question remains, how did these children come to utter their claims of having previously been monks? How did they develop ideas or images which they spoke of as they would of any other memories? We have no way of directly experiencing the images that may go through their minds, or directly testing whether they are making these stories up. We can only test their accounts against objective realities in the lives of some persons who lived recently, and we can compare their behavioural characteristics and interests with those of these past personalities. In the case of Duminda we find that his statements fit important facts in the life of the abbot Gunnepana. In the case of Ruvan the behavioural features are dominant. Of the memory items his statement about the clay monkey in Pitumbe, his very religious parents and his statements of leading the flower offerings, organizing religious processions, and motivating people towards meritorious living fit the life of Pannasekhara. The behavioural traits and interests of Duminda and Ruvan show a good deal of resemblance with the respective abbots.

No normal physical connection or interaction could be traced between these children's families and the abbots. If we tentatively assume that these children have in their minds genuine images or memories of real events or of someone's past subjective experiences, this must have taken place through some unknown processes. An alternative interpretation would be that, by chance, the statements of the children correspond with the life histories of the abbots concerned. If these cases only consisted of alleged memories, we might find such explanation a reasonable solution.

What complicates this hypothesis is that these three boys have deep-seated, unusual behavioural features, which unfolded at a very early age. They display behaviour that would fit dedicated monks who might be found worthy to be elected to high positions by their peers. From a young age these boys displayed a religious commitment and life-style of devoted Buddhist monks. For example, witnesses unanimously agree that they expressed calmness, dignity and devotion rarely found in young children. Also at a very early age they wanted to dress as monks; furthermore they quickly knew the Pali words and phrases used in some religious ceremonies, and they knew the general behaviour appropriate in the setting in which monks live. Not only that; two of the three persistently requested that they be allowed to become monks again. Grudgingly, their parents gradually accepted their wishes, and they have now joined Buddhist monasteries at the earliest age possible. Apparently the children did not show any emotion when they left their parents, whereas the parents were sad.

We have described one way to approach these cases. One should also explore more natural explanations. For example, some boys at an early age want to enter a particular profession, such as that of a policeman or a pilot, when they grow up. For such an idea to develop the child needs some exposure to the profession of their choice. Perhaps such children may sometimes express behaviours and characteristics that are typical for such professions, but they definitely do not claim that they have been policemen or pilots before they were born, nor would they identify with particular individuals of the past or express knowledge of their histories.

The sagas of these boys might lead us to describe them—perhaps a bit too dramatically—as heroically resisting and fighting the constraints they found in their respective families. They apparently developed, quite early, ideals and goals of a possessive strength, which was not in line with life in their families (particularly in the case of Ruvan and Sandika). In addition, they had no immediate familiarity with monks with whom they might have identified.

There are many pitfalls to guard against when investigating and interpreting cases of this kind. Researchers, however vigilant they may try to be, look through their particular mental glasses. Witnesses may have biases that distort their perception of things, they may not tell the whole truth, they may embellish or exaggerate, their memories may be distorted, and so on. These potential distortions we have tried to minimize by interviewing many witnesses, and the crucial ones on more than one occasion, and by avoiding at all times leading questions. Our research work has been extensive and in each case we carried out our investigation over a period of three years. For example, in the case of Ruvan, we conducted 29 interviews with 21 persons.

There are different interpretations of the data once they have been collected as objectively as possible. Some favour reincarnation, others do not. In Sri Lanka there are differing assumptions among those who are open to the possibility of reincarnation about what may constitute evidence for reincarnation of a particular personality. For example, the monks who knew Ven. Pannasekhara best did not consider Ruvan to be his reincarnation because he did not recognize any of them. For them Ruvan's behavioural features and some correct statements that would fit Pannasekhara were not sufficient evidence, although the same evidence was sufficient for most laymen who knew Ven. Pannasekhara and for some other monks.

Obviously our conclusion can only be very tentative. If we assume for a moment that a reincarnation process is involved in some cases of children who claim previous-life memories, it seems likely that the number and qualities of memories, behavioural features, etc. that come through, would vary widely among the children. These could range from distant echoes and unclear shimmerings to full-blown images/memories and stable behavioural and motivational characteristics that emerge at an early age. Perhaps our cases are a mixture of these.

The case of Duminda is among the best cases but the other two fall well behind the best cases that have been investigated in Sri Lanka.[21] They all, however, have strong behavioural features. The memory aspect is rather poor in all of them. Only one of our cases fulfils the requirement that the statements of the child are recorded before the case is 'solved', namely the case of Ruvan. The case of Sandika is not specific enough to allow any attempt of verification although it includes the most common feature of cases of the reincarnation type, i.e. alleged memories of a violent death. None of these cases includes personal names, only place names, but that is common in Sri Lankan cases.

In all Buddhist traditions reincarnation is taken for granted, also that some persons may have previous-life memories. In Theravada Buddhism there exists considerable literature on the theoretical aspects of reincarnation, in ancient Pali texts and in books and articles written in this century.[22] However, there have been no systematic studies—using empirical methods—of children who are considered monks reborn, or who make such claims.[23] Ours is the first in-depth study and attempt at verification. We do not claim that our cases contribute greatly to the issues of this debate but the questions raised by them are an invitation to the reader, the investigators and the critics to speculate and ponder.

ACKNOWLEDGEMENTS

We gratefully acknowledge grants from Institut für Grenzgebiete der Psychologie and Psychohygiene, Freiburg; The John Björkhem Foundation, Stockholm; Division of Personality Studies, University of Virginia, and the University of Iceland. Prof. P. D. Premasiri, Hector Samararatne, Tissa Jayawardane, Ven. Revata and Ven. Wimalakirti assisted us in various ways.

Notes

1. This article was originally published in the Journal of Psychical Research, Vol. 63, No. 85. Minor editorial changes have been made.
2. See E. W. Cook et al, "A Review and Analysis of Unsolved Cases of the Reincarnation Type. II. Comparison of Features of Solved and Unsolved Cases," *Journal of the Society for Psychical Research* 77 (1983): 115-135 and I. Stevenson, *Children Who Remember Previous Lives: A Question of Reincarnation* (Charlottesville: University Press of Virginia, 1987).
3. I. Stevenson, *Cases of the Reincarnation Type Vol. 1 Ten Cases in India* (Charlottesville: University Press of Virginia, 1975), I. Stevenson, *Cases of the Reincarnation Type Vol. 2 Ten Cases in Sri Lanka* (Charlottesville: University Press of Virginia, 1977), I. Stevenson, *Children Who Remember Previous Lives: A Question of Reincarnation* (Charlottesville: University Press of Virginia, 1987), I. Stevenson, *Reincarnation and Biology: A Contribution to the Etiology of Birthmarks and Birth Defects*, Vols. 1 and 2 (Westport: Praeger, 1997), I. Stevenson, *Where Reincarnation and Biology Intersect* (Westport: Praeger, 1997), A. Mills, "A Replication Study: Three Cases of Children in Northern India who are Said to Remem-

ber a Previous Life," *Journal of Scientific Exploration* 3, 2 (1989): 133-184, A. Mills et al, "Replication Studies of Cases Suggestive of Reincarnation by Three Different Investigators," *Journal of the Society for Psychical Research* 88 (1994): 207-219, S. Pasricha, *Claims of Reincarnation: An Empirical Study of Cases in India* (Delhi: Harman Publishing House, 1990), H. H. J. Keil, "New Cases in Burma, Thailand and Turkey: A Limited Field Study Replication of Some Aspects of Ian Stevenson's Research," *Journal of Scientific Exploration* 5 (1991): 27-59, E. Haraldsson, "Children Claiming Past-life Memories: Four Cases in Sri Lanka," *Journal of Scientific Exploration* 5 (1991): 233-261, E. Haraldsson, "Personality and Abilities of Children Claiming Previous-life Memories," *Journal of Nervous and Mental Disease* 183 (1995): 445-451, I. Stevenson and G. Samararatne, "Three New Cases of the Reincarnation Type with Written Records Made Before Verifications," *Journal of Scientific Exploration* 2 (1988): 217-238, E. W. Cook et al, "A Review and Analysis of Unsolved Cases of the Reincarnation Type. II. Comparison of Features of Solved and Unsolved Cases," *Journal of the Society for Psychical Research* 77 (1983): 115-135.

4. F. Story, *Rebirth as Doctrine and Experience* (Kandy: Buddhist Publication Society, 1975).
5. P. Edwards, *Reincarnation: A Critical Examination* (Amherst: Prometheus Books, 1996) and I. Wilson, *Mind Out of Time? Reincarnation Claims Investigated* (London: Gollancz, 1981).
6. For details on methodology, see E. Haraldsson (1991), op cit. and I. Stevenson (1975 and 1987), op cit.
7. For a detailed discussion of unsolved cases, see E. W. Cook et al, op cit.
8. E. Haraldsson, ibid and I. Stevenson (1977), op cit.
9. P. D. Premasiri, "The Theravada Buddhist Doctrine of Survival After Death," in *Concepts of Transmigration: Perspectives on Reincarnation*, ed. S. J. Kaplan. (New York: Edwin Mellen Press, 1995): 133-188.
10. Ibid: 8.
11. B. J. Gould, *The Jewel in the Lotus* (London: Chatto and Windus, 1957), H. Harrer, *Seven Years in Tibet* (London: Rupert Hart-Davis, 1953), T. J. Norbu and C. M. Turnbull, *Tibet* (London: Chatto and Windus, 1969), M. Pallis, *The Way and the Mountain* (London: Peter Owen, 1961), C. Trungpa and E. Roberts, *Born in Tibet* (London: George Allen and Unwin, 1966).
12. B. J. Gould, op cit.: 214.
13. T. J. Norbu and C. M. Turnbull, op cit.: 228.
14. Ibid.

15. Ibid.

16. H. L. Seneviratne, *Rituals of the Kandyan State*. Cambridge Studies in Social Anthropology (Cambridge: Cambridge University Press, 1978).

17. As always, we conducted our interviews in an open-ended fashion and refrained from asking leading questions. Mr. Sedaraman volunteered the information about the red car.

18. At the request of Sandika's parents only personal names are used.

19. R. Gombrich, *Precept and Practice: Traditional Buddhism in the Rural Highlands of Ceylon* (Oxford: Clarendon Press, 1971).

20. It should be noted that we are here only considering statements that were definitely made before the case was considered 'solved' by Ruvan's parents. There are also further statements that fit Pannasekhara, but we exclude them as they may have arisen out of contamination with knowledge of Pannasekhara's life by persons around Ruvan or by Ruvan himself, after he became associated with Pannasekhara.

21. E. Haraldsson (1991), op cit., A. Mills, et al (1994), op cit., I. Stevenson (1977), op cit., I. Stevenson and G. Samararatne, op cit.

22. V. F. Gunaratne, *Rebirth Explained* (Kandy: Buddhist Publication Society, 1971), P. D. Premasiri, op cit., F. Story, op cit.

23. In this connection it is interesting that there have been some Buddhist scholars who have emphasized the relationship between empiricism and Buddhism (Jayatillaka 1963, Kalupahana, 1976). See K. N. Jayatillaka, *Theory of Knowledge in Early Buddhism* (London: Allen and Unwin, 1963) and D. J. Kalupahana, *Buddhist Philosophy*: A Historical Analysis (Honolulu: University of Hawai'i Press, 1976).

Acharya Godwin Samararatne

Ven. Bhikkhu Bodhi

In late March death snatched from our midst, too soon, one of Sri Lanka's most beloved Buddhist teachers, Godwin Samararatne. For close to twenty years, Godwin had been the resident meditation teacher at the Nilambe Meditation Centre near Kandy. He had also taught meditation within Kandy itself, at the Lewella and Visakha Meditation Centres (two affiliates of Nilambe) at the University of Peradeniya, at private homes, and at the Buddhist Publication Society. But Godwin did not belong to Sri Lanka alone.

He belonged to the whole world, and he was loved and esteemed by people clear across the globe. Thousands of people from many lands came to Nilambe to practise meditation under his guidance, and they also invited him to their countries to conduct meditation courses and retreats. Thus over the past two decades Godwin, in his own quiet way, had become an international Buddhist celebrity, constantly in demand in countries ranging from Europe to Hong Kong and Taiwan. He was also a regular visitor to South Africa, where he conducted his last meditation retreat earlier this year.

What was so impressive about Godwin, however, was not what he did but what he was. He was above all a truly selfless person, and it was this utter selflessness of the man that accounts for the impact he had on the lives of so many people. I use the word "selflessness" to describe him in two interrelated senses. First, he was selfless in the sense that he seemed to have almost no inner gravitational force of an "I" around which his personal life revolved: no pride, no ambition, no personal projects aimed at self-aggrandisement. He was completely humble and non-assertive, not in an artificial self-demeaning way, but rather as if he had no awareness of a self to be effaced. Hence as a meditation teacher he could be utterly transparent. This inward "emptiness" enabled Godwin to be selfless in the second sense: as one who always gave first consideration to the welfare of others. He was ready to empathise with others and share their concerns as vividly as if they were his own. In this respect, Godwin embodied the twin Buddhist virtues of loving-kindness and compassion: *maitri* and *karuṇā*.

Even without many words, his dignified presence conveyed a quietude and calm that spoke eloquently for the power of inner goodness, for its capacity to reach out to others and heal their anxiety and distress. It was this deep quietude and almost tangible kindness that drew thousands of people to Godwin and encouraged them to welcome him into their lives. The trust they placed in him was well deposited, for in an age when so many popular "gurus" have gained notoriety for their unscrupulous behaviour, he never exploited the confidence and goodwill of his pupils.

Though Godwin taught the practice of Buddhist meditation, particularly the way of mindfulness, he did not try to propagate Buddhism as a doctrine or religious faith, much less as part of an exotic cultural package.

His inspiration came from the *dhamma* as primarily a path of inner transformation whose effectiveness stemmed from its ability to promote self-knowledge and self-purification. He saw the practice of meditation as a way to help people help themselves, to understand themselves more clearly and to change themselves for the better. He emphasised that Buddhist meditation is not a way of withdrawing from everyday life, but of living everyday life mindfully, with awareness and clear comprehension, and he taught people how to apply the *dhamma* to the knottiest problems of their mundane lives.

By not binding the practice of meditation to the traditional religious framework of Buddhism, Godwin was able to reach out and speak to people of the most diverse backgrounds. For him there were no essential, unbridgeable differences among human beings.

He saw people everywhere as just human beings beset by suffering and searching for happiness, and he offered the Buddha's way of mindfulness as an experiential discipline leading to genuine peace of heart. Hence he could teach people from such different backgrounds—Western, Asian, and African; Buddhist, Hindu, Christian, and Muslim; Sri Lankan Theravādins and Chinese Mahāyānists—and all could respond favourably to his guidance.

If it was not for a chronic liver condition that he had patiently endured for years, with hardly a word of complaint, Godwin might well have lived on to actively teach the way of mindfulness for at least another decade. But this was not to be, for in late February, almost immediately upon his return from a teaching engagement in South Africa, his illness flared up and a month later claimed his precious life. Those of us who have been touched by him will long bear in our hearts the memory of his calm, gentle personality, and of the impact his life had on our own. May he quickly attain the Supreme Bliss of *nibbāna*.

Contributors

Anne M. Blackburn has been conducting research in Sri Lanka since 1986. She is now Assistant Professor in the Department of Asian Studies at Cornell University. Anne Blackburn has received research funding from organizations including the National Endowment of the Humanities and the American Council of Learned Societies. Her first book, *Buddhist Learning and Textual Practice in Eighteenth-century Lankan Monastic Culture*, was published by Princeton University Press in 2001.

Bhikkhu Bodhi is an American Buddhist monk, ordained in Balangoda, Sri Lanka, in 1972. He has been the long-term president and editor of the Buddhist Publication Society in Kandy. He has translated a number of works from the Pāli Canon and commentaries. His publications include *The Middle Length Discourses of the Buddha*, *The Connected Discourses of the Buddha*, and *A Comprehensive Manual of Abhidhamma*.

George D. Bond is a Professor of Religion at Northwestern University and a recipient of the Charles Deering McCormick Professorship of Teaching Excellence. He teaches courses on Buddhism and the history of religion. He is the author of several books including, *The Buddhist Revival in Sri Lanka*, and *The Word of the Buddha* and has also written numerous articles on Theravāda Buddhism. Currently he is working on a book about contemporary lay Buddhist movements in Sri Lanka.

John Ross Carter is Professor of Philosophy and Religion, the Robert Ho Professor in Asian Studies, and the Director of Chapel House at Colgate University. He has lived in Sri Lanka on several occasions, travelled there many times, and has taken Colgate students on study tours there three times in the 1980s and 1990s. Recently he has received the D.Litt degree (honorus causa) from Kelaniya University in Sri Lanka. He has published numerous articles and works on the Theravāda tradition (Hokuseido Press, SUNY), was a co-translator with Mahinda Palihawadana of the Dhammapada (Oxford) and has published studies dealing with the thought of the Pure Land tradition in Japan (Otani and Book East).

Richard Gombrich was born in London in 1937 and has spent most of his adult life in Oxford as a student and teacher at the University. Since 1976 he has held the Boden Chair of Sanskrit. Most of his early publications were on Buddhism in Sri Lanka; in recent years he has concentrated on early Buddhism and Pāli texts.

Erlendur Haraldsson, Ph. D. is Professor of Psychology at the University of Iceland in Reykjavik, and has been visiting professor at universities in the USA and Germany. He has published four books that have appeared in many translations, has been an active researcher, and contributed numerous articles in international psycholological journals, particularly on paranormal or psychical experiences, and recently on his studies of children who speak of memories of a previous life. He made an extensive study of Sai Baba which he published in his book *Miracles are My Visiting Cards* (US edition: *Modern Miracles*).

Gananath Obeyesekere is Emeritus Professor of Anthropology at Princeton University where he has taught for twenty years. He has also taught and lectured in many universities in the US, Sri Lanka, England, Europe and Australia. He has published six books and numerous scholarly articles and his most recent book is *Imagining Karma: Ethical Transformation in Amerindian, Buddhist, and Greek Rebirth* (University of California Press, 2002).

P.D. Premasiri, B.A. hons. Sri Lanka; B.A. Hons. Cantab; M.A. Cantab; Ph.D. Hawaii, first graduated with a Bachelor's degree majoring in Pāli at the University of Peradeniya, Sri Lanka. Later he graduated from the University of Cambridge majoring in Western philosophy. He did his Ph.D. in comparative philosophy at the University of Hawaii. Presently he is the Professor and Head of the Department of Pāli and Buddhist Studies, University of Peradeniya, Sri Lanka. He has contributed a number of articles on Buddhism to the Encyclopedia of Buddhism published by the Ministry of Cultural Affairs, Government of Sri Lanka. His special area of research interest is Buddhist ethics.

Susan A. Reed is a cultural anthropologist at Bucknell University. Since 1986, she has spent almost four years in Sri Lanka, conducting research on a range of topics including Kandyan dance, ritual, nationalism, Buddhism and mental health. Her most recent publications focus on the anthropology of dance and middle class nationalism in Sri Lanka. In addition to teaching at Bucknell, she is currently the Co-Director of the Race/Gender Resource Center.

Jeffrey Samuels is an Assistant Professor in the Department of Philosophy and Religion at Western Kentucky University where he teaches courses on Asian Religions. His areas of research are Pāli texts and modern Sri Lanka Buddhist practices. He is currently studying contemporary monastic training and education in Sri Lanka.

Donald K. Swearer is the Charles and Harriet Cox Professor of Religion and Philosophy at Swarthmore College where he teaches courses in Asian and Comparative Religions. His special field of research is Buddhism in

Thailand. His recent books include *The Buddhist World of Southeast Asia* (1995), *The Legend of Queen Cāma* (1998), and *Becoming the Buddha: Image Consecration in Northern Thailand: Sources and Interpretation* (forthcoming).

ASANGA TILAKARATNE is Professor and Head of the Department of Buddhist Philosophy at the Postgraduate Institute of Pāli and Buddhist Studies, University of Kelaniya, Sri Lanka. His publications in English include: *Nirvana and Ineffability: A Study of the Buddhist Theory of Reality and Language* (1993: Colombo). His most recent publication in Sinhala is a translation of and a commentary on the Mūlamadhyamakakārikā of Nāgārjuna (2001: Colombo).

Index

Page references followed by *t* indicate a table.